Y2K

A REASONED
RESPONSE TO
MASS HYSTERIA

DAVE HUNT

HARVEST HOUSE PUBLISHERS
Eugene, Oregon 97402

Except where otherwise indicated, all Scripture quotations in this book are taken from the the King James Version of the Bible.

Cover by Terry Dugan Design, Minneapolis, Minnesota

Y2K A REASONED RESPONSE TO MASS HYSTERIA
Copyright © 1999 by Dave Hunt
Published by Harvest House Publishers
Eugene, Oregon 97402

Library of Congress Cataloging-in-Publication Data

Hunt, Dave.
  Y2K—a reasoned response to mass hysteria
     p. cm.
    ISBN 0-7369-0167-1
    1. Year 2000 date conversion (Computer systems)   I. Title.
  QA76.76.S64H86   1999
  363.34'97—dc21   98-35638
                                    CIP

Printed in the United States of America.

99 00 01 02 03 04 05 / BC / 10 9 8 7 6 5 4 3 2 1

Contents

This is not a prediction, it is a certainty—there will be a serious disruption in the world's financial services industry...it's going to be ugly. It will start with a millennium-induced crash of the world's stock markets around the middle of 1999.

—*Sunday Times*, London, England[1]

A bank run like no other will bankrupt banks all over the world in 1999. A worldwide panic is now inevitable. It has literally been programmed into the banks' computers....*All banks are at risk if most of them aren't Year 2000-compliant by December 31, 1999....When depositors at last figure this out, the mother of all bank runs will begin.*

—Gary North[2]

Failure to achieve compliance with the year 2000 will jeopardize our way of life on this planet for some time to come.

—Arthur Gross, chief information officer for the IRS[3]

The year 2000 represents...a cyber nightmare that could...[throw] our entire high tech civilization into total chaos and gridlock....Guaranteed to occur, beginning at midnight on December 31, 1999, is the coming computer crisis....It could trigger a wholesale U.S. and global run on the banks and stampede into cash and gold: a collapse in the U.S. securities markets..., the biggest global depression since the 1930s..., and political/social turmoil (especially in major cities).

—Donald S. McAlvany[4]

The failure to get it [Y2K] right will affect the integrity of the payment system, financial markets, and the performance of the domestic and the global economies.

—William McDonough, president, Federal Reserve Bank of New York[5]

The ability of international banks to operate effectively after the Year 2000 is, in our estimate, *seriously in question.*

—Larry Martin, president of Data Dimensions[6]

CHAPTER ONE

Worldwide Chaos and Disaster?

Historically, the turn of every century, especially the approach of a new millennium is accompanied by alarmist rumors, the current equivalent of Chicken Little's "The sky is falling! The sky is falling!" Yet there seems to be concrete evidence for a number of today's gloom-and-doom predictions: the solar storms coming around Christmas 1999 and continuing for months, which could disrupt communications and other electronics on earth; the predicted alignment of planets May 5, 2000, which some scientists believe could disrupt the tilt of the earth's axis or dislodge one or both polar ice caps; the increasing frequency and intensity of killer earthquakes and other upheavals in nature; and the mysterious invasion of lethal microbes, which are untouchable by any known medical weapons.

The threat of widespread disaster that has received by far the most attention as the year 2000 approaches, however, is the Y2K computer problem. Experts dealing with this subject are almost unanimous in predicting unbelievable catastrophe worldwide. Although both the exact nature of the problem and the solution are known, many of the most knowledgeable professionals believe there simply is not enough time left in which to do the necessary work to fix the problem. Popular television prophecy commentator Jack Van Impe calls Y2K "one of the most serious topics" he has ever dealt with and warns that it will "affect all of our lives." On a video he recently released Van Impe says:

> After studying 250-300 major reports from experts globally, I can honestly say I'm shocked, startled, and stunned. If they are right, then Luke 21:25 [cites the signs heralding the Second Coming of Christ] is just ahead of us....This could be the prelude of the final sign before the return of Christ.... This is an emergency video....[7]

This author disagrees with that appraisal. Unfortunately, many of those dealing with this topic have adopted a sensationalist approach, which we believe is creating unnecessary anxiety and could lead to panic that would fulfill their worst predictions. We strongly oppose the pessimistic conclusions of great disaster that so many are promoting. That Y2K presents a serious problem we do not deny. However, the problem is well known and so is the solution that is being effected right now.

It is our firm opinion, after much careful investigation, that those now crying disaster will shortly be proved wrong. And those who, on the basis of such warnings, have stocked up on large amounts of food and emergency supplies, purchased diesel-powered generators, sold city property and moved into the country, and otherwise prepared for a collapse of the power grid (infrastructure) and banks, will have endured needless anxiety and disruption of their lives, from which some may have difficulty recovering.

Before giving our reasons for this contrary view, however, we must in fairness present the predominant position as fully and objectively as we can in the limited space available. In fact, the doomsayers are not crying wolf—they have solid evidence to support their worst fears.

What It Is—How It Began

Numerous experts with the highest credentials in the computer world warn that Y2K will usher in one of the worst crises mankind has ever faced. Y2K stands for "Year 2000." It is firmly believed that the dawn of the new millennium, January 1, 2000, will bring almost indescribable chaos and disaster because of a computer crash precipitated by that date.

The root of the problem goes back to the early days of computers, when the technology was in its infancy and memory space was limited and expensive. In order to save space, computer programmers used only two digits for the year: i.e., 65 instead of 1965. For every date given, computers interpreted the unseen first two digits as 19. Thus, when the year 2000 rolls around and 00 turns up, many computers and embedded chips will decode the date as 1900. That could create serious problems, depending upon the type of information being generated and the function that time plays, if any, in the system. Some computers could conceivably freeze up because 1900 wouldn't make any sense. Others might start to generate false data, which might not be immediately recognized as such and could possibly do considerable damage.

No one is really certain exactly what may occur in those computers or embedded systems in which the problem has not been fixed. Computer programmers, however, are not willing to accept blame for the extreme difficulty this problem poses. In letters to the editor responding to an article in the *San Francisco Chronicle*, two computer programmers said:

> As a former programmer, I must insist on this phrase: "Programmers were forced by management to use two digits" to represent the dates in computer software. We all knew that the problem was coming. We complained, and management refused to listen. Stop blaming us programmers. We were not allowed to program with four digits for the date.
>
> —*Mary Danlon, Hayward*

> As a mainframe programmer of 10 years' standing,
> nothing infuriates me more than to be...[blamed for
> Y2K] when I have spent most of those past 10 years
> trying to get management to do something about this
> problem.
>
> For your edification, programmers used two
> digits to represent the year to save companies
> money. In the '60s and '70s, mainframe memory was
> exceedingly expensive....
>
> The first article warning about the Year 2000
> glitch was written in 1979. That's right, almost 20
> years ago. Management has had 20 years to get its
> house in order.
>
> In my own experience, whenever the issue was
> raised, it was deemed either too expensive to do now
> or too far in the future to worry about by—guess
> who—corporate management. The real answer is
> that the inertia and myopia of managers is the cause
> of the Year 2000 glitch.
>
> —*Mark Turrell, San Francisco* [8]

Painting the Grim Picture

Whoever is to blame, we are faced with a December 31,
1999, deadline by which time this error from the past must be
corrected or else. The problem is well known and so is the solution. Then why worry? Latest estimates put the cost of fixing
Y2K computer problems in the United States at nearly $900
billion. Not only is it impossible for many companies to come
up with enough money to make the necessary repairs, but also,
it usually takes so long that they tell us there simply is not
enough time remaining. These shortcomings occur to an even
greater extent in many countries less affluent than the United
States. In addition, the computers of Wall Street-based financial networks and American and European multinational companies (even if they all could be made Y2K compliant) are tied
together in an international network with thousands of computers which are not likely to be fixed in time.

Consider only the time factor. The Social Security Administration worked diligently for more than ten years before achieving Y2K compliancy near the end of December 1998. But many companies, even here in the United States, have just awakened to the fact that Y2K is a real problem. They are only in the beginning stages of investigating what they ought to do (and many overseas are not even aware of it). Not enough time remains for these latecomers! Moreover, all too many companies have neither the funds nor the knowledgeable personnel even to begin addressing the problem. Never mind Indonesia, India, or China. As of early November 1998, 40 percent of European companies hadn't gotten around to planning what to do about Y2K![9]

On the other hand, here in the United States one would have to be almost deaf and blind to remain ignorant of Y2K. The media is being deluged with books, magazines, videos, the internet, and radio and TV programs on this subject. All are quoting the same "experts" and one another to the effect that the year 2000 is going to bring the world to a halt and probably usher in the worst worldwide financial crash in history (along with accompanying civil unrest and the death of millions). Indeed, the chaos will be light years beyond anything imaginable until now.

In his bestselling book, *The Millennium Bug*, computer expert Michael S. Hyatt paints a grim picture. Hyatt recently was on James Dobson's "Focus on the Family" radio program as a panelist and is highly recommended by Dobson. Notice that Hyatt isn't hedging at all. He is assuring us of a disaster so complete that it boggles the rational mind:

> *12:01A.M. JANUARY 1, 2000:* Your electricity goes off. Phones aren't working. The computer at your local bank crashes. Police and 911 are nowhere to be found. The illusion of social stability is about to be shattered...and nothing can stop it....The results will be catastrophic.

Social Security checks will stop coming. Planes all over the world will be grounded. Credit card charges will be rejected. Military defense systems will fail.... There will be massive, long-term power failures. Bank funds will be inaccessible. Insurance policies will appear to have expired....Telephone systems will fail to operate. IRS tax records and government funds will be unavailable.

The Federal Reserve will be unable to clear checks. Time security vaults will fail to open or close on time. Traffic signals will fail to function. Office systems will fail and your employer will go out of business.[10]

Why Hide Our Heads in the Sand?

If such predictions turn out to be only half true, utter chaos will reign and civilization as we know it will collapse causing a return to the law of the jungle! Yet those whom we are tempted to call alarmists are not, as a whole, wild-eyed fanatics with no comprehension of what they are talking about. Their ranks include many of the top business, government, and military leaders, who assure us that we are facing a worldwide collapse of civilization as we have known it. And they are joined by leading Christian computer and business experts who are pronouncing the same doom.

Considering the fact that today's modern world is almost totally dependent upon computer technology, it is not far-fetched to believe that our present civilization could collapse with a worldwide crash of the computers which run it. And there are more than a few Christian leaders who, from their study of Bible prophecy, would consider this to be a very appropriate judgment upon our technology-worshiping world by a righteous God whose patience with rampant evil has finally worn thin.

The Government Accounting Standards Board (GASB) has issued new rules requiring state and local governments to report their costs in fixing Y2K problems. Those costs are rising rapidly as the process of repair proceeds—costs which most states haven't even included in their budgets. The Board is concerned that "if governments don't correct their Y2K problems in time, major disruptions could occur in fire departments, law enforcement agencies, and municipal water and sewer systems."[11] The latest surveys, as shown by the few expenses reported, indicate that state and local governments and their agencies are not doing well at all.

Almost everyone is finding that in the process of attempting to exterminate the pesky millennial bug the larger the problem grows and the more costly it becomes. This unpleasant fact has come home to the state of Oregon, one of the less populous states, so it must be even more troublesome for states which are many times its size. In mid-September 1998, the following news was released from Salem, Oregon's capital:

> The price tag for state agencies to fix the millennium bug in state-owned computers has risen to $99.7 million—up nearly $8 million from January's estimate. Staff assigned to deal with the problem keep stumbling on new glitches while trying to fix the programming defect....
>
> "It's extremely high anxiety," said Don Mazziotti, the state's chief information officer. "Each week we see a new facet to this problem and it does affect my sleep."[12]

Nor is the progress toward Y2K readiness by the federal bureaucracy anything to give us much comfort, in spite of President Clinton's attempts (in public at least) to sound a note of optimism. GASB project manager Terry Patton, as late as November 1998, described Y2K as "a very pervasive problem in government computer systems."[13] Representative Stephen Horn "(Congress's most avid [Y2K] Bug-watcher) handed the Feds a report card on their Year 2000 effort. The overall grade was D-, with Defense and Transportation getting flat Fs."[14]

With so many enemies around the world—from Iran and Iraq to terrorists of all kinds, some of whom have nuclear capabilities—defense both for our country and for Americans traveling abroad is vital to our continued existence. It is therefore troubling to learn that this Y2K computer problem could put us in jeopardy. The end of November 1998 saw this disheartening report hit the papers:

> The U.S. agency managing the nation's nuclear weapons stockpile is testing its most critical computers, after Pentagon inspectors discovered nobody had verified whether key systems could withstand year 2000 problems. The Defense Special Weapons Agency wasn't alone in certifying computers Y2K safe without independent testing, said the Pentagon's Inspector General's office, which found only 25 percent of the agency's "mission critical" defense computer systems had been tested.[15]

Newsweek magazine for June 2, 1997, had a feature article titled "The Day the World Shut Down." It raised the possibility of power plants being unable to operate, Social Security checks failing to arrive on schedule, and bank accounts disappearing on January 1, 2000. Nearly a year later *Newsweek* was still pessimistic, declaring that "unless the Bug is purged, the air-traffic-control system will do a total Cinderella on New Year's Eve [1999]. The FAA insists that the fix will come in time, but recent...congressional testimony concluded that 'at its current pace, it will not make it in time.' If so, the Bug could transform the friendly skies to the lonely skies."[16]

President Clinton and Vice President Gore have tried to put the best face on Y2K and have sounded an optimistic note in recent press conferences on the subject. Nevertheless, even White House Y2K czar John Koskinen "has admitted that not everything will be fixed and that his goal is to keep disruptions down to a manageable level. Some of the worst problems will be international....Koskinen... wants the State Department to...warn citizens about countries that will be badly hurt by the bug."[17] Obviously, considering the interconnectedness of today's world, problems in a few countries affect all of the rest.

Major Components of Disaster

A major key to survival, of course, is electrical power, the backbone of our modern world. Without electricity, the Y2K problem is of no significance because computers wouldn't work anyway. Consequently, those concerned about Y2K give a great deal of attention to the power grid (also called the infrastructure) that channels electric current to every corner of the United States. Every country, even the most backward, has a similar infrastructure. The experts agree (and common sense affirms) that "if one link in the chain breaks, it becomes rather painful and expensive (and sometimes impossible) to reroute electrical power."[18]

When multiple parts of the grid go down, as so many are convinced will happen just after midnight December 31, 1999, a power blackout all over the country could result, so there is certainly some justification for the fears being expressed. To add to the seriousness of the problem, January 1 comes in the dead of winter for half of the world. Ross Anderson of Cambridge University's computer laboratory explains the consequences simply but grimly: "Electric power is the critical utility. After more than about three days [of failure] everything just folds up. Trains, heat, refrigeration, water supplies all go. We'd be straight back to 18th and 19th century, and it would take 20 years to regain the lost economic capability."[19]

The millions of embedded chips hidden and even forgotten throughout the electrical power system pose a seemingly insurmountable problem. It is a massive job to run down every component which needs to be corrected for Y2K within each electric-power generating facility, much less in the vast interconnected grid across the country. Can it be done? Most experts have not been very hopeful.

Senator Christopher Dodd (D-Conn.) commented on June 12, 1998, "Quite honestly, I think we're no longer at the point of asking whether or not there will be any power disruptions, but we are now forced to ask how severe the disruptions are going to be."[20] Julian Gregori comments that "systems are not yet failing, because utilities are afraid to test or because they are putting it off....The failures will [begin to] come late in 1999." And David Hall, an embedded-systems consultant at Cara Corporation, warned Congress in May 1998 of "certain-to-come power outages":

> Every test I have seen done on an electrical power plant has caused it to shut down. Period. I know of no plant or facility investigated to this date that has passed without Y2K problems.
>
> Things like this come out and the mass media get hold of it—you're going to have shortages [of food and supplies] because of panic. How to communicate this to the public needs to be addressed.[21]

Water, of course, is the most essential item for life and well-being that would be affected by a failure in the electrical grid. Drinking water everywhere depends upon electricity to run the pumps that deliver it, whether from large water systems in the city or from an individual well in the country, with the exception, of course, of those run by windmills. On November 18, 1998, Gary North summarized his analysis of the latest survey of water companies conducted by the American Water Works Association:

> Without water, you're dead in five days. Without water, no modern city could survive a year. Water is the lifeline. Where will cities get water? This survey indicates that the industry will not finish on time....

36% [of water companies] have no formal y2k plan....

Over 70% have not completed the repairs and testing; 6% refused to respond....

69% had not surveyed their suppliers and vendors....

72% have no contingency plans for internal breakdowns.

What about emergency contingency plans for external problems? 83% said they had none...but 65% said they are confident that they will be ready in 2000.[22]

Based upon this report, North concludes, "A disaster looms." We cannot argue with the statistics he gives, but those statistics are changing rapidly in favor of success. Furthermore, the fact that water utilities are not *yet* ready for the year 2000 does not warrant the conclusion that they *will not* be ready. The statistics are presented, however, in a manner intended to lead the average person to conclude that a disaster does indeed loom and that there is little if any hope of preventing it. Two of the most desperate needs in this whole matter of Y2K are calm appraisal and sound reasoning based upon actual facts. Unfortunately, few of the "experts" in this area are applying these principles.

Like everything else, the water situation is more complex than most people realize. Even if all the power plants were functioning to provide the necessary electricity, there are other serious Y2K-related computer problems inherent within any city's system for supplying drinking water. Here is what one programmer, Dick Brich, of the city of North Platte, Nebraska, discovered:

The [North Platte] water system now has year 2000 compliant software controlling its valves. In contrast, software that controls valves to prevent backflow of lawn fertilizer through residential sprinkler systems, waste in hospitals, and sewer runoff into the drinking water, has not been updated. The software which records inspections of these systems will not accept dates past May 25, 1995,...[and] the software supplier...is out of business...,[so] records are kept manually at this point.[23]

Though the situation is not good, it does show that at least in some cases manual operation is a viable alternative to prevent a breakdown of systems that cannot become compliant by January 1, 2000. Of course, there are many systems so highly computerized that manual operation is no longer possible. Nevertheless, most of those sounding the Y2K alarm pass right over the possibility of manual operation because it detracts from their disaster thesis.

Worldwide Banking/Financial Collapse

Although not as vital to life in the short term, over the long term the banking system is essential to the equilibrium of our modern world. Most people seem unaware that banks operate largely on credit and trust. Banks are allowed to lend out several times more than the funds they have on deposit. Moreover, there is never much cash in the system (just enough for normal in-and-out circulation) because those who take cash out normally return it very quickly in purchases or other payments. If enough customers were suddenly to start hoarding cash because they had lost confidence in a particular bank, they would quickly bring that bank down. The entire banking system would collapse when lack of confidence became general and depositors started to convert their accounts into cash.

Here we encounter another serious problem. Panic does not run on facts but on rumor. The very alarm being sounded by the Y2K crusaders, of possible (never mind probable) collapse of bank computers and unavailability of cash withdrawal or clearance of checks, could become a self-fulfilling prophecy by creating the panic that would bring it about. Furthermore, it wouldn't require many computers going down to provide the hard facts for a bank run. Hong Kong management consultant Robert Lau has warned:

> It is our prediction that it will only take 5 to 10 percent of the world banks' payments to not work on that one day [January 1, 2000] to create a global liquidity lock-up. I don't think the [stock/financial] markets have quite grasped the implications of what will happen if the entire system goes down.[24]

Senator D'Amato warned of banking "catastrophes which could endanger the financial well-being of hundreds of millions of Americans" because the computers upon which "the world's banks are dependent" are going to crash. The threat, he says, "is not only real, it is now inescapable."[25] On September 9, 1997, the central bankers of the G-10 (top ten industrialized countries) "met in Basel, Switzerland and issued a statement warning of the potential for chaos and an international banking system failure...: '*The year 2000 issue is potentially the biggest challenge ever faced by the financial industry. Weak links could pose a risk even to banks and businesses whose computer systems are functioning smoothly.*'"[26]

Fear and panic breed upon one another, and as the rumors gather momentum it is almost impossible to turn the tide. Already we are getting more than rumor to the extent that one wonders why the panic attack hasn't already begun. In his February 1998 *Intelligence Advisor*, Donald S. McAlvany warns:

> The entire global financial system is intertwined like a giant spider web—the stockmarkets, bond markets, derivatives markets (totaling $56 trillion), the commodities markets, the banking system, governments (which issue and trade in debt), and telecommunications. *This gigantic global financial network is all tied together by computers—many of them non-Y2K*

compliant.....If any of these systems go, they can take
down all the rest.[27]

If McAlvany's assessment is accurate, then real trouble
lies ahead and we'd better start to do something about it.
Larry Burkett tells us what to do. Founder and director of
Christian Financial Concepts and the most highly regarded
economic advisor among evangelicals, Burkett has offered
this alarming counsel on the Internet: "Stash some cash.
Prepare now for the possibility that you may be unable to
get your money from your bank. Paper money in small
denominations and coins, enough for one month, might
prove very helpful."[28]

Burkett is forced into a corner. He is a very conservative
financial advisor for Christians, the James Dobson of fi-
nances. He has an excellent reputation; he is not an alarmist.
But what if he fails to tell people to prepare for Y2K and
something drastic does happen? So, in addition to considerable other advice, he tells everyone to get enough cash to
last a month. That in itself, if everyone were to follow his
advice, would break the banking system. There simply isn't
a month's supply in print for everyone! Others dealing with
Y2K are advising people to withdraw much more than that,
even to the extent of withdrawing everything they have on
deposit. It would be difficult to find an excuse for not taking
this advice, if for no other reason than to get some cash
before it is no longer available.

It is amazing that such advice coming from so many
"experts" hasn't already brought down the banking system,
especially considering the fact that those sounding the alarm
tell everyone to pass the word (and rumors) along. Larry
Burkett says, "Pass on what you learn about Y2K to friends,
family, neighbors, and others. Nothing will delay midnight,
December 31, 1999."[29] Apparently relatively few have heeded
the experts' advice until now, but that could change quickly
at any time. It may only take a bit more public awareness.

Banking analyst Mike Phillips provides some interesting and disconcerting information:

> It seems clear…that any initial Y2K impact will not originate with the major New York banks. They should be compliant. However, there are hundreds of banks in this country, many of which don't appear to be on track to compliance. Once one bank gets cash demands which exceed its ability to pay, it must begin calling in loans or close. Either action tends to spread the problem to other banks, regardless of whether or not they are computer compliant.
>
> Okay, what about the FDIC? Don't they guarantee deposits? Yes, and they have been very good over the years at swooping in to small banks in trouble and making a public show of paying off the depositors. However, it's largely a bluff. They only have enough to cover about 1 or 2 percent of the deposits in the banking system. Y2K has the potential to affect much more than this.
>
> Even worse, Y2K doesn't have to directly impact the banking system in order to cause problems. Suppose a large number of small and mid-sized businesses have difficulty dealing with the banking system [i.e., making loan payments on time], even temporarily, because of [their own] Y2K computer problems. In order to stay in business, they turn to [asking their customers for] cash. Their customers, wanting what they have to offer, go to their banks and demand cash from their accounts in excess of previous demands. This is enough to start unwinding the debt pyramid, even if the banks are 100 percent computer compliant.[30]

As late as mid-November 1998, the *Wall Street Journal* was still expressing grave concern over foreign banks, suggesting that they were caught by a calendar that "is ticking its relentless way to a potential electronic Armageddon.…Western bankers and financial experts say that Asian banks are way behind in fixing their computers, cannot afford to complete the task, and pose a great risk of infecting anyone doing business with them after the year 2000 [arrives]."[31]

A Prudent Course of Action?

Former defense industry top executive and pioneer in the computer business Chuck Missler, highly regarded both in secular and Christian circles, has often said that those who speak lightly of the Y2K problem simply have not given it serious study. Missler has served on the board of several large defense corporations involved in electronics and is extremely concerned. So concerned did he become, that by mid-1998 Missler was devoting a major portion of his time and ministry to sounding the Y2K alarm. He was not declaring that the disaster many predict is inescapable, but he felt compelled to warn of the possibility and to recommend that reasonable precautions be taken. Others go much further than Missler in their warnings.

It is not comforting to discover that some of the top experts seem to be the most pessimistic. None is more convinced of impending disaster than Ed Yourdon, who has published 27 books in the field, many used as texts in university computer science courses. Yourdon has moved out of New York City into the country in preparation for the unbelievable chaos and disaster he is convinced is inevitable. Gary North has done the same, and Missler has said that he is carefully studying the possibility of making such a move as well. In his article "Sayonara Washington," Yourdon bluntly stated: "Nobody seems willing or able to say it in simple language, so let me be the one: the federal government is not going to finish its Y2000 project....How Washington expects to continue functioning after 1/1/2000 is a mystery to me."[32]

When someone that knowledgeable makes such extreme statements and backs up his firm convictions by moving out of the city and setting himself up in a self-sustaining property far out in the country, it makes those of us who haven't yet (or can't, which includes most people) look more than foolish. Nor is Yourdon the only expert who has already taken such drastic steps to protect himself and his family.

Christian Y2K experts often quote Solomon's twice-repeated wisdom in this regard in trying to stir their fellow believers into appropriate action: "A prudent man foreseeth the evil, and hideth himself; but the simple pass on, and are punished" (Proverbs 22:3; 27:12).

But what is a prudent person to do in this situation? That is an extremely important question, but finding an answer is not easy. We hope to provide that answer by the end of this book.

Embedded Chips, the Achilles' Heel

Nearly all of the experts, Christian and non-Christian, express special concern regarding the most difficult and potentially dangerous problem: embedded computer chips. Computer consultant Mark A. Frautschi explains: "Embedded microprocessors...are silicon integrated circuits, generally with permanently coded instructions (firmware) that are not designed to be easily changed, indeed if they can be changed at all. These monitor, regulate or control the operation of devices, systems, networks or plants."[33]

A major problem is that many of these chips were placed years ago; locating and correcting them could consume far more time and manpower than is available. Furthermore, "many embedded systems are considered 'black boxes,' since they are bought ready-made from vendors, without businesspeople's knowledge of their inner workings and code."[34]

At a ministerial association-sponsored meeting in a small central Oregon town, Jack Anderson attempted to alert a group of church leaders to the seriousness of the problem we all face together. Mr. Anderson, who has been associated with Larry Burkett's organization for more than 20 years, declared:

I've seen estimates...up to about 40 billion embedded chips....In some cases they will be Y2K compliant, in some cases not....There's one in every transformer, by the way, on the power poles out here...[and] what about the 27 million of them that are in the Alaska pipeline? If one of those shuts down and the pipeline is stopped for one hour in January it will not be operational until August because it will take that long to thaw it out. There are another several million chips in the oil wells in the North Sea, same problem there.[35]

After that bit of misinformation (see page 49, "Contradictions and Misinformation"), Anderson continued:

Those two things impact on our supply of crude oil coming into this country, which results in your gasoline and diesel and all the things we use for transportation, leading you to the conclusion that maybe there's going to be a problem there.... There's not a truck on the road that's Y2K compliant [because of embedded chips], and those are the folks that deliver all the stuff to the supermarkets. ...It might be a good idea, possibly [he says, tongue in cheek], to store up a few things, I suppose.[36]

Participating on a panel on James Dobson's "Focus on the Family" radio broadcast in late October 1998, Chuck Missler also pointed to embedded chips as the gravest problem: "What frightens them—and I'm speaking in this case of one of the international oil companies—is the embedded chips, because they know they won't get them all. And they just hope the ones they don't get won't sink the company. But the embedded-chip problem is the big enigma."[37] Donald S. McAlvany elaborates on this Achilles' heel of our modern world:

There are billions of embedded computer chips all over the world....If the chip has its program embedded into it, it cannot be revised by software...*and it is estimated that 8 to 20 billion chips are presently in use throughout the industrialized western world....All* chips must be tested, one by one, system by system. This is not possible between now and 12/31/99....

Embedded processors are found in cars, elevators, traffic lights, security systems...telecommunications, medical, navigational, and military systems. ...Many will fail or give erroneous data which could have catastrophic results....

One such piece of medical equipment (a respirator) was tested by a hospital by turning up the clock to midnight 12/31/99. It stopped cold and would not start up again. How would you like to have been a patient on that respirator? Happy New Year—goodbye world![38]

The answers to this seemingly insurmountable problem and our own opinion to the contrary will be presented in a later chapter. Here we want to give a fair hearing to the Y2K scenario from the viewpoint of those most concerned. And to do so we will quote extensively from the panel discussion of the Y2K problem hosted by Dr. James Dobson of "Focus on the Family."

Sounding the Christian Alarm

In late October 1998, James Dobson aired the first series of programs in which he attempted to address Y2K through what he described as a "*powerhouse* panel" of top experts. The announcer introducing the program said, "Today we're going to attempt to sort through a topic that's receiving more and more attention these days because of the potential it has to affect each and every one of us in the not too distant future."[39] Dobson began by saying,

For the past year or so, I've been reading and studying about what is known as the Year 2000 problem, or more simply, Y2K, which refers to the potential for a worldwide economic and social upheaval that *may* occur—no one is sure exactly what's coming-—as computers begin to crash....And during that year I frankly have not been sure what our response here on the broadcasts ought to be.

I didn't want to create panic in our listeners; but neither did I feel right about withholding information that could be useful to people. And so, frankly, I have kind of avoided this subject until I could deal with it in maybe a rational and calm manner, and I hope today is that day....

The truth of the matter is, no one knows [what will actually happen on January 1, 2000]. I mean, there's evidence that would lead us in one direction or another...and personally I put myself in the camp of those who think there will be some tough times before we're through with it.[40]

Dobson introduced his panel of Christian experts that day as follows:

Michael Hyatt...has spoken all over the country..., appeared on more than 100 radio shows, even testified recently before Congress about Y2K....[He is] senior vice president and associate publisher of Thomas Nelson Publishers..., the one who helped get me into computers in the first place...; next we have Shaunti Feldhahn..., author of a book that's due out next month called *Y2K, The Millennium Bug: A Balanced Christian Response.* Prior to founding The Joseph Project...she worked at the Federal Reserve Bank in New York...; Chuck Missler..., founder and chairman of the board of Koinonia House, a ministry on the cutting edge of technology for spreading the gospel worldwide..., author of six books, including one that's due out soon... *What to Do When the Chips Are Down...*; Reverend Steve Hewitt..., founder and editor-in-chief of *Christian Computing* magazine..., hosts his own radio show called "Christian Computing Live,"...a leading expert in the use of computer technology in ministry...; Ron Blue..., founder and managing partner of Ronald Blue and Company, a financial investment and estate planning firm...[with 3,000 clients and $1.5 billion of their money invested around the world].[41]

The lone dissenting voice on the panel belonged to Steve Hewitt, who does not believe that the effect of Y2K will even come close to being the worldwide chaos and disaster that so many are projecting, but considers it more like a bad snowstorm. He suggested to Missler that it would be unthinkable for any profit-oriented company not to be taking this problem seriously (including the matter of embedded chips) and working on it diligently. Missler countered:

> Make no mistake. They're working...hard. In many, many board rooms they're near panic, because they recognize as they go through the arithmetic and as they look at the progress (here and there, there's some progress made that's a little ahead of schedule)...but in general it's behind schedule and there aren't enough [software computer] programmers or dollars to *really* accomplish the total task.[42]

At this point, Shaunti Feldhahn interjected her thoughts:

> Can I respond to that...? One of the Y2K writers and speakers who has analyzed this thoroughly—his name is Jim Lord...has a good analogy....Y2K at its core is a very simple problem and it's easy to fix. That's one of the reasons why there are a lot of people who really are not that worried. He likens it to...if I had 20 marbles to polish by Friday, it would be very easy....But now imagine that I took you to

the rim of the Grand Canyon…it's filled with marbles and I said, "Polish these marbles by Friday." It's
the same exact task, very easy, we know exactly what
needs to be done to fix it. There's just too much of
it to get done by the deadline. And that's where I
disagree with Steve, respectfully, because, quite
frankly, I just do not see that we have the ability to
get it completely fixed in time, and because of that
there are going to be certain problems. And because
of the interconnectedness of our economy and our
society we have to at least be concerned….You know
how Proverbs…says that a prudent man sees trouble
coming and does something about it.[43]

It is rather disconcerting when, as ordinary individuals,
we hear experts warning us that there is neither the manpower nor the time to finish the Y2K readiness job satisfac-
torily. One feels rather hopeless realizing that there is
nothing we can do to prevent the disaster. Apparently all we
can do is to see to our own preservation—but there we face
further questions concerning exactly what we ought to do.
On that subject, too, the experts differ.

For many business and government agencies, as well as
individuals, at least part of what needs to be done to solve
the Y2K problem is apparently going to be left undone, and
that could be dangerous. Computer expert William G.
Phillips has said, "The Millenium Bug is such a formidable
opponent that programmers are concentrating on fixing
only the computers critical to a business operation."[44] But is
that enough? Time will tell.

Pervasive Sense of Hopelessness

Bruce Webster organized a "Year 2000 Group" of experts
to meet monthly in Washington to discuss the Y2K problem.
He tells us that "the longer people work in this area, the
more pessimistic they are." He is convinced that we will face
"political crises, regional supply/infrastructure problems

and social disruptions."[45] In the previously cited February 1998 *Intelligence Advisor,* McAlvany elaborated with this grim assessment:

> As of the end of 1997, there was not one single Fortune 500-size company that was compliant, and some had been working on Y2K for five years. ...Purdue University and Oklahoma State University have been working on it since 1985, and neither is presently compliant....U.S. and global banks are interdependent....If 80% of the banks become compliant, and 20% don't, the 20% can bring the 80% down.[46]

And let's not overlook hospitals which, of course, pose a special problem. Most of them have standby diesel engines in case of an electrical power failure. But they don't stock enough diesel to continue this source of power indefinitely. Moreover, many pieces of equipment in hospitals, vital to the moment-by-moment survival of patients, contain embedded computer chips. There is a danger, according to the experts, that embedded chips that are not Y2K compliant could shut down a respirator keeping a patient alive, or some other piece of equipment equally crucial.

As one would expect, with lives literally depending upon their efforts, hospitals have been in the forefront of dealing with the Y2K computer problem. In the medical field, especially, much of the equipment both for monitoring and for life support as well that which is used in diagnosis and treatment relies upon calendar dates and is, consequently, more likely than nonmedical systems to be affected by Y2K considerations. It is therefore helpful to learn what medical experts' concerns are and what they have been doing. Following is a brief summary:

> Medical experts say that most of the medical technology in hospitals...should work safely [January 1, 2000 and thereafter in the new millennium] and that hazards to

patients will be rare. But the thought of even a few incidents is enough to cause anxiety.

"You have to look at the numbers, and this makes me worry," says Dr. Kenneth W. Kizer, undersecretary of health for the Veterans Health Administration, which annually cares for about 3 million veterans at more than 1,100 hospitals, clinics and other facilities nationwide.

"How many patients are treated in America every day? About 3.8 million in a hospital or outpatient setting," Kizer says. "Those in intensive care, for example, are having hundreds to thousands of interactions with technology a day. Say there's just a tiny fraction of the devices or systems that don't work that could cause harm—the numbers are still bothersome."

Hospitals across the country are bracing for millennial problems of a scope and complexity that no one fully understands. Anything from a small $800 medication pump to a $1.6 million nuclear accelerator that kills tumors may be suspect....

Ken Kleinberg of Gartner Group..., technology consulting firm, predicts the cost of trouble-shooting millennial software problems across all industries worldwide could total $300 billion to $600 billion. He figures that the U.S. health-care system's tribulations could account for $10 billion to $20 billion....For individual hospitals, the millennial challenge is enormous. For large hospital systems, equipped with tens of thousands of various machine makes and models, the job of locating a weak link is a mind-numbing task....

Cedars' [-Sinai in Los Angeles] 1,000-bed hospital, research center and outpatient offices house as many as 20,000 pieces of equipment....[Marc Beauchesne, software developer hired last year to run Cedars-Sinai Health System's Y2K project, says] his handpicked team of a dozen technical specialists—including six biomedical engineers—has made its way through about 70% of the inventory. Thus far, they've turned up 1,700 pieces of clinical equipment with date-related problems....

"If you take an X-ray of someone's heart, for example, it must be dated appropriately so doctors can take the necessary action," Beauchesne says....

Experts guess that a small percentage of the medical equipment in use—some say 10% to 20%—faces millennial problems. Only about 2% to 3% of those could harm somebody directly. But the cost of rooting out and replacing culprits can run into the tens of millions of dollars for large hospital systems.[47]

Many of the millennial difficulties faced by hospitals relate to embedded chips. As Chuck Missler explained on the Dobson program, these chips were mostly purchased for their function and were not part of a designed system. Some are date sensitive and others are not. And a hospital (as well as an electrical power plant or other business) which doesn't need date-sensitive components in a particular application could nevertheless unwittingly have purchased chips that are date sensitive without knowing it because the manufacturer had not labeled them as such. In that case, the date-sensitive nature of the chip might not be discovered until a malfunction occurs January 1, 2000—and that is why the big search is on in hospitals across the country. Late in 1998, William G. Phillips presented a shocking picture:

> Only 30 percent of U.S. hospitals have formal remediation plans, yet the effects of Year 2000 could be dire: Not only could medical records be lost, but IV feeders could malfunction and dialysis machines could shut down. On the positive side, pacemakers and other medical implant devices are not affected, contrary to popular belief, says leading manufacturer Medtronic.[48]

The Grave Consequences

Remember, these dire warnings come not from a few fanatics but from a host of experts who all agree on the following: the stockmarket will crash and the world will sink into a great depression as bad as or worse than in 1929.

> [IBM] will be dead...interest rates will skyrocket ...Medicaid will go under on January 1, 2000...there will be a major breakdown in all ATMs...the banks, insurance companies, and even public utilities may be headed for a breakdown...so are the governments...stockmarket mania will turn into panic... [there could be a] breakdown of the West's entire defense system...[and] a breakdown in the payments system.[49]

To support this scenario, Gary North offers this sobering explanation:

> AT&T has 500 million lines of code to go through. The typical programmer can go through about 100,000 lines a year and fix any bad lines. So, AT&T needs around 5,000 programmers (deadline for testing 12/98). At the same rate of repair, Citicorp (400 millions lines) needs 4,000. Chase Manhattan (200 million lines) needs 2,000. And so on....
> Where will any nation find tens of thousands of skilled mainframe programmers who are not already engaged in keeping existing systems going...? One researcher recently identified a system with 70 languages in its programs. The temps [temporary employees hired for emergency] must be familiar with these other languages, too. Forget it. It's impossible....
> For three decades, the best and the brightest of the programmers...did not write documentation— i.e., summaries or manuals. Those who now must piece together what those genius programmers did decades ago have less than two years to get it done, ready for testing. It's impossible.[50]

Early in 1998, Edward Yardeni, highly respected chief economic forecaster of New York-based international investment banking firm Deutche Morgan Grenfeld, warned, "The Y2K virus has infected all the vital organs of our global body. A failure in one system could corrupt other systems....There is no silver bullet."[51] Yardeni originally "estimated the odds of a Bug-based recession at 60 percent."[52] He has since raised the odds of a "severe global Y2K recession...[to] 70 percent" and warns that in the stockmarket crash that he predicts investors "easily could lose $1 trillion."[53]

Jerry Falwell's *National Liberty Journal* has served for years as an excellent source of reliable information for Christians. It is therefore not to be taken lightly that Falwell's *Journal* repeats some of the same predictions we have already seen. Perhaps they bear repeating. The *Journal* adds another trusted voice on this important subject, along with further insights :

> Experts predict that millions of computer programs and countless numbers of embedded computer chips—in everything from cars to police dispatch centers to nuclear reactors—could fail on, or before, January 1, 2000....[54]

> The cost of repair to the world's computers is now estimated to be between $600 billion and $1.6 trillion. However, the chief problem programmers now face is time...; experts say there isn't nearly enough time...to avoid crisis...: consequential effects on banking, insurance, telecommunications, transportation, oil production and Wall Street....

> What's more, fallout from Y2K, including lawsuits, could shake the proverbial rafters of the insurance industry, costing billions of dollars and burying insurers with a torrent of claims from individuals and companies suffering Y2K losses....Lloyds of London has estimated that Y2K litigations in the U.S. alone will cost a staggering $1 trillion....

Despite upbeat language from the White House, the Federal Aviation Administration probably will not be able to upgrade all of its traffic-control systems....[A] frightening posting on the National Air Traffic Controllers Association's web page on June 11 [1998] reported, "NATCA perceives the overall condition of the national Airspace System to be catastrophic."[55]

Chaos from PCs to Mainframes

There have been articles declaring that PCs (personal computers) are not affected. At least one expert, however, British computer consultant Karl Feilder, warned in September 1997:

> If you can sleep properly at night, you don't understand the significance of the PC problem....We conducted the largest-ever independent testing of PC programs and hardware. We have tested the Basic Input/Output System, or BIOS, on over 500 types of PCs, and of those machines made before 1997, 93% failed the BIOS test. This is very real and will have a far-reaching effect. I think that this problem is going to be far worse than anyone expects.[56]

As for calling the problem to the attention of those who need to do something about it, Feilder added, "I'm taking bookings into the middle of next year for awareness programs. What am I going to tell them? Hey, guys, wonderful you're here. It's too late!"[57]

Donald S. McAlvany reminds us of what we have already learned and adds another warning:

> Virtually the entire United States and most of the industrial world is...completely dependent upon computers. So is the federal government, all state governments, most local governments, our military and most others around the globe. The national

power grid (a complex matrix of public power utilities, dams, nuclear power plants, etc.) is completely
computer dependent and may be the most important system at risk. Every participant in the grid must
be Y2K compliant if the system is to be compliant.
If 20% of the grid goes down, it could pull down
the rest of the grid with it, giving us the "mother of
all electrical blackouts."...A major depression, social
upheaval in American cities, widespread food shortages, and a state of national emergency would only
be a few of the results of such a failure.[58]

Michael S. Hyatt gives some examples of failures that have
already occurred. These seem trivial in comparison to the
chaos and disasters which loom ahead if so many experts are
right in their appraisal of the Y2K problem. But these few
examples of what has actually happened give us some prac-
tical insights into what could occur on an international scale:

1. An electric utility ran a series of tests on the city
power grid to see what would happen on January 1,
2000. The power system simply stopped working.
2. Some credit cards with expiration dates three
years hence had to be recalled—the machines
reading them thought they had expired.
3. Computers have already mistakenly ordered
the destruction of tons of corned beef, believing
they were more than 100 years old.[59]

Gary North was one of the first to sound the Y2K alarm;
few have sounded it louder or more persistently than he. In
a special report to promote his newsletter, *Remnant Review,*
North had this to say:

On January 1, 2000, the world's computers will
either shut down or go haywire. So will everything
dependent on them: banks, Social Security, Medicare,
and (if you don't take action soon) your retirement
plans. In 1999, depositors all over the world will

figure this out and will pull their money out of the
banks: the ultimate bank run![60]

As we have already noted, it is speculation of this kind
(or advice from a Larry Burkett to "stash cash"), stated with
the authority of a recognized expert, which could trigger
the panic that will create the very bank run North warns will
come. Here is a very real problem. And, oddly enough,
those warning of a Y2K disaster seem strangely unaware that
they could literally be the ones creating it. Runs on banks
and supermarket shelves caused by panic from hearing Y2K
warnings give us far more concern than Y2K itself. We are
told that suppliers of freeze-dried food, kerosene lamps,
diesel generators, and other survival items can't keep up
with the demand, and that some of them are 12 to 18
months behind on deliveries already. When demand gets so
far ahead of supply that people can't obtain what they desperately want, who knows what could happen?

Nuclear power plants, of course, pose an especially worrisome problem.
—*Business Week,* March 2, 1998

It wouldn't surprise me if certain plants find that they are not Year
2000-ready and have to shut down.
—Jared S. Wermiel, Nuclear Regulatory Commission[1]

One company involved in doing deeply classified government work has
a two-day training course for all of its employees, instructing them that
*they should prepare for a national power blackout—not a brownout—of up to 90
days due to Y2K.*
—Chuck Missler[2]

I am amazed by the lack of concern about Y2K by our political and business leaders, journalists, and the general public. The widespread
mantra I hear over and over again is "Bill Gates will fix it...." It is too
big and overwhelming for even Microsoft.
—Edward Yardeni[3]

John Koskinen is in charge of making sure the U.S. government's computers don't crash come January 1, 2000. Koskinen's task is not just
daunting: it's impossible.
—*Time* magazine[4]

Even with the strong efforts being made...it is clear that all non-com-
pliant computers and software simply cannot be upgraded or replaced
before the non-negotiable deadline.
—The Joseph Project, quoting Larry Burkett's
position paper[5]

Don't panic....There is a middle ground between panicking and doing
nothing.
—Dr. James Dobson, "Focus on the Family"[6]

Chapter Two

Panic,
Stock Up, and Arm?

As we noted in the first chapter, if the estimates of so many experts turn out to be even half true no one can afford to wait another minute before plunging in earnest into the task of preparing for the coming disaster. Furthermore, many of the experts are leading the way in getting ready for the worst. We learned that Ed Yourdon has moved out of New York into a self-sustaining country property in New Mexico, and he is one of the most knowledgeable, yet conservative, computer experts. Is he crazy? Or are we the crazy ones for not doing likewise?

Gary North, who is probably one of the most knowledgeable Christians working in this area and the first to sound the alarm, has "moved to a rural property with its own private natural gas well. He has installed three 10kw natural gas generators in reserve."[7] Bob Reinke is a 49-year-old computer programmer and Year 2000 consultant who has worked for several federal agencies in the Washington, D.C., area in the course of a 29-year career in this field. He is convinced we will face "global chaos lasting as long as six months. He's stocking up on food and water, expects to be without electricity for days, maybe weeks, and plans to take much of his money out of the bank. 'January 1, 2000,' he says, 'will be remembered as Black Sunday.'"[8] For those who believe what these experts are saying and have the courage to act upon their convictions, North offers the following advice, together with a rather compelling argument:

> The June 2, 1997, issue of *Newsweek* ran a front-cover story on the looming computer crisis of the Year 2000—called Y2K....In the week the article appeared (late May), the Dow Jones Industrial Average set a record new high. (It was beaten a week later.)
>
> If investors believed the information reported in the *Newsweek* article, the world's stockmarkets would have collapsed. But they have risen. Clearly, people don't believe the story.
>
> That's why a small handful of people can get out now—out of the stockmarket, the bond market, and any city over 25,000....
>
> Not everyone can get out at the top of a bull market. This includes the "bull market" known as modern industrial society. Pull the plug on the local power utility for 30 days, and every city on earth becomes unlivable. What if the plug gets pulled for five years?
>
> How do you rebuild the shattered economy if the computers go down, taking public utilities with them? Without electricity, you can't run the computers. Without computers, you can't fix computers. How can you assemble teams of programmers to fix the mess? More to the point, how do you pay them if the banks are empty...?
>
> My conclusion is simple: it is time for you to begin taking Y2K seriously—a lot more seriously than the public. The public's apathy is the only thing that allows you a little more time to get prepared.[9]

Act Now, Before It's Too Late?

When presumably conservative and level-headed experts are taking such precautions it seems only reasonable for the rest of us to do likewise. It would be disastrous to find oneself without electricity, food, and water and to have delayed doing anything for so long that such items can no longer be found. Julian Gregori suggests that the panic-driven run on banks and stores for food and supplies could come well before the year 2000. Like Gary North, Gregori says that for some unknown reason the general public hasn't yet awakened to the danger lying ahead and, like North, he adds, "That's good news for the readers of this book [because supplies are still available]. Once the public realizes the vulnerability of every family, there will be a run on...resources...and many families will have to do without the things they desperately need because there are not enough to go around."[10]

Even those who believe that Y2K will not be the widely expected disaster of chaotic proportions admit that no one has just made up a wild tale. *Something* is going to happen out of the ordinary here, there, and everywhere on January 1, 2000. The problems may begin before then and could continue sporadically for some time thereafter.

The difficulty we all face, however, is to make enough sense out of contradictory reports and opinions to come to a definite and timely conclusion and act upon it. There can be no doubt that we must give considerable attention to this matter of Y2K. Where there is so much smoke, there must be some fire. Everybody can't be crazy. In its Special Anniversary Issue, *Computer Shopper* carried an article stating what we have heard many times:

> The year 2000 bug is the most dramatic problem in the history of computing, and alarmist hype notwithstanding, the consequences of ignoring it could be dire....The truth is that no one can accurately predict the outcome or the severity of the Y2K problem until it occurs. So in the meantime, educating yourself about the challenge..., then taking the appropriate actions...is the smartest course....
>
> An August 1998 report by ZD Market Intelligence analyzed the progress of 24,000 enterprise sites (those with 1,000-plus employees)...[and] found

that...only 18 percent of sites contacted had actually completed a Y2K project.[11]

A "Conspiracy" to Take Over?

With his usual insight and candor, Chuck Missler has pointed out another dimension to this problem: the likelihood that unscrupulous leaders already in power either in the United States or elsewhere could use the crisis to take dictatorial control. He is not suggesting that there is a plot to do so but has wisely pointed out the possibility. Here is his cautioning voice of reason to one audience:

> Most of you are probably aware that we actually operate under the Emergency War Powers Act of 1944, I think it is. FDR put it into office and each president has renewed that, which means that the chief executive of the United States can—if he deems it a national emergency—put the United States under martial law...there's a whole bunch of executive orders...that give the chief executive of this country absolute power. When you go through those...you can get very uncomfortable.
>
> Now one of the questions that we can give some thought to is...long before the year 2000 it's likely that there will be a broadly recognized crisis brewing. This crisis can take many forms....The economy of the United States is delicate and as various manufacturers or other participants in that economy stumble...there can be a real loss of confidence, which will affect the investment market, a real loss of earning power, etc. etc. And so one of the things, in practical terms, that shouldn't surprise us is if the government, either in the forms of its agencies or from the chief executive, doesn't exploit these opportunities to increase power.
>
> It's not fanciful to imagine...[that] the federal government will adopt some *drastic* action to deal with the civil unrest and chaos and so forth that could emerge from this strange problem that we're facing [i.e., Y2K].[12]

During the question-and-answer period that followed, Missler responded in the affirmative to a question concerning whether, in the event of a crisis, President Clinton could suspend the Constitution and elections and remain in office. This same question surfaced during the Dobson panel discussion, and it was generally agreed that the president has the power to suspend constitutional law and impose martial law by declaring a national emergency. This concern comes up often with those who are sounding the Y2K alarm. Unlike Missler and the others on the Dobson program, there are many who suspect that Y2K could fit too neatly into the plans of the globalists for coincidence. Donald S. McAlvany writes:

> However, the most ominous aspect of the Y2K crisis is how the global socialists who run America and most Western (first world) countries will try to use the crisis to push us in one quantum jump toward global government—which *they* call the New World Order. Could Y2K be that *"right major crisis"* that David Rockefeller talks about—wherein the peoples of the world will accept a new global order in return for a promise of stability or a return to normalcy?
>
> *If the banking industry collapses, if banks close their doors...President Clinton will declare a national emergency.* Banks will be crying for help; individuals...will be crying for help, and the government will step in to help. This is not merely likely. It is a dead certainty.
>
> Since a banking/financial crisis is likely to be a major element of the Y2K upheaval, the potential for declaration of a national state of emergency by Bill Clinton...is very high....The year 2000 elections would also be suspended...leaving Bill Clinton in office....
>
> Could the Y2K crisis and the financial/banking crisis it is likely to precipitate be the excuse the global socialists use to launch a preemptive strike against cash and the overnight mandating of a total electronic money system? It could![13]

McAlvany is very astute. His *Intelligence Advisor* often makes valid points and provides information that most of us have overlooked or to which we don't have normal access. But the fear of Y2K has a way of unhinging the best of us if we aren't careful. Obviously, Y2K could not push us into a cashless electronic money system if the computers have crashed and the electrical power is off. If that is not the case, then there is no Y2K emergency and no basis for pushing us into anything, including the proverbial one-world government of Antichrist. The truth is that we are already well on the way to a cashless system, and it would seem, rather, that Y2K would turn us back to a more primitive way of doing business if power is off for an extended period of time or computers have crashed and the Y2K problem has proved too difficult to handle.

Global Conspiracies and Common Sense

Recently President Clinton joined those calling attention to the Y2K problem and arousing America to do something about it. Was he sincere and can his voice of reason be trusted? Perhaps a country totally engrossed in preparing for the year 2000 will forget about Clinton's personal problems and credit him with leading the way out of a potential disaster. Interestingly, however, the president was not trying to build Y2K into something so huge that it would take all the attention away from questions about his moral conduct. Amidst the cries of alarm, his was a more reasoned voice.

On July 14, 1998, in an address at the National Academy of Sciences, the president called upon businesses to help one another to achieve compliance by the year 2000. He said, "We've worked hard to be ready. I set a government-wide goal of full compliance by March of 1999. The American people have a right to expect uninterrupted service from government, and I expect them to deliver." Was Clinton responding to Jerry Josinowski, president of the

14,000-member National Association of Manufacturers? Just two weeks earlier Josinowski had complained, "[Y2K] is a large global disaster in the making....President Clinton and Vice President Gore have failed to make the problem a national priority."[14]

Cynics suggest that Clinton simply found a new subject to lie about. The motive? He was painting an unwarranted rosy picture in order to allay the public's fears and to prevent the panic that pessimistic reports could very well create. They think Clinton himself knows better but is only trying to sound positive for political reasons. If so, he chose a strange place to tell his lies—in front of a group of top scientists who, common sense would indicate, were hardly the easiest audience to deceive. And they all took in what the president said with straight faces.

Then there is the equally cynical argument that Clinton actually wants Y2K to devastate the country so that he can declare a national emergency and establish himself as dictator. It hardly makes sense for several reasons. First of all, Clinton himself and his family and friends would be victims just like anyone else. If the power grid is down, it's down for everyone; Washington is unlivable, and that includes the White House. What is the point in hoping to become dictator over a devastated country that has suddenly fallen to worse than third-world status—when the would-be dictator sitting in Washington can neither communicate with the rest of the country nor even know what is happening, much less control it? Who would deliberately plot to bring *that* scenario about?

Again, McAlvany's reasoning is faulty when he suggests that the government will step in to help the banks or anyone else. Y2K involves a computer crash, and that includes the government's computers. Clinton and the Rockefellers and other wealthy and influential leaders who, for all we know, may very well be plotting to usher in a one-world government, could hardly use Y2K to bring that about. They would be its victims just as much as anyone else. Obviously, they have as much motivation as anyone to see Y2K solved—even more motivation, because they stand to lose a whole lot more than the rest of us.

Conflicting Voices: Whom Can We Trust?

In that same address at the National Academy of Sciences, Clinton commended the Social Security Administration for being more than 90-percent ready. That news seemed to be in complete contrast to the predictions we have heard so often, and which are still being repeated to this day by alarmists, that the SSA is too far behind schedule to ever catch up and become Y2K compliant, that after January 1, 2000, Social Security payments will be suspended. It's beginning to look as though the checks will be in the mail after all—but the Y2K extremists have yet to admit it.

There is no doubt, of course, that the president wanted to avert loss of confidence in government and the panic that would follow—and he could hardly be faulted for that. Before an intelligent, well-informed, discerning audience, he presented sound factual information to support his statements. Nor did he deny the problem. He acknowledged it, but at the same time encouraged Americans to believe that even if not all computers were corrected, the predicted worldwide financial and economic collapse and social and political chaos would not materialize because other means would be found to deal with and get around whatever problems might arise: "No one will ever find every embedded microchip, every line of code that needs to be rewritten. But if companies, agencies and organizations are ready, if they understand the threat and have backup plans, then we will meet the challenge."[15]

Gary North, of course, strongly disagrees. In contrast to his usual extreme alarmism on this topic, North seems to bend over backwards to be conservative and reasonable. He generously assumes that 99 percent of the Y2K problems will be solved in time (though he doesn't believe that). He then shows that a mere 1-percent margin of error will create chaos:

> I have deliberately...assumed...only the following: in every industrial nation, the public will figure out in 1999 that they are utterly dependent on the services of organizations, including governments, whose computers will begin to produce erroneous information in 1% of their operations by 2000. Not 10% or 20%, let alone a complete shut-down. Just 1%. *This is not a far-fetched scenario....*
> Kathleen Adams of the Social Security Administration... says that if the Social Security Administration has a 1% failure rate, it will mean that local SSA offices will get somewhere between 430,000 and 500,000 phone calls on the same day...this would overwhelm the system....
> This 1% scenario, if it comes to pass, will paralyze *every* mainframe computer-driven organization on earth....Panic hits a large group almost without warning. I saw this back in 1974, when the Arab oil embargo produced lines in front of gas stations. One day there were no cars lined up. There was no panic. The next morning, the lines were long, and they were permanent. City by city, the panic spread like a plague. It will happen again, but on a scale unimaginable, beginning sporadically at least one year before 2000....
>
> ### THE MILLENNIUM CLOCK KEEPS TICKING
>
> There is nothing we can do to delay it. *This disaster is programmed.* If you think to yourself, "This just won't happen," ask yourself this question: "Exactly what is going to prevent it...?" Time is running out. *Don't sit there, immobilized, like a deer caught in the headlights of an oncoming truck.* [16]

Despite many good points, a major problem is that North seems to be averse to paying attention to or advising his readers of any positive developments. There is the tendency to leave a terrifying statistic or statement on record even after the situation has changed for the better. While it is true that on his website one can access the latest news items on both sides of the issue, North comes up with so few positive articles that they are almost lost in a sea of bad news. Nor does the good news seem to affect his opinion, which has remained unchanged since he first began warning about Y2K more than a year ago.

One good reason we have for doubting many of the alarming conclusions concerning the deep problems we will face one nanosecond after the clock strikes midnight December 31, 1999, is the fact that so often they are based upon outdated information. The picture is constantly changing but never seems to be brought up to date by alarmists, especially if that would tend to weaken their case. For example, early in September 1998 we were told that the FAA was only 30-percent ready and would never make it in time. But by early in October, the FAA announced that it was already 90 percent compliant. In December 1998 a special news conference was held to announce that SSA was certified 100 percent compliant. We are still waiting for North, Hyatt, Gregori, and others to admit to these and other improvements.

As of November 20, 1998, North's website was still presenting old quotes of pessimistic assessments of the Y2K problem from early in 1998 and even 1997. What is the point of continuing in November to quote, for example, Rick Cowles, saying in February that the electrical industry isn't going to make it; in fact isn't even going to come close?[17] Has nothing changed since then? Of course it has, and the reports from most of the major utilities in the country of what they are doing to become Y2K compliant by early 1999 are available to anyone, certainly to Gary North. Yet in his editorial comments he chooses to give no credit to recent developments which give valid cause for optimism. Instead, he continues to recycle the same outdated pessimism from the distant past.

Fomenting Terror by Error

While factual data is being offered which gives any thinking person reason to take Y2K seriously, one must distinguish fact from fancy. There is a high volume of pure alarmism, much of which doesn't even make sense. For example, according to Jack Van Impe, this whole Y2K problem is one huge and very clever satanic plot. In fact, it couldn't be anything else because, as Van Impe informs us with the air of one who is letting us in on a dark secret, Satan "is the prince of the power of...electricity, the currents! And that's why we wrestle against evil, wicked spirits in high places (Ephesians 6:12)...." Apparently the Amish have been right all along: electricity is inherently evil and we should have nothing to do with it. No wonder, then, that electronics has led us into this trap! Lest there be any doubt, Van Impe goes on to say: "I believe that the one who causes all this mass confusion is the Satanic being who has power over the atmosphere, over space...and, yes, I want to repeat it, electricity!"[18]

Amazing! Is electric current giving Satan an entrance into our homes? This is but one example of some of the extremism we are currently hearing with regard to the Y2K computer problem. This is a once-in-a-millennium opportunity for rumormongers that won't last forever, so jump aboard quickly and ride it as far as it will go!

We have great respect for Noah Hutchings and Larry Spargimino of Southwest Radio. However, the very title of the book they coauthored is enough to awaken fear if one believes the authors are well informed and sincere: *Y2K = 666?* In that book they elaborate on that question:

> The Y2K problem could very well produce a totalitarian police state of universal proportions *that will be welcomed by everyone.* Totalitarian regimes are always unpopular *unless* they are perceived as solving some common problem that can only be resolved by

such drastic measures. Might the Y2K problem be
that common problem?[19]

How could Y2K be resolved by a totalitarian regime taking
control? In fact, it couldn't. Y2K is a computer problem that
can only be repaired through a lot of hard work on the part
of thousands of computer programmers—and that is exactly
what is happening and which I contend (with few exceptions)
will be carried to a successful conclusion before January 1,
2000. Furthermore, Y2K as it is being hyped will not and
cannot be the means of putting Antichrist in power.
Obviously, Antichrist cannot correct millions of computers.
Without computers, how can he take over the world, control
all banking and commerce, and make everyone take his mark
and worship his image? He can't.

So anyone who believes that Antichrist is going to take
over the world, as the Bible clearly says, would be highly suspicious about the possibility that Y2K will be the undoing of
our computerized world. Indeed, it would seem to require
computers for the biblical prophecies in Revelation 13
regarding Antichrist to be fulfilled; and that fact makes those
prophecies from 1,900 years ago all the more remarkable.

Extreme statements continue to be made, and speculation is passed off as fact. For example, we are being told on
websites and by speakers at Y2K conferences that the
Russians and Chinese have stolen our software to use with
their missiles but don't have the know-how to make it Y2K
compliant. Consequently, moments after December 31,
1999, their missiles, already pointed at our cities, could start
heading in our direction—and we, in all probability, will be
without computers either to warn us of attack or to assist in
our defense.

Common sense says that the Chinese and Russians can't
possibly be that stupid, especially if they are clever enough
to steal our software and to make it work. In any country
having nuclear capabilities there are multiple safeguards to

prevent missiles from being launched prematurely for any reason. Rich Hoffman, Army consultant, explains that missiles don't just fire away because of a computer glitch:

> Though these and other weapons have embedded chips, a malfunction would disable the weapon, not deploy it. The bigger issue is the possibility of a mistaken offensive [i.e., for a country to receive false computer data saying it was under attack]. Recently the Clinton administration appointed a commission to raise awareness in the international community about this issue.[20]

Contradictions and Misinformation

Eventually, one begins to suspect that there may be some exaggeration and considerable misinformation involved. The so-called experts seem to quote one another without checking to verify the story. And sometimes they don't get it straight. For example, in his talk to the ministerial association, Jack Anderson referred to a nuclear power plant in Florida that ran a test by turning the clocks forward to 2000, which shut the whole thing down. Jack told the wide-eyed ministers: "They spent weeks trying to find the problem on that. It turned out there was one noncompliant chip all the way up in the top of the smokestack, one that tested for the particulates in the smoke as it was leaving, and it shut down the whole plant right there. So you've got all these little bugs that are running around."[21]

We asked Larry Burkett's office for the name of this nuclear plant and they were unable to provide it. John Davis of the Nuclear Energy Institute (NEI) said he had never heard of this event and doubted that it had ever happened. Furthermore, he stated that the NEI had established Y2K guidelines way back in 1977. Any problems he has been notified of were caught in following the protocol for reaching compliancy. When we finally reached Anderson, he said that the power plant was actually in England but could give no further details. On Dobson's program, Chuck Missler stated, "In Great Britain a power plant went down because a chip in a smokestack was...taking data from two different points and subtracting and it had a date function."[22] At this point he was interrupted by Dobson.

We checked with Missler's office and they provided the origin of the story, but it didn't match what Anderson had said. It was not a nuclear power plant, and the sensor in the flue stack had nothing to do with testing "particulates" as Anderson said, but was programmed to integrate and average temperature over a specific time period. The story was first told during a Year 2000 Embedded Systems Workshop sponsored by the Electric Power Research Institute (EPRI) September 10-11, 1997, in Scottsdale, Arizona.[23] Nothing was stated concerning how long it took to locate and correct the problem, so we have no notion where Anderson derived the idea that "they spent weeks trying to find the problem."

Rick Cowles' website carries a story apparently about the same plant being shut down during a test in England, but rather than being in a smokestack, one of those "little bugs running around" was part of a generator temperature-controlling system.[24] The story may well be true, but we have been unable to discover the name of the power plant or the date of the incident or which version is factual.

Cowles' website where this alleged incident was cited had the impressive heading, "Electric Utilities and Year 2000: Real-Life Examples of Date Related Problems for Electric Utilities." Yet there was nothing else, beyond this story, of any substance. Steve Hewitt reminds us:

> Basic high school journalism teaches that any good report includes who, what, where, when and how! Many of the most alarmist articles on the Y2K problem have one thing in common. They quote "experts" and "reports" without giving us the names,

places and dates. Such reporting should never be trusted, especially when it comes in an article that is predicting dire consequences and the destruction of our present society....

A Christian radio evangelist has a book out about Y2K. In his newsletter he made this statement, "Out of the Y2K debacle, could there come a universal software program that would assign every individual an individual code mark and number? Some secular computer sources are even advocating this solution so that the present problem (Y2K) will never occur again." I have called his office and asked him for his source on this statement (What secular computer sources..., etc.) but no one ever called back.[25]

Anderson also told those church leaders gathered at that ministerial association-sponsored meeting that he had been informed that Florida Power and Light had issued a statement to the effect that beginning January 1, 2000, they would be without power between 4 and 13 months. If true, that would be disastrous. Simple logic, however, told us that was a false rumor. First of all, it would be out of character for a large power supplier to make such a statement, and certainly it was too far in advance for any official declaration to be so pessimistic. Moreover, such a statement is directly in conflict with everything being presented on the Internet by other electric utilities. When we checked this story with Florida Power and Light, they denied that it was the case or that such a statement had ever been made. One wonders why the story wasn't checked out before passing it along.

Furthermore, the idea that wide sections of the United States will be without electricity for weeks or months beginning in the new millennium is contrary to the latest information coming out on the websites of the electric utilities. On September 17, 1998, the North American Electric Reliability Council (NERC), in an investigative report to the U.S. Department of Energy—"the first comprehensive review of where the electric industry of North America is in its efforts to identify, fix, and test for the Y2K bug"—indicated that the industry was on track to provide "sustained operation of electrical systems into the year 2000."[26] In reference to widely circulated predictions of widespread and long lasting power outages across the United States, NERC had this to say: "Are these predictions true? One thing we do know—these predictions are not based on facts or rational analysis of information from the industry."[27]

Those Pesky Embedded Chips Again!

While explaining the problem allegedly posed by the billions of embedded computer chips, Anderson declared, as quoted in Chapter 1, "There's one [an embedded chip] in every transformer, by the way, on the power poles out here." He followed that announcement with the rhetorical question, "And do we have time between now and the year 2000 to go out there and climb that pole and check that chip in that transformer? If we had enough people we could do that."[28] The obvious implication was that embedded chips pose a hopeless problem because there is just not enough time or available manpower.

It is disconcerting that such misinformation would come from an expert who was brought in from a distance to inform this large group of Christian leaders. The number of alarmist errors given out on the subject of Y2K is prodigious. Unfortunately, the misleading data the trusting audience received on this occasion was rather typical of what occurs in such meetings. To verify our own perception, we asked an acquaintance (who happens to be a lineman who actually climbs these poles) about embedded chips in transformers on power poles. He looked at us as though we had lost our mind. "Transformers are just hunks of dumb metal," he informed us. "There's nothing like a computer chip in any of them on a power pole." To make doubly certain, we checked with the engineering department of our local power company and were told that some very large transformers at power stations might possibly have embedded chips in them, but that those on top of utility poles had none.

Anderson's statements are alarmist, misleading, and betray a lack of understanding of the basic elements of the subject on which the speaker was supposed to be an expert. Simple logic would tell you that if it is necessary to climb every pole and individually inspect each transformer to find and check out the embedded chips, then it must also be necessary to trudge the entire length of the Alaska pipeline to find each of the 27 million chips Anderson said were scattered in or along that conduit. Or dive under the North Sea to find the chips in the oil wells he said were out there. Obviously, physical inspection of every embedded chip would take years.

Even if there were an embedded chip in each transformer on power poles, it is the height of uninformed naivete to suggest climbing the poles to look at them. The function of these extremely complex devices is not apparent from a physical inspection, even with sophisticated electronic equipment. In fact, the hardware manufacturer often protects the actual workings of the device to prevent others from stealing its firmware. Furthermore, even without such measures, the very nature of the electronics in an embedded chip is such that the world's greatest computer and electronic expert could not tell its function by simply looking at an embedded system, much less whether or not it was Y2K compliant.

McAlvany's statement is equally false—that "*all* chips must be tested, one by one, system by system. This is not possible between now and 12/31/99."[29] Although it certainly is not possible to check each chip, it is possible to go to the engineer's schematics and firmware sourcecode and there learn whether an embedded system is compliant or not. If the engineering drawings do not reveal that information, they at least reveal that there are hundreds or even thousands of chips of exactly the same kind. Test one of these and they have all been tested. To suggest that every chip must be tested individually not only betrays a naive lack of expertise, but it also paints a picture far more hopeless than the facts warrant.

No embedded system could have been built and installed except as part of an engineering design, the basis of which is a series of engineering drawings comprised of circuit schematics, printed circuit board layouts, an embedded firmware sourcecode, mechanical drawings to describe the packaging, and also the associated test data that validates the design. Embedded systems don't drop out of the sky; they are carefully designed for specific purposes and placed according to an engineering plan.

Nor could some engineer simply design something and have it installed on a pole or along the Alaska pipeline. The product designed must first be tested by both simulation and real-world input and the test results validated and placed in an engineering notebook for future reference. Of course, if it is an old system, the plans could have been discarded or lost—and the designer may no longer work for the company, or may even be dead. Those circumstances could create a real problem, but such cases would be the exception. Logically, the sourcecode would be archived on a magnetic tape or floppy disk, or other permanent backup device. The engineers who built the Alaska pipeline should have all of the original design data in the form of detailed engineering drawings both as hard copy and in electronic form. These drawings would tell where every embedded controller or monitoring system is located, and from them one could tell whether or not it is Y2K compliant, and if not, how to repair it.

Betraying a Trust

As another example of misinformation, Gary North, along with other Y2K alarmists, has declared that if everything isn't ready by June 30, 1998, it will be too late because the testing procedure takes about 18 to 24 months. We checked this out with an electrical engineer who designs the most sophisticated military systems and the test equipment that completely checks them out for readiness. He stated that the *development* of a guided missile could take 24 months, but testing could be done in a few days, and no system, no matter how large and complex, should take more than a few weeks at most to see whether or not it is Y2K compliant and functioning as such. It is true that Hewlett-Packard, for example (which is already Y2K compliant and checking out all of its suppliers), is planning to spend all of 1999 testing and retesting, just to make certain. That is because they have that time for extended testing—but it wouldn't be necessary.

Someone responds, "Windows 95 has been out there for nearly five years and they're still finding new bugs in it." But how does that apply? No software is ever bugfree, but always requires maintenance for fixing bugs. Windows 95 has also been operating well for millions of users during all of that time. Its bug list is compiled from customer complaints. A glitch showing up now and then does not shut down the whole system. Nor is it reasonable, even though a system is not Y2K compliant and will presumably crash on January 1, 2000, to assume that some kind of makeshift solution couldn't be patched in at that time.

One Valid Fear: Panic Created by Misinformation

Anderson also told his trusting audience (as the expert invited from afar):

> The IRS's computer system was a total mess to start with...; they've spent millions...and made a mess of it. They were hoping that the Social Security

Administration would get all their problems fixed
so they could piggyback on them, and to find out
that the Social Security Administration was not
going to be ready was bad news for them. It forced
them into a very unfamiliar corner...they have now
become advocates of the flat tax...they see that as
their only salvation.[30]

Referring to the Social Security Administration, Anderson said:

Just to give you an idea of the magnitude of the
problem, the Social Security Administration, when
they surveyed the problem back in 1989, found out
that they had 30 million lines of code. So they put
400 programmers to work on it and as of this year
(1998) they've gotten through 6 million lines of
code, leaving them five times as much to go through
as they've already gone through. So the likelihood of
Social Security to be ready is something between
slim and none.[31]

Barely one month after Anderson made that statement
the IRS announced that it is totally Y2K compliant and as
noted above, SSA became compliant in December. In fact,
SSA is now being held up as a prize example for other government agencies to emulate. The sad thing is that Anderson
made that erroneous statement several months after
President Clinton boasted that the SSA was over 90-percent
compliant and would be ready well ahead of time.

How could such rapid improvement be possible? One
means would be the adoption of new products such as
StepWise Solutions. StepWise claims:

The major risk in Y2K projects is the *time-to-com-
plete* the identification and modification of year
numbers and the time that it takes to compile and
test the resulting modifications. Using the "StepWise
Solution," this major risk is eliminated because once

> the tool has identified the necessary changes, the
> actual code is modified at the rate of up to *4 million
> lines of code per hour! The resulting code compiles fully and
> cleanly and is ready for testing.*[32]

The time necessary for correcting Y2K problems has shrunk substantially. Yet the alarmists seem unaware of these promising developments. And as for that flat tax? I wouldn't count on it—it would put too many IRS people out of work! But Anderson, though traveling around the country and speaking as an expert on Y2K, hadn't kept up to date (like so many others sounding the Y2K alarm).

It is tragic not only that so much valuable time is being spent on needless speculation about the year 2000, but that so much that passes for truth concerning Y2K, and is accepted as such by a concerned public eager to be informed, simply does not reflect reality. Unfortunately, it doesn't take facts to create panic. Rumors spread quickly and are usually far more alarming than truth. On the program we have already referred to, James Dobson put it well: "If the technical impact of this [Y2K problem] turns out to be nothing…, if it is *perceived* as a problem, you have a major social disruption because people begin running to the bank to get their money and selling their houses and heading for the hills—and who knows what."[33]

And here we confront a genuine possibility of real disaster. It seems amazing that panic hasn't already been created. After all, it is repeatedly stated by presumably reliable experts that there will be no cash available from banks and ATMs, that the check transfer system won't be functioning, that this could go on for weeks or months, and that everyone ought to "stash some cash" as Larry Burkett advises. That in itself should be sufficient to cause a run on banks that would shut them all down. But it hasn't happened—yet.

Undoubtedly, a large number of individuals have already started to accumulate cash. We don't know how many, and as yet there have been no reports from banks that would identify the extent of beyond normal withdrawals. Apparently in anticipation of this very problem, the Federal Reserve (Fed) is planning to put an additional $50 billion cash into circulation early in 1999. How did they come up with that figure? The Fed decided that $500 was a reasonable amount for a family to withdraw and there are 100 million families: "Clyde Farnsworth, the Fed's director of payment systems, said that amount would allow most families to purchase basic necessities over a period of a few days....To prevent possible consumer panic, the Fed intends to make sure all of its banks have sufficient cash inventories."[34]

Attempting to allay any fears the public may have picked up from extremists, a spokesman from Chase Manhattan Corporation, the nation's second-largest bank, stated, "In reality, the ATMs are not going to crash."[35] Steve Hewitt, who does a good job of keeping up on all the developing Y2K news, writes:

> When you hear reports about how our banks will not be able to function, try to keep calm. Solutions are constantly being developed that cause old projections to be inaccurate. During the month of July, Citibank, NationsBank and others began using a new program from Data Integrity. According to Bob Osmond, a consultant making Year 2000 fixes for Citibank, this latest program has allowed them to fix in one day a system with over 100,000 lines of code. ...[Previously] it would have taken them 30 days using other tools. More programs and solutions continue to reach the market each week.
>
> Now I realize I am going to get a lot of E-mail and letters on this subject. I am not trying to say we are out of the woods, or that Y2K will not be affecting each and every one of our lives, because I think it will. However, I just want to assure you that there are solutions.[36]

The lack of panic to date is reassuring. Alarmists have reported that the small freeze-dried food industry is swamped with orders backed up for months. On the contrary, this author found no problem as of mid-January 1999 in ordering the best quality freeze-dried food by the ton for prompt delivery. Emergency generators suitable for a household, however, were in short supply with some models not available for six months. Even in this arena it seems that alarmists have been guilty of exaggeration

Lowering the Anxiety Level

A major problem which becomes apparent as soon as one gives some serious thought to Y2K is that very little is stated for certain. Yes, there are a few alarmists, such as Julian Gregori, who make their pronouncements of doom without any ifs, ands, or buts. For most of those who sound the alarm in this area, however, there is always a big "if" or "unless" or "could": *if* the national power grid goes down (or *unless* remedial action is taken in time, the power grid will go down), *if* the banks are not Y2K compliant (or *unless* remedial action is taken in time, banks *could* be unable to function); *if* the Department of Defense doesn't get its critical systems all ready for the year 2000....*If—unless—could.*

But in the aura of fear surrounding Y2K, the conditional part of the statement is usually overlooked and possible future failure is taken as inevitable. For example, a typical report dated October 22, 1997, stated: "*Unless* timely corrective action is taken to address the Year 2000 problem, the Social Security Administration (SSA), like other federal agencies, *could* face critical computer system failures at the turn of the century." [Emphasis added.][37] Hearing that, many, if not most, people take it to mean that corrective action won't be taken and that there *will* be critical computer system failures in the SSA. Yet SSA became compliant more than a year before the deadline.

The level of anxiety is substantially lowered as soon as one realizes that all of the doom being predicted *could* occur only *if* millions of hardworking and intelligent people fail to do their jobs—or it will happen *unless* they do their jobs. But America is built upon the tradition of people doing their jobs, and doing them well—in fact, each one trying to do the job better than someone else in order to get a competitive edge. AT&T cannot possibly afford to let Sprint or MCI show up on January 1, 2000, operating more efficiently than it does and thereby stealing its customers. Nor can either Sprint or MCI afford to let AT&T get the edge.

And so it is with banks and public utilities and food chains. General Motors cannot afford to be down for a day. Nor can Japanese and European automakers. One hears frequent repetition of concern that there is very little understanding, let alone preparation, for the year 2000 outside the United States. In reality, there is a great deal of understanding and preparation worldwide.

At the ministerial board meeting, Jack Anderson said, "Even Japan...where a lot of computers are built, hasn't really started to fix their own Y2K problem yet."[38] That may have been true a one time and perhaps Anderson was repeating older information. The current fact is, however, that the Tokyo Stock Exchange recently surveyed a number of Japanese companies and found that 98.2 percent expect to finish Y2K repairs by December 1999.[39]

How Bad Will It Really Be?

A major reason this author cannot believe the scenario of doom that is being promoted is the fierce competition among power plants, automakers, banks, credit card companies, and others in business to make money. We continue to learn of new techniques being developed for speedily and automatically locating and fixing the Y2K problem in various systems. American business, industry, the financial and medical sectors, the military, and everyone else now knows about Y2K; they know what the problem is and how to fix it, and they are working diligently at doing so. No matter how seemingly impossible the task, in the vast majority of cases it will be accomplished.

The Y2K alarmists, on the other hand, refuse to believe that American ingenuity, determination and competitiveness will win the day. But can we deny that those who continue to warn of coming disaster make some valid points? Listen to Gary North once again:

> I am making my personal plans based on what I understand. What I understand is this: (1) there is not one compliant [power] plant in the U.S.; (2) power plants must be supplied with fuel, which requires trains (coal) or nuclear power; (3) power plants rely on suppliers (up to 6,000); (4) things wear out; (5) it takes power to generate power, i.e., the suppliers that make power generation possible. In short, it takes the division of labor. I think the division of labor will collapse in 2000. If the power grid goes completely down, it will stay down. The division of labor will collapse to early 19th century levels, except that we have lost early 19th century skills. This is unthinkable, of course, but I keep thinking about it.[40]
>
> On February 4 [1998], President Clinton signed an executive order on Y2K. It warned that government agencies are now [were then] at risk. This executive order set up a commission to discover ways to pressure government agencies to get 2000-compliant. Not one cabinet-level federal agency is compliant today.
>
> In the same week, the U.S. Department of Defense's Acting Secretary for Command, Control, Communications and Intelligence resigned. He was in charge of the Department's Y2K repairs. Two other senior staff members also resigned.
>
> We are still waiting for any money center bank—or any other bank—anywhere in the world to announce that it is 100% Year 2000-compliant. The same is true of every phone

company, power generation plant, and major city water utility. Yet the public just sits there, as if nothing were at risk. But everything is at risk.[41]

One cannot argue with his facts, but the facts keep changing in the face of new developments. And as we have documented in part and will do so more fully, the situation continues to improve rapidly. One reason for that improvement is the development of new and greatly improved methods for rapidly locating and repairing Y2K problems in computer systems. StepWise Solutions's material states:

> *Year 2000 compliant.* Our patent was granted in September 1997. We completed the development of our product in June of 1998....
>
> Due to the *fully-automated* nature of the StepWise Solution, the time necessary to complete remediation of existing code is reduced by an *estimated 70% or more!*[42]

Not only do North and other Y2K alarmists ignore the new developments which make it possible for any company or government agency to become quickly and inexpensively ready for the year 2000, but some of their conclusions involve speculation which we don't believe reflects the facts. In contrast to North's inflexible adherence to the scenario of disaster he has held from the very beginning, others who had been sounding the alarm equally as loud have begun to change their views. In mid-November 1998, the *San Francisco Chronicle* ran an informative article, which said in part:

> Some experts who have been warning about a technological Armageddon caused by year 2000 computer problems now are telling Americans...[it's] not necessary to stockpile months' worth of food and water, convert bank accounts into cash, squirrel away guns and ammunition or buy generators to weather power outages....

As a precaution, they're advising people to put aside enough food, water, fuel, medical supplies and cash to last a few days....But at the same time they saw a growing Y2K paranoia....

Four experts interviewed last week [early November 1998] softened statements they made earlier in the year. Some had predicted that year 2000 problems would shut down banks and bring the American infrastructure tumbling down....

Even Canadian computer programmer Peter de Jager, who is generally recognized as the first to bring the year 2000 problem into the public arena and has been an alarmist on the issue, said that now there might be too much alarm.

"The people who say buy a cabin in the woods and take your money out of the banks and the markets, they're not only silly, these are self-fulfilling prophesies," de Jager said.[43]

Even Utah Republican Senator Robert Bennett, chairman of the Senate Special Committee on the Year 2000 Technology Problem, who has been extremely pessimistic, now says that he feels much better about the outlook for the year 2000. Others previously convinced that Y2K would be a huge disaster are also now saying that it won't be as bad as they had thought. How bad will it *really* be? Let's try to reach a rational conclusion based upon facts.

──────────── *What they are saying...* ────────────

America has never seen a really widespread...blackout....One programmer wondered aloud if electrical power might be off for fifteen years, and then he added, "maybe for good."

—Julian Gregori[1]

Wall Street took the lead Monday [July 13, 1998]...launching a series of tests to see if U.S. markets will run into disaster in less than 18 months, when 1999 turns into 2000.

"At this point, I haven't seen glitches," said Arthur Thomas, Merrill Lynch vice president and chairman of the Securities Industry Association's Year 2000 steering committee....

The test by 29 securities firms and 12 exchanges was the first in a $2 million, two-week dress rehearsal. It was a precursor to more comprehensive testing in the spring.

—Michael Diamond[2]

Frankly, I don't lose any sleep on worrying about being Year 2000-ready.

—Eric Benhamou, CEO of 3Com Corp, large network-equipment maker[3]

Dealing with the Year 2000 problem is a simple software task. It is clear when the problem arises (at the end of the century). It is clear what it will do (confuse calculations performed with dates). The places where the problem arises are easy to find in software code....The corrective action to be taken is straightforward.

—Nicholas Zvegintzov, Technical Editor *Software Management Technology Reference Guide,* co-founder Software Maintenance News, Inc.[4]

It's still unclear how much pain there will be.

—Bill Gates, Microsoft founder and CEO[5]

The public faces a high risk that critical services provided by the government and the private sector could be severely disrupted by the Year 2000 computing crisis.

—Joel Willemssen, Director, Accounting and Information Management Division, U.S. General Accounting Office[6]

──

CHAPTER THREE

Could It Really Be That Bad?

We are not attempting to downplay the seriousness of the Y2K problem. Make no mistake, it is a very serious one and poses an extremely difficult challenge—but not an impossible one. The solution is well known, has been completed by many business and government departments, and is in the process of completion by others. In fact, Nicholas Zvegintzov says, "Most real world software problems are much harder; they are problems in which [unlike Y2K] neither the context, the symptoms, the evidence, [nor] the treatment are so plain. If an organization cannot handle the Year 2000 problem, it is a dangerous organization indeed; avoid it!"[7]

Zvegintzov would surely consider statements such as the initial one on the facing page to be dangerous and irresponsible. The United States and the world may never be able to restore power again? Such a statement is completely irresponsible, yet it reflects so much of the misinformation and wild imagination surrounding the entire Y2K, as exemplified in some of the statements we have already cited.

The Incredible Complexity of Interrelationships

At the same time, however, we dare not ignore the incredible interrelated complexity of the problem we face. Consider as one example the key role played by the railroads. Without railroads to deliver coal, the power stations that depend upon coal for generating electricity would be shut down. That could shut down much if not all of the rest of the power grid. But without electricity the trains can't run because they are all controlled by computer. Without computers the switches won't work, nor can the cars be routed or tracked—and that includes not only cars carrying coal to power plants, but railroad cars taking raw materials or parts to manufacturers, produce and livestock from farm to processor, and packaged food from processor to market—and on and on it goes.

Without computers and the electricity to run them our entire food chain breaks down, including the raising of many poultry, hogs, and livestock. Naturally, frozen and refrigerated foods would perish if the power were off for very long. But even such hardy foodstuffs as raw grains, oranges, or apples would be at risk without computers to monitor and regulate temperature and moisture. It is this kind of interconnectedness which makes Y2K so complex and the consequences so grave should computers fail in the year 2000.

The manufacturing of products we take for granted, from automobiles to dishwashers, involves thousands of parts coming from tens of thousands of suppliers who in turn rely upon thousands of others to provide the still smaller parts which they assemble. Most of our manufacturing plants, even those that may not look automated, rely upon computers in ways most of us haven't even imagined. Consider the following brief explanation showing the dependence upon dates and thus the vulnerability of manufacturers to Y2K:

> The average manufacturer uses dates—and calculations based on them—to drive all manner of business processes that take place inside plant walls. These range from product-data tracking and bar coding to scheduling and monitoring of preventive maintenance, instrument calibrations, and

environmental systems....But relatively few manufacturers are as yet aware of the complex Year-2000 date-change problems that can disable many crucial factory operations. Some companies, in fact, use time-and-date information for as many as 40 different purposes on the shop floor....

David Waddington, information manager at Unilever NV, Rotterdam [says], "It's really quite a nightmare scenario...."

And make no mistake about it, the impact of Year-2000-caused interruptions to business could be catastrophic, experts say...."It could bring an entire supply chain to a screeching halt, because some plants will not be able to deliver," says Bill Swanton, director of plant-operations research at Advanced Manufacturing Research (AMR), a Boston-based research firm. "One little guy not taking [the year 2000] seriously could shut the whole supply chain down...."

With some of the embedded shop-floor software widely in use today, companies will have to do some serious digging just to get to the bottom of the problem....Freudenberg-NOK...ranks among the top 50 suppliers to North America's automakers, with global sales last year of $6 billion....By November 1997 the company had sent letters to its customers and its approximately 1,000 active suppliers to impress the importance of Year-2000 issues upon parties not sufficiently aware of them....[At the same time it] completed a survey of all the equipment [at risk] used at its 17 facilities throughout North America and embarked on the process of summarizing these data in order to determine exactly how many different pieces of inventory would have to be tested for compliance problems....

"What they [manufacturers] are finding at the plant-floor level is really squirrelly," says AMR's Swanton. Some of these systems that are affected are fire protection, safety, and security, many of which have timing devices that include calendars.[8]

Y2K: An Opportunity Knocking?

The Y2K computer problem is complex, time-consuming, and expensive beyond imagination, and some have complained that it becomes more complex the deeper one delves into it. But life is about overcoming difficulties and adversity rather than accepting defeat. It has been the meeting of such challenges that has made America the world's leader, with its technology and products setting the pace on every continent.

Yes, conquering Y2K isn't cheap or easy, but it can be done. Nissan Motor Co.'s Smyrna, Tennessee, plant has been working toward Year 2000 compliance since 1995. It would have been fully compliant years ago had some of the time-saving techniques recently invented been available earlier. Nissan uses about 1,800 devices in its automated operations, all of which must be checked and corrected if necessary. There is no question that Nissan intends to and will complete everything in good time. Other smaller manufacturers may not.

Moody's Investors Service refers to preparing for Y2K as a new kind of competition that will weed out companies that can't handle the challenge. Moody's says, "what might sound to some companies like a bomb ticking could be perceived by others as opportunity knocking."[9]

So, while Y2K is difficult, complex, and staggering in its scope, it does not present so great a challenge that well-financed and soundly managed companies will be overwhelmed by it. It can be handled efficiently and effectively. In fact, a number of shortcut alternatives have been developed that will keep the operation running into the next millennium and buy time until the problem can be solved permanently. Freudenberg-NOK, for example, has placed into effect a technique called "windowing," which is only one of several recently developed and now available shortcuts to a viable temporary solution. And more ingenious ideas are being invented all of the time to simplify and speed up the Y2K repair process.

In "windowing," one simply instructs the system that any year 50 and lower belongs to the twenty-first century; while all years 51 or higher belong to the past century. This simple maneuver allows continued operation into the next century, still using only two digits to indicate the year. This will not work, of course, for banks or the Social Security Administration, where a real date of birth or the date of origin or expiration of a contract comes into play. But it will work for many military applications, where the computer couldn't care less what year it is.

So we find that in contrast to gloomy predictions of collapse, many companies, as Moody's says, look upon the whole Y2K problem as a great opportunity to get a competitive edge over rivals. The confident attitude that Y2K difficulties can be conquered is exemplified by David Imming, manager of integrated solutions and Year-2000 project team leader for Fisher-Rosemount Systems, Inc., Austin, Texas. He says:

> To me, there has been so much hype on this Year-2000 situation. Certainly if you look at it worldwide, for government organizations and financial institutions where they have all sorts of date calculations, they have many issues that need to be resolved. And while it needs to be taken very seriously in our industry, there are a vast number of our products that don't care at all what century it is.[10]

Will Y2K Leave America Defenseless?

We are still receiving a plethora of discouraging reports concerning the lack of preparation for the year 2000 on the part of the federal government, in spite of President Clinton's assurances to the contrary. In interpreting such reports, however, one must avoid the pitfall of taking statements which are intended to motivate to greater diligence as though they were factual statements concerning what must inevitably occur. Let's consider, for example, the declaration by Congressman Stephen Horn's subcommittee on government operations, September 9, 1998. Based upon the General Accounting Office's August 15, 1998, quarterly report, the subcommittee declared the federal government "not on track to complete necessary year 2000 preparations before January 1, 2000." Horn's subcommittee report stated in part:

> As of August 15th, only 50 percent of [the 7,300 mission-critical] systems were Year 2000 compliant. At the *current rate of progress*, the percentage compliant would climb only to 66 percent by March 1999, the President's deadline to fix noncompliant systems and still have enough time to test and implement the systems....
>
> The August 15, 1998, quarterly reports were the primary basis for the subcommittee's September 9, 1998, report card. Overall, the Executive branch of the Federal Government earned a "D,"...a modest improvement from the "F" earned on the June report card....The Department of Defense earned a "D" and simply is *not on track* to complete Year 2000 compliance efforts before January 1, 2000. The committee is encouraged, however, by the strong leadership demonstrated recently by Defense Secretary Cohen and Deputy Secretary Hamre. They are making the Year 2000 problem a top priority, and the importance of this kind of executive leadership is the key to success. But the leadership *must develop an organization that can do the job*. [Emphasis added.][11]

Note the phrases in the committee report that we have italicized. The report is gloomy, but *only* if the *current rate of progress* is not increased sufficiently. This is a wake-up call; it is not a doomsday pronouncement, yet the alarmists present it as such. The phrase *not on track* only indicates the condition at that time; it does not say that the DOD can't get on track. In fact, the report is telling them that they *must* do so. The new leadership is commended for vigorously attacking the Y2K problem. And the statement that the leadership *must develop an organization that can do the job,* far from saying that it can't, actually indicates that the committee believes this to be possible. With this kind of urging, GAO auditors looking over their shoulders and Horn's committee watching like hawks, it is unthinkable that DOD will fail to come through with the necessary effort to accomplish the task on time.

One of the most serious concerns often repeated by the doomsayers involves government's ability to send secret messages to our diplomats or troops. The suggestion is continually made that the Y2K computer problem could leave our top secret communications open to access by enemies and even by computer hackers. In their book, Hutchings and Spargimino quote credible sources without realizing that the information is either false or outdated:

> The Y2K problem promises to pose a security risk. *USA Today* (June 25, 1998) reported that "the Year 2000 computer glitch could help adversaries penetrate critical U.S. businesses, government, and defense computers. CIA director George Tenet stated: 'We are building an information infrastructure, the most complex the world has ever known, on an insecure foundation.'"
>
> In seeking to "fix" the Y2K problem, companies and government agencies must open their computer systems, and that "provides all kinds of opportunities for someone with hostile intent" to plant viruses that would cripple the systems and gain highly sensitive information.[12]

Actually, fixing Y2K problems in a system would no more open it to access by outsiders than would the normal day-to-day operations. Of course, if someone who was hired to come in and do the work planted a bug or stole confidential material, that is another matter. But that could be done also by a regular employee of the CIA or some disloyal officer in military intelligence. It is such statements as the one just quoted that alarm the public. We need factual data, not wild speculations. Unfortunately, the aura of mystery that has grown up around Y2K seems to inspire the latter.

Again, the newly developed procedure of StepWise Solutions is able to solve even this concern about outside programmers coming in to effect the essential Y2K compliance. In a personal letter to the author, Ellen M. Steinlauf, StepWise director of marketing, wrote:

> The StepWise solution is probably the only Y2K solution which could be used by the DOD itself to remediate most of the code *without help from outside vendors.* DOD would not need to expose any vendor staff to secrets. Their [DOD] staff could be trained in 2 or 3 days to utilize the tool independently and do the work itself, with minimal additional assistance. The power of that is enormous![13]

What Is DOD Accomplishing?

As we explained previously, the CIA director's statement was a wake-up call to get moving; it was not a declaration of hopelessness describing a condition that must forever remain the same. Yet this particular quote is used to support dooms-day prophecies and is repeated in various newsletters or on websites month after month as though failure were a foregone conclusion when the tick of the clock ushers in that dread moment right after midnight December 31, 1999—a moment, presumably, for which we will all be unprepared.

The CIA director was honestly presenting a problem in order to spur on those who were working on the solution. And the solution to that particular problem has been found— ahead of schedule. In mid-October, the Boeing Company's in-house newspaper (Boeing is the world's largest aerospace company and one of the largest defense contractors) offered the following information under the heading, "Boeing Gets Intelligence Community Y2K Ready":

> A government-mandated test has proven that the Boeing system used to send and receive secure electronic intelligence communication, the Automated Message Handling System (AMHS), is now ready for the year 2000.
>
> Intelligence organizations have been using the system— a collection of message handling tools for use with computer and satellite networks—since 1992. AMHS is installed at 25 sites around the world.
>
> The test was "the culmination of eight months of intense work" by over 25 members of the Boeing Information Processing Systems Team in Fairfax, VA, said Jono Evans, AMHS program manager. A directive from an assistant secretary of defense set December 1998 as the date the product had to be Y2K ready. The team beat the deadline....
>
> Besides running the system well past January 1, 2000, the test also turned the clock forward to other important dates. Sept. 9, 1999 could be critical because some computer languages use a string of nines as an error or default code. Other tests were designed to ensure that the system realized the year 2000 was a leap year....
>
> "The Y2K problem is a top priority for the Air Force and the Boeing team really came through," said 1st Lt. Todd Siemers, of the 497th Intelligence Group.[14]

Note that the Department of Defense had set a deadline of December 31, 1998, for this system to be Y2K compliant and that the supplier met that deadline. Obviously, DOD has set such deadlines for all of its suppliers. Yet the fact that there was a need has been reported by alarmists as though the situation were hopeless and the problem could not possibly be solved in time. Time, in fact, is proving the emptiness of much Y2K rhetoric. That the Department of Defense would fail to keep itself at top readiness is unthinkable.

Nevertheless, pessimistic reports persist. Don McAlvany reported that Representative Stephen Horn's Y2K Committee "projects that the Defense Department cannot be compliant until 2012."[15] Obviously this is a worst-case scenario that would be realized only by DOD *not doing* what Horn tells them must be done in order to be compliant. We are told also that Horn has complained that the DOD is overstating its progress in becoming Y2K compliant. Reportedly, the Inspector General's office sampled computer systems which the Pentagon claimed were ready for the year 2000 and found that many systems reported to senior management as compliant had not been properly certified.[16] Whatever the exact status, at least we know the DOD is working on the problem and someone is checking up on them to make certain the job gets done properly and on time.

Furthermore, in contrast to pessimistic reports from several months before, at the defense industry's annual 10-Year Forecast in McLean, Virginia, the end of October 1998, some 225 military and industry officials were told by one of the speakers, Lt. Gen. Albert J. Edmonds (Ret.), that according to the latest estimates "only 29 percent of our mission-critical systems are not Y2K compliant."[17] Skeptics say he is fudging to make it sound better than it really is.

The DOD is not asleep. It knows what the problem is and is working to meet the deadline. Here is an example of what is being accomplished: "The U.S. Army's White Sands Missile Range on July 2, 1998, successfully tested an F4 Phantom jet. They rolled all of the 100+ computer critical systems to the year 2000 and put the plane through an extensive series of tests. All systems checked out just fine, revealing no Y2K problems."[18] So DOD is making significant progress. We may be certain that America won't be sitting here defenseless January 1, 2000, helpless prey to the Chinese or to Islamic terrorists. In late November 1998 it was reported that "the Defense Department has conducted more than 200 audits in the past year to ensure officials are conducting proper tests."[19]

One thing we do know: The DOD is responsible for the defense of America, they have done the job well in the past, and they will meet this challenge even if, for some systems, they must adopt windowing temporarily, as mentioned previously, or the U.S. Navy's proposed 28-year solution. Either of these temporary fixes could be used by any of our defense units for those systems which they don't have time to make fully compliant. Moreover, as we have documented, there are now other solutions which cut repair time to a small fraction of what it used to be. To effect the 28-year solution, clocks are turned back 28 years (a full leap-year cycle) so that the days of the week coincide correctly with the date, in case that is essential. While this method, like windowing, cannot be used by banks or insurance companies or other entities dealing with dates of birth and origin or expiration of mortgages, it is viable for most mission-critical defense systems. Assuredly, neither the Army nor the Navy will fall back upon temporary make-do solutions unless necessary, and then only to the extent required. Nevertheless, the fact that these methods are viable and available, especially to the electrical power industry, effectively minimizes the scenario of disaster we are being offered.

Alarmists Are Hanging Tough

In spite of many improvements in methods and software for handling Y2K problems, and in spite of great progress being made, Y2K disaster forecasts were growing worse during the writing of this book, toward the end of 1998.

Most of the alarmists, far from backing off in the face of encouraging developments, were actually toughening their position. Gary North continues to ignore any good news. As of November 20, 1998, his website was still warning readers, "When you hear good news about some organization that is y2k-compliant, recall Ronald Reagan's statement with respect to disarmament treaties: 'Trust, but verify.' Get a signed letter on letterhead stationery that the organization is 100% compliant."[20]

On the one hand, that sounds like good advice; but on the other hand it imposes an unreasonable condition which betrays a lack of the very trust that makes all business and commerce possible. Obviously, it would be most imprudent for any company to declare itself 100-percent certain that no glitches could occur. All anyone can do is to examine everything and repair everything that seems to need it. No one can guarantee 100-percent compliance any more than North can guarantee that he never makes an honest mistake.

North is only one of many who, having announced destruction through Y2K, will apparently persist in that posture until it becomes so obvious that they are mistaken that they have no choice but to back down. That probably won't be until January 1, 2000. The following, apparently originally posted some time in August 1998, was taken from Donald S. McAlvany's website of November 20, 1998:

> With less than 17 months to the turn of the century, the Y2K/Millennium Bug Crisis is looming larger and larger with every day that passes. The more the experts learn about it, the more spooked they become....
>
> MIA [McAlvany Intelligence Advisor] believes that the problem is huge, that it could (indeed is likely to) precipitate a financial collapse, and is likely to create severe economic, financial, and social dislocations for a number of weeks or months. The biggest financial bubble in world history could well

be burst by Y2K in combination with the Asian financial meltdown. And, a power-hungry Clinton Administration could use the crisis to try to usurp a tremendous amount of financial and political power—much as Franklin Roosevelt did in 1933.[21]

Notice the use of *could* and *likely*. The doomsayers won't guarantee 100 percent that what they predict will occur, so why should they demand 100-percent assurance from those who think we'll make it? By "biggest financial bubble in world history," McAlvany probably is referring to the unprecedented bull market in stocks and prosperity the West has been enjoying year after year. Such a financial bubble could always burst at any time for a variety of reasons other than Y2K. As for the "Asian financial meltdown," that is probably near its end, with Japan beginning to see the light at the end of the long, dark tunnel. China is certainly booming, and this communist country promises to set a new standard of competition for the capitalist world—a challenge, again, which the West will have to meet.

Alarmists are becoming more numerous, more vocal, and more urgent. Websites, books, and magazines are springing up like mushrooms, far too numerous to list. James Dobson has joined the ranks of those sounding the alarm. While Dobson is trying to bring balance and reason into the discussion, he is promoting at least one of the most extreme alarmists, Michael Hyatt, author of *The Millennium Bug*.[22]

"Mother of All Blackouts"?

McAlvany rightly describes electrical power as "the heart of Western Civilization." He uses that fact as a launching pad into an orbit of pessimism based upon outdated reports: "If the power generation plants fail because of the effects of the Millennium Bug, it's literally over for the West....Most electric utilities are still, for the most part, in the awareness/

inventory stage of Y2K....*Not one electric company has started a serious remediation effort on its embedded controls. Not one....Here's my main message—the electric industry doesn't have the time left to lick this thing.*"[23]

It's hard to imagine where McAlvany, who is usually so well informed, picked up that information. He could not have talked directly to anyone at the major power generating companies. In fact, many if not most of the electrical power companies are well on the way to being Y2K compliant, and that includes tracking down and verifying embedded chips (and correcting those that need it) as well as establishing contingency plans for any imaginable emergency arising from any cause. Power companies are keeping the public informed through their websites. Commonwealth Edison of northern Illinois recently announced that it expects "to have all systems ready and running in plenty of time for the Year 2000 scare."[24] The same is true of other large electrical power companies, as we document elsewhere in this book. The North American Electric Reliability Council has gone on record that fears of widespread electric outages due to Y2K "are unsubstantiated."[25]

Nevertheless, despite abundant available evidence to the contrary, there are many who continue to sing the same dirge as McAlvany, not the least of whom is Julian Gregori of The International Crisis Management Center. No one seems to have studied the problem in more depth or to have better credentials for understanding it, and no one paints a more hopeless picture than he. Rather than hedging with "maybe" or "could" or "possibly," Julian Gregori confidently and without equivocation pronounces doom. In the last chapter of his book *What Will Become of Us? Counting Down to Y2K,* Gregori provides in straightforward language what he calls his "Official Prediction." It is horrifying:

> Dan Looper is the y2k manager for one of the nation's most respected auditing firms....He was asked in June 1998

if there were any companies anywhere in the U.S. who were ready. There were none. Their "finished" code is riddled with problems. As for compliance [by January 1, 2000], "It's just a dream," Looper said....[26]

The prognosis is not encouraging....By December, 1999,...computers won't be ready and it will be too late to fix them....My prediction...is based on an 18-month study...and reduced to language we can all understand.

Summary: Because our civilization waited too late to begin the y2k repair process, every developed nation will fall into a seven-to-eight year economic collapse followed by a slow, delayed, awkward recovery....Families who are unprepared will be at risk for hunger, disease and lasting hardship. Fear of the future will increase every year until some light is seen at the end of the tunnel in 2006....

I predict that serious y2k computer ambushes will begin surprising Americans in mid-1999...the majority of Americans will finally come to grips with urban and suburban vulnerability by early September, as a number of computer systems begin to falter, causing an economic uncertainty that results in a drastic correction in the stockmarket (by the end of September 1999), and the closing of some banks. The closing of some nuclear power plants in October will quickly increase apprehension....

I predict that...largely because of failures of electrical power...in urban North America, in the year 2000...people will die from cold...from hunger, and...perhaps as high as three percent will die from crime and disease. (That percentage will rise in 2001 and again in 2002.) Most y2k victims will be refugees who are attempting to flee anarchical conditions in the cities....

Even if partial electrical power is restored by the summer of 2000, economic implosions will continue, and...by April 2000, *at least seven out of every ten Americans will lose their jobs or their present level of income.*...There will be no unemployment payments or benefits available....

> The U.S. government...in early 2000, will find it necessary to impose martial law in some areas, and may announce it for the entire nation....
>
> History will remember the y2k crisis as one of the most traumatic upheavals of civilization ever....
>
> "New York, Chicago, Atlanta, and a dozen other cities are going to resemble Beirut in January 2000. That's why I moved out of NYC to rural New Mexico a couple months ago....The government of the U.S. as we currently know it will fall on 1/1/2000. Period."
>
> That's computer programmer guru Ed Yourdon talking. And he's one of the more conservative Y2K experts. There's growing alarm in computer programming circles.[27]

In fact, anyone could go on the Internet and find reams of material from electrical power plants across the country declaring that they have been working on the Y2K problem and will have it conquered well ahead of January 1, 2000. We quote some of these reports elsewhere. In contrast to McAlvany's pessimistic appraisal and Gregori's dogmatic insistence upon a failure of the power grid, the North American Electric Reliability Council (NERC) recently said in relation to Y2K, "At this point, the perceived operating risks are manageable." As for the pessimistic reports one continues to hear, that there will be widespread electricity outages beginning in 2000, NERC said they "are unsubstantiated." The following is excerpted from a NERC report to the U.S. Department of Energy, September 17, 1998:

> The...impacts of Y2K on electrical systems appear to be less than first anticipated. With continued work toward finding and fixing components that may be Y2K deficient and with properly coordinated contingency planning, the operating risks presented by Y2K can be effectively mitigated to achieve reliable and sustained operation of electrical systems into the year 2000.[28]

Recycling Old Material

One reason for the perpetual pessimism is the recycling of outdated information. One can look at a current news item or article, not realizing that it is quoting old reports, or that new and encouraging developments are missing. For example, as late as November 20, 1998, Don McAlvany was still quoting gloomy and obsolete estimates six and seven months old from IRS Commissioner Charles Rossotti, Edward Yardeni, Steve Forbes, Senator Robert Bennett, and others. Yet in citing outdated material he repeatedly uses the term "recently."

Even someone as well informed as Chuck Missler can fall victim to this problem. On the Dobson panel, Missler referred to "the head of General Motors who said if tomorrow is the first of January of the year 2000, General Motors would not be able to build one car for a year." That information came from an April 1998 *Fortune* magazine. However, when Steve Hewitt consulted the article, he discovered that the author had used old information. In fact, a June 1998 article in *Computer World* indicated that GM was doing very well on Y2K and expected to be in good shape when the year 2000 arrived.[29]

In contrast to outdated pronouncements of doom, there are increasing numbers of encouraging developments that deserve to be publicized in order to prevent the panic based upon false information which we believe is the greatest danger—and a very real one. Hewitt often reminds us that "reports continue to come in stating that we are getting closer to solving the Y2K problem."[30] Here are some recent encouraging developments:

> A special report by the Gartner Group [who previously had been very negative] dated October 7, 1998...states: "Embedded systems will have limited effect on Year 2000 problems, and we will see a minimal number of failures

from these devices. Only 1 in 100,000 free-standing micro-controller chips is likely to fail due to Year 2000...and of those that fail, the majority will fail right at the millennium, and the majority of these will only fail once—if they are active when the clock ticks over."

How valid is this recent report? In Michael Hyatt's book, *The Millennium Bug: How to Survive the Coming Chaos,* he states on page 12, "The Gartner Group, which is arguably the most respected and highly quoted Y2K research company in the world..."

CMPNET reported, October 7, 1998: "Lifesaving equipment in major metropolitan hospitals will continue to work when 2000 rolls around, the CEO of a Washington, D.C. hospital said Tuesday." Philip Schaengold, George Washington University Hospital CEO, went on to state, "I don't think any patient should go into the hospital Dec. 31, 1999, worried about medical devices working...."

[In mid-1998], Chicago Federal Reserve Bank President, Michael Moskow, stated, "The Year 2000 computer problem will have a mild impact on the U.S. economy and cause the nation's businesses a modest loss of productivity for reprogramming.[31]

The Federal Reserve's electronic funds transfer network, known as FedWire, appears to be in "good shape" for making the transition to Year 2000, according to Carl Gambs, head of the Fed's Century Date Change Project. Mr. Gambs said tests of FedWire since June have revealed "no Y2K problems."[32]

Searching for the Truth

One need not listen to many speakers or read many books on the subject of Y2K to detect an underlying bias toward pessimism. Disaster is far more exciting and sells many more books and newsletters, to say nothing of survival food and supplies, than a calm and factual appraisal. Assurance that the year 2000 will dawn without any serious problems would dampen sales of books, freeze-dried foods, and emergency supplies.

A statement by some responsible representative of a power plant, large business, or government department that they face very difficult problems with Y2K (which admittedly most of them do) is almost invariably interpreted to mean that the problem is insurmountable and will remain so. The truth is that someone in a responsible position is making a clear declaration of the difficulty of the Y2K problem in order to identify it as needing immediate attention. That it could and even will be solved, however, is not allowed to soften the rhetoric of the doomsayers.

We have carefully checked the realistic potential of Y2K for disruption from every possible angle and from many authoritative sources. In so doing, we have been unable to justify the sense of disaster that is being portrayed. If this problem had suddenly come upon us without any warning, perhaps the predicted chaos might make some sense. Surprise, however, is not the case. Many companies have been working on the Y2K problem for five or more years, Bank of America and some other banks for more than 20 years.

In contrast to the great concern being expressed by many Christian leaders (Pat Robertson recently did a gloomy one-hour special on Y2K), there is little concern among knowledgeable business leaders. One of the top computer experts whom we interviewed at the end of November 1998, commented:

> I deal with seven to ten IT [Information Technology] managers of major corporations each week and always ask them about Y2K. I have never found even *one* that was worried. Everyone I deal with feels they have finished, they've done what they needed to do, and Y2K is now history. Actually, they haven't found that much to deal with.[33]

Based upon the information we have discovered in our investigation, it is inconceivable that airlines, banks, large grocery chains, public power companies, and others who have known of this problem for years and are in business for a profit will allow themselves to lose any customers because of Y2K. They have reputations to maintain; customer relations are of the utmost importance. Nor is it conceivable that county, state, and federal governments will shut down because of a computer problem. As for foreign countries being caught by surprise, the level of awareness worldwide is high and increasing.

In mid-1998 BBC ran a special about Y2K that exceeded in quality and information anything we have seen to date on American TV. The Organization of Economic Cooperation and Development (OECD), in conjunction with the World Bank, is holding Global Year 2000 Summit conferences to keep responsible leaders in all nations informed. Both organizations are monitoring progress worldwide. Furthermore, American multinational companies are keeping their customers and suppliers in foreign countries apprised of Y2K and are assisting them in becoming compliant. For example, Hewlett-Packard (HP), with 29,000 products and 1997 fiscal year revenues of nearly $43 billion, derives more than 56 percent of its business from outside the United States including not only Europe but Japan, Australasia, the Far East, and Latin America. As we document elsewhere, HP offers to its customers a complete list of its products, identifies those with Y2K problems, and provides the necessary assistance, some of it by phone, to make everything ready for the year 2000.[34]

We mentioned that all of the alarmists agree that the matter of embedded chips is the biggest problem we face. However, "Steve Rosenstock of the Edison Electric Institute, which represents America's publicly owned utilities," says that "the chances are very slim that [an embedded chip] would shut down the system."[35] The alarmists speak as though it would take forever to go line by line through billions of lines of computer code, or to locate every embedded chip and test it to see whether it was date sensitive, and if so, whether it was Y2K compliant. Somehow, they fail to mention the new developments which are constantly making it easier to conquer Y2K difficulties, including the locating of embedded chips. For example, Tava Technologies of Englewood, Colorado, has developed a tool "for automatically finding year 2000 errors in manufacturing's embedded systems."[36]

In bringing its secret-message handling system up to Y2K standards, Boeing reported that it "ran a tool called 'Y2K Sniff,'" which is able to quickly "identify areas with a date or time component."[37] That eliminated the necessity the alarmists repeatedly stress of examining every chip or every line of code. In fact, a plethora of new technology is becoming available to speed up the process of identifying those areas that will pose problems in the year 2000 and making them Y2K compliant. On the Dobson radio panel, Steve Hewitt declared:

> There's two reasons why I think we are doing well. Six months ago you talked about how much code the Social Security has to do; but then you look at a new program that Citibank is using, for example, just three months ago, that they're saying now does 30 days of work in one day. And that's continuing [i.e., such developments]. Oracle's now coming out with new software that's 100 times faster than that....
>
> The second reason...[is] what we are discovering in the time factor, Dr. Dobson. Companies that are only 25 percent into the embedded chip and into the studies...are starting to discover that the damage here is not that bad.[38]

Dr. Dobson responded, "Every one of your colleagues here, Steve, are shaking their heads. They obviously disagree with you."[39] It is not easy to change with changing developments when one has publicly and repeatedly announced that Y2K will bring dreadful disaster upon us. In his magazine, Hewitt provides some useful insights for evaluating what is being said:

> As we draw closer and closer to the year 2000, the estimation of the effects of Y2K on our society has begun to be more positive. Yet most of those [Christians] that originally started their "cry of danger" have refused to change their tune. Why? I believe there are several reasons.
>
> First, some think that we have made a god of technology, and they love the thought of it all failing. Second, some think that Y2K is a punishment from God, and America and the world are in moral decay and therefore we NEED Y2K. Third, others feel that even if Y2K is a non-event, they did a good thing by scaring Christians into storing up food and water for other potential disasters. Fourth, some actually refuse to believe the good reports because they hold to a conspiracy theory that the government is going to use Y2K to declare martial law and do away with elections. And finally, there are some that believe Y2K is a "sign of the time" and believe that somehow Y2K will bring about the second coming of Christ.[40]

Y2K Has Become Big Business

Sounding the Y2K alarm can be very profitable, depending upon what one has to sell. There is money to be made in Y2K, big money, and it is attracting opportunists. The crisis coming upon us provides a once-in-a-millennium opportunity for selling newsletters and books, and some of the promotion is blatant. For example, Jim Lord, favorably mentioned on the Dobson program and highly regarded in Christian circles, runs this ad:

WHO CAN SHOW YOU HOW TO GET READY FOR THIS MESS?

His name is Jim Lord. He is a technical profes-
sional who, for thirty-nine years operated, maintained and designed complex military electronics
systems....Currently he is a full-time writer, speaker
and analyst of the *Year 2000 Computer problem*....
With the way this crisis is developing, don't you think
you should be calling on Jim Lord for his expertise?[41]

While Lord's motives may be good (desiring to pass on
a warning which he sincerely believes everyone ought to
heed), the above has all the earmarks of a hard-sell promotion. We have a genuine concern that, in their desire to make
money out of Y2K, entrepreneurs could engage in such
aggressive advertising to promote their products that panic
could be created, including runs on banks, possibly putting
some out of business, and even disrupting the entire
banking system. Steve Hewitt writes:

As if the situation were not bad enough already, many
individuals have deduced that Y2K can help them get rich!
People are trying to sell emergency survival food and Y2K
books covering everything from growing your own medicines (because all of the pharmacies will close) to how-to-
books on growing your own Y2K garden. People are even
selling real estate based on the Y2K panic. (You can lease a
half-acre lot for $10,000 in "Heritage Farms 2000," a self-suf-
ficient Y2K village in South Dakota....)
I have been reading scare tactics warning of everything
from our nuclear missiles taking off by themselves, to suggestions that Russia's nuclear power plants are going to melt
down.[42]

It was inevitable, of course, that Y2K would be exploited
for personal gain. Many alarmists are making money from
their gloomy Y2K predictions. The worse it sounds, the more
books and tapes and newsletters they sell. In most cases they
probably have the best of motives, desiring to inform as

many people as possible of what they consider to be a genuine danger and to offer helpful advice. Yet the sales pitch inevitably becomes an almost integral part of many warnings. Somehow, it just "happened" by apparent accident that someone showed up in a small Oregon town at a ministerial association meeting involving Y2K—someone known to the invited outside speaker—who was selling freeze-dried foods, glass jars for water storage, and other items that would be needed in a Y2K crunch. What a fortunate coincidence!

Indisputably, Y2K has become big business. Larry Burkett reported on his weekly e-mail in November 1998,

> At least a portion of the American public isn't taking Y2K lying down. *Wired* magazine reported that companies specializing in bulk foods, generators, and solar cells are doing a booming business, as people prepare for possible Year 2000 disruptions in food supplies and power availability. "Orders are up 1,000 percent since the first of the year," said Loren Day, president of China Diesel Imports, a generator dealer. Meanwhile, at Walton Feed, one of the nation's largest bulk food suppliers, demand is so heavy that orders placed now won't be delivered for six months. "It's not just survivalist-types who are stocking up on Y2K supplies," said Steve Portela of Walton Feed. "It's common everyday folks."[43]

A new canning factory was started in 1998 in Bozeman, Montana, specifically to supply Y2K special survival foods. Countless websites on the Internet warn of Y2K and offer recommended products that, according to these entrepreneurs, one needs for weathering the coming storm. Magazines have sprung up which specialize in this whole concern. The ad for *Quit You Like Men* magazine reads, "Y2K: Our subscribers worry less."[44] *Y2K News Magazine* claims to be "the world's leading bi-weekly magazine & information source for the Year 2000 computer problem," according to an ad in

Jerry Falwell's *National Liberty Journal.* The ad declares, "Noah built the ark. People scoffed. Today experts and church leaders tell us Y2K will be devastating to our way of life….[To] subscribe call toll free 1-888-Y2K NEWS."[45]

The same issue of the *Journal* contained an ad for "Y2K Solutions" of various kinds, urging readers to "Order Your Emergency Food Supply Today!" For $85 one could purchase "The Countdown to Chaos, a six [audio] tape series and preparedness manual."[46] Ads for *The Millennial Bug* by Michael Hyatt, one of the Dobson-invited panelists, include what may be intended as helpful urging but (like Jim Lord's and so many other ads) comes across as an opportunistic hard sell:

> The Year 2000 crisis is approaching fast. If you want to protect yourself and your family, it's crucial that you get *The Millennial Bug Personal Survival Kit* as soon as possible. Don't delay. To order, send your check or credit card information (VISA, Master-Card, Amex) payable to: Y2KPrep, 251 Second Avenue, South, Franklin, TN 37064.
>
> Or, for faster service, phone your order by calling toll free 1-888-Y2K-PREP (1-888-925-7737). *Remember, it's better to be safe than sorry!*[47]

While we can't argue with the old adage "better safe than sorry," the question is, how safe do you want to be? Safe for a few days? A few weeks? A few months? Or even years? How much food and water can you store, or even afford? How much money will you take out of the bank?

The question is not only *how safe* but *safe from what?* What is the realistic threat for which one should prepare? Is it true that the only safe place will be on a self-sustaining property in the country far from a city of any size?

Year 2000 is an annoyance, a speed bump. We're overassessing the end-of-the-world aspect of the Year 2000 problem.

> —Tony Hampel, group manager for Year 2000
> Marketing, Sun Microsystems Inc.[1]

We view Y2K as a tremor, not a quake....Economies are resilient and can adjust quickly to temporary shocks, especially when such shocks are anticipated, as is the case with Y2K.

> —Alex Patelis, economist, in an analysis for Goldman
> Sachs, investment bankers[2]

The impact would be similar to the economic effects of a snowstorm.

> —Rick Egelton, economist,
> Harris Bank/Bank of Montreal[3]

FAA administrator Jane Garvey, insisting the organization will be ready, recently announced plans to fly across the country shortly after midnight January 1, 2000. Boeing and Airbus say their aircraft have no Year 2000 safety issues.

> —William G. Phillips, in *Popular Science*[4]

When it comes to the fizzle factor—the degree to which an expected event fails to live up to its hype—the "millennium bug" (aka Y2K) will prove to be the standard against which all other overhype is measured. Not for 1,000 years or so has so much dread been provoked, and so much money made, in preparation for something that will amount to so little.

> —Fred Moody, *ABC News* commentary[5]

Y2K preparedness is becoming a hot topic in the mainstream press. However, I suggest you DO IT rather than just talk about it. Before long there will be so many people trying to prepare that prices are likely to rise and availability will become an issue.

Prepare early and beat the rush. By waiting until the last minute, you become part of the problem. By preparing now, you are part of the solution.

> —The Y2K Weatherman[6]

CHAPTER FOUR

A Calm Appraisal

The quotations on the facing page, as well as many others we have given in previous chapters, show that the experts are by no means in agreement concerning Y2K. Many who are knowledgeable in computers and business are confident that the gloomy predictions about Y2K will prove to be a false alarm. On the other hand, there are many others (by far the majority within the Christian community) equally qualified, who are just as convinced and are sincerely warning, based upon the information they have, that the greatest disaster in history is about to descend upon us. We could go on quoting experts on both sides, but it would prove nothing.

What we need to do is to take a deep breath, calm down, and think logically based upon the information we have. Too many people let emotion rather than reason rule their thinking. Many Christian leaders writing and speaking on this subject are convinced that the computers upon which our world has become dependent, and in which we have put our trust, are about to fail. It seems to them to make such good sense. That belief, however, rather than facts or logic, becomes the lens through which they view Y2K.

The evil of our world is cited to show that God's judgment ought to fall—and indeed, it should. But the world has been evil for its entire history, and God is "longsuffering..., not willing that any should perish, but that all should come to repentance" (2 Peter 3:9). God inspired Peter to write those words for us "in the last days" (verse 3) to explain why judgment hasn't yet fallen. Okay. But today's evil is so great that it cries to heaven for God to pour out His wrath. That is true, and God surely will pour out His wrath upon this world. The Bible makes that clear, but in this author's opinion the time for the outpouring of God's wrath, beginning in Revelation 6, has not yet come. Y2K seems so made-to-order that many are swayed on that basis to believe that Y2K will turn out to be a major way in which God will judge our wicked world, rather than what the Bible teaches.

Is Y2K God's Fitting Justice?

That Y2K should be the means of bringing about God's judgment upon mankind seems fitting, indeed, for those expecting it. Surely this would be poetic justice to the max. Computers have created a new world of conveniences and luxury unimaginable to past generations. That these same computers would turn out to be our downfall could not be more appropriate. We have made a god of technology. What greater justice, then, could there be than for this god to fail us and indeed to bring us down with it?

In fact, the poetic justice seems too neat, too apropos to be believable. Richard Landes, professor of medieval history at Boston University and director of the Center for Millennial Studies, agrees with our appraisal. Landes suggests similarities between what he calls "millennial behavior" brought on by the approach of the year 2000 and that which occurred at the end of the first millennium. Then the expectation was for the end of that world and the Last Judgment; now the expectation is for a great crashing of the very technology that has built our world and in which we trust. Author Fred Moody argues the same point in an *ABC News* commentary:

The thing that has always bothered me about the various Y2K doomsday scenarios—ranging from massive nationwide power failures to the collapse of world financial markets and, eventually, worldwide famine and widespread death—is that it has always been too perfect a bug for our times. It is too apt a symbol to be real, too ingenious and appropriate an end to 20th century civilization to be credible.

The notion that the world will end because of a careless bit of programming of computing machines—machines, moreover, that have become the 20th century's false gods—is something that belongs in the realm of fiction or art rather than reality or science.

It is, in other words, too good to be true.[7]

The question whether Y2K might be God's judgment upon America came up during the panel discussion James Dobson hosted in October 1998. Steve Hewitt said that when he voiced that possibility in his magazine, he received "Email from Korea and from Australia and from around the world saying, 'Look, Y2K is a worldwide problem. If you think USA deserves its hand slapped by God, don't take us down with you, we don't think our country deserves that.'"[8] Hewitt commented:

It's a good point. Y2K, if it is the judgment of God, it's an unusual way for God. The walls of Jericho didn't fall down because 25 years ago they used the wrong kind of straw with the wrong kind of clay..., it wasn't a technological blooper....It would be an unusual way for God to work..., it wouldn't be only to slap America but to slap the world....It's not just this nation that deserves to be slapped.[9]

There are a number of reasons why Y2K, even if it happens, could not be God's judgment. Obviously, we refer to the catastrophic disaster predicted by North, Gregori,

Yourdon, and others. If Y2K doesn't turn out to be a disaster of that magnitude but merely causes some serious but manageable disruptions, it would not be severe enough to be called *judgment from God*. It is our considered opinion that the results of Y2K will be disruptive and annoying but fairly mild. But even should it become a worldwide catastrophe, it still would not be a judgment from God. We will develop that argument from the Bible in Chapter 6.

Is the Situation Actually Worsening?

Judgment from God or not, some of the supposed experts are convinced that the situation is worsening, not getting better. One reason for the continued pessimism is that problems continue to surface even after an organization thinks it has fixed everything and is finally Y2K compliant. The Y2K Weatherman has pointed out, "As more and more companies start bringing their new 'Y2K compliant' systems on line, screw ups...may become more common. It is a good sign that we're making progress, but as millions of software systems all over the world are hastily converted and slammed into real world 'production' environments, I expect to see a lot more problems....It will not be a smooth transition."[10]

An October 1998 conference sponsored by the Center for Strategic and International Studies was titled "Y2K: An International Perspective." One of the speakers, Ed Yardeni, voted the top economic forecaster of 1997 by *The Wall Street Journal*, made this disheartening statement: "Based on what I heard today it seems to me that, clearly, the [Y2K] situation is not improving, and it's just as clear that...we're going to go into this thing largely blind."[11]

We certainly do not have the credentials to match Yardeni's, but one wonders how he could possibly say we are going into this "largely blind." In fact, we know precisely what the problem is and what the solution is; many organizations and even government departments have been working on this

for years, knowing exactly what they have to do to fix it—
and many are already Y2K compliant. Gary North, also, is
not backing down from his earlier predictions. His electronic
mail in October 1998 had this to say:

A BILLION LIVES LOST IF THINGS GO FAIRLY WELL

I have been unable to persuade the vast majority
of my readers, after almost two years, that if the division of labor collapses, we will lose millions of lives.
Joe Boivin, who was the Y2K director for Canada's
Imperial Bank and Commerce until he quit, estimates that a billion people will die in 2000. He limits
his discussion to the third world. I think we could
lose half a billion in the urban West.

Unthinkable? All right, show me how any large
city will survive if the power goes off for 60 days, all
railroad deliveries of grain and coal stop, all gasoline station pumps shut down, and there are no
banks. Go on. I'm serious. Sit down and outline a
scenario that will keep an urban population alive
without mainframe computers.[12]

Liability for Failure to Provide

We're trying to take a calm and reasonable approach to
Y2K. Utilities providing electricity have an obligation to do
so and would be liable for failure to fulfill that obligation.
This is a powerful incentive. No provider of electricity could
afford not to be fully Y2K compliant on January 1, 2000.
They would be out of business. There are attorneys licking
their lips right now and hoping for plenty of action—and
the lawsuits would bankrupt any company that failed the Y2K
test. "Everybody is going to sue and be sued," said consultant
Joel Ackerman at a November 1998 conference on millennial planning for hospital managers in Orange, California.[13]
As one report has put it:

In a litigious world, it's hardly a shock that lawyers and their clients have begun climbing all over the year 2000 bug....The big explosion of shareholder and insurance-related claims—so-called Y2K lawsuits—is probably more than a year away, but lawyers are already busy.

Lou Marcoccio, a year 2000 research director at the Gartner Group who keeps tabs on about 375 law firms around the country, already knows of 183 disputes attorneys have managed to settle without filing suits. "They were all customer–vendor situations," he says. "There's a lot of animosity developing against large computer and software companies over this."[14]

Interestingly, because the year 2000 hasn't yet come, none of these settlements involved a Y2K problem that had actually occurred. The plaintiffs were objecting to paying anything either to have their software upgraded or to purchase new software or equipment. They knew that with what they had, they would face serious problems January 1, 2000. Therefore, they argued that the need to upgrade either software or equipment constituted a "latent defect" existing at the time of purchase and ought to be covered by warranty.

We can't possibly know every state law that may mitigate damages for providers of certain services. But in the case of gross negligence and dereliction of duty there is an implied obligation that cannot be escaped. No legislation should be allowed to exempt a utility or the government itself from such a failure. Every state has common-law negligence laws, under which if a person or a company acts unreasonably in the circumstance, it can be liable for damages. That includes a public utility providing electrical power.

Y2K is not something which arises suddenly on January 1, 2000, and catches everyone by surprise. This problem has been known for at least 25 years. With that much advanced warning, any utility failing to make Y2K repairs would be liable for damages, depending upon the harm that resulted.

If failure to provide a service, such as electric power, is due to a natural disaster over which a provider has no control, then, of course, there is no obligation on its part—unless its negligence contributed to the disaster or it failed to use due diligence in mitigating the damage and restoring the service. In the case of Y2K, there have been at least 20 years of advanced notice, including the fact that the task *must* be completed by January 1, 2000. It would be gross negligence not to finish the task in time, with people dying as a result for lack of heat in the dead of winter, or for lack of food and water because there was no power to pump water, or to preserve food, or to operate switches on railroads; and on and on it goes.

No insurance companies, not even Lloyds of London, offer Y2K insurance. The reason is obvious: the only way a liability could arise would be due to gross negligence on the part of the provider. Who is going to insure someone for that! As Nicholas Zvegintzov, cofounder of Software Maintenance News, Inc., and technical editor of *Software Management Technology Reference Guide* (whom we have already quoted), said way back in early 1996: "Dealing with the Year 2000 problem is a simple software task....The corrective action to be taken is straightforward...an exercise for the software novice....If an organization cannot handle the Year 2000 problem...avoid it!"[15]

Thus we may be certain that when January 1, 2000, arrives, no utilities, banks, or any other providers are going to fail to provide the services they are obligated to provide. And surely they would not lie about their preparedness, for that would increase their liability. Yet one of the statements one hears repeatedly from alarmists is that employees of utilities or banks or other service providers are told to lie by saying that they are fixing the Y2K problem and will be ready for the year 2000, when in fact they are not going to be ready in time. That rumor not only impugns the integrity of those whose livelihood literally depends upon their reputation and reliability, but it makes no sense.

However, some corporations have been petitioning the federal government to enact a new law that would largely exempt them from liability. We can understand the fear involved, but it would not be fair for the government to enact a law that would relieve anyone of the obligation to be Y2K compliant. As of the publication of this book, that issue was up in the air and we can only hope that it will be resolved in a just manner. One reliable source stated:

> "Because of fear of litigation, many companies are afraid of sharing information" about their readiness, says Harris Miller, president of the Information Technology Association of America. President Clinton agrees, and plans to send a bill to Congress this week designed to get companies to reveal how Y2K-OK their computers are, in exchange for partial protection from lawsuits. "The maker of any such statement shall not be liable" for it if the company made an effort to tell the truth, a draft obtained by *Time* says.
>
> But skeptics argue this lets businesses off the hook. "It's an invitation for sellers to tell their customers a product is Year 2000 compliant when it isn't," says David Friedman, professor of law and economics at Santa Clara University.[16]

Electric Power the Key—What About It?

Electricity is indeed the most important part of the picture. Without power even computer systems which have been made compliant won't function. In our modern world, almost nothing works without electricity. If all power is off for 60 days throughout the entire world, we would have a disaster of the proportions Gary North describes. But this is an extreme view which is contrary to everything this author has been able to learn through contact with those in charge of implementing Y2K compliance at the major power suppliers. We have not found anyone of any responsibility in that industry who even suggests that there will be any substantial disruption of electricity or gas or water.

In complete contrast to North's assertions, for example, is the notice sent out in November 1998 by Central Electric Cooperative (CEC), which supplies power to central Oregon. Bear in mind, as we have just noted, that (except due to a natural disaster or "an act of God" beyond its control) failure of any utility to supply its customers with power due to its own negligence would open it to lawsuits claiming damages of astronomical proportions. Failure to become Y2K compliant on time would be gross negligence, leaving any public company clearly culpable. Furthermore, to tell customers that all is well, as the following notice did, and then to fail to provide the promised service after customers have reasonably relied upon that promise, would greatly increase the damages. Yet here was the notice:

WHAT WILL HAPPEN IN 2000

Dear Member,

We have received several calls and letters from members who are worried about what might happen to their electricity service on January 1, 2000. This is widely known as the "Y2K" problem.

Many people have speculated that at midnight on January 1, 2000, some computerized equipment might not function properly because it won't be able to distinguish between "00" as in 1900 and "00" as in 2000.

I want to assure you nearly all our computer software is Y2K compliant—and when we install new software next year, all of it will be. Furthermore, most of our main transmission/distribution equipment does not rely on computers. Nevertheless, our Corporate Information Officer has been reviewing our entire system to ensure we are in no way vulnerable to any problem stemming from Y2K.

Another question we receive is, "Will the Bonneville Power Administration (BPA) be Y2K compliant?" [BPA supplies power to CEC.]

The BPA—from which we buy most of our electricity— is out in front of the Y2K problem, having been working on it for the last two years. The BPA has devoted a significant amount of manpower and money to making sure its system runs properly when the year 2000 arrives.

The BPA is now testing all its critical equipment and expects to finish the process by July of 1999. In addition, it is developing elaborate contingency plans, allowing for possible component failure, while ensuring reliability can be maintained. It is also developing a comprehensive emergency plan, just in case of trouble, and plans to have a host of additional operations personnel on hand when the clock strikes "12" on January 1, 2000.

In September, the BPA project manager for Y2K compliance said, "We've examined about 40 percent of our system and we've only found a handful of things. None of them would have taken the system down, but we do have to be careful. On a scale of 1 to 10, we're treating the Y2K problem as a 10. But we're expecting that when we get to 2000, it will be a 1."

It's a long time between now and January 1, 2000. We will keep you informed of our progress on this issue in the coming year.

(Signed)
Al Gonzalez
President[17]

National and International Power Grid Failure?

Anyone seeking factual information may simply access the Internet for the major power company supplying their area. For example, the Bonneville Power Administration (BPA) in charge of the system providing electrical power for the Northwest and much of the West Coast can be reached at [http://www.bpa.gov/Corporate/CI/Y2K/Y2K.html].

BPA's summary sheet in October 1998 stated:

> No one can predict what will happen with 100 percent certainty. But we are taking action to help the Northwest's electric power system make a smooth transition into the 21st century....
>
> BPA's transmission system connects to many utilities' networks, so the computer systems of other utilities are also of a concern to BPA. We will be working with our customers and suppliers...to provide for reliability at our interconnection points....
>
> We are putting Y2K contingency plans into place in case any system fails. Even though we are taking action to provide for power system reliability on January 1, 2000, we expect to have some problems and will alter operations if necessary.[18]

The website of any of the major power companies provides an almost inexhaustible list of articles, briefings, and newsletters on the subject of Y2K, revealing the fact that power companies are not only well aware of the problem but have been working on it *together in a cooperative effort* for years and are determined that there will be no interruption to the power they supply. This information is available to anyone who wants to take the time to access it.

In contrast to the predictions of power blackouts of not just days but weeks and even months, the suppliers of electrical power assure us that they have the situation well in hand. It makes no more sense to imagine that they are lying than it does to think they would subject themselves to the lawsuits and economic disaster of failing even for days, much less for weeks and months, to provide uninterrupted service. Here are a few representative statements to show what the major electric utilities have been saying and doing about Y2K:

COM/Electric Is Readying for Year 2000

COM/Electric shares your concern about the Year 2000 computer bug and we want to assure you that our business plan calls for a seamless transition into the next century.

COM/Electric has been working on Year 2000 compliance since 1996....While some of our systems have already been updated, tested and put into operation, we expect to complete the balance of the renovations during 1998 and early 1999.

We've also requested Year 2000 compliance verification from all vendors doing business with us. Our purchase orders and contracts now clearly state the requirement of Year 2000 compliance.

COM/Electric is confident that we will be fully compliant regarding all Year 2000 issues and will continue to provide uninterrupted electricity and related services through the millennium change.[19]

Facts: Western Power Administration, Year 2000

The Western Area Power Administration is concerned about the approaching Year 2000 century rollover and its potential impact on our operations and business functions.

To ensure that we will continue to serve our customers without disruption, Western is engaged in a project to address potential date problems in all our systems, software, hardware, and other equipment....

Western knows that much work remains to be done. We must get our key replacement systems installed on schedule and we need to conduct validation testing. Year 2000 problems are complex and widespread....However, Western is taking appropriate steps to address concerns and ensure that we continue to provide power and services to our customers.

For additional information, please contact Don Nord, Year 2000 Project Manager, at (303) 275-1466 or [nord@wapa.gov].[20]

NATIONAL POWER PLC–UNITED KINGDOM
YEAR 2000

The Company has a project designed to ensure that the universal problem of the date change to the year 2000 in computer systems is resolved without material impact on its operations. The project...includes not only National Power's own information technology and plant control systems but also suppliers, customers and other external contacts of the Company. It covers the UK and overseas....The project is well advanced in identifying the problems and in taking positive steps to implement solutions for critical systems, where possible, by the end of 1998, and others in the following year....Appropriate management control is being exercised at a senior level to ensure risks are mitigated and that resources are available to deal with any issues that might arise in the new millennium.[21]

In order to maintain their high level of concern, those who are loudly sounding the alarm view such statements by major providers of electricity with skepticism. In fact, they come right out and say the utilities are lying. For reasons already given, that is unthinkable.

Early in 1998 there was a U.S. Senate hearing on the impact of the year 2000 computer bug on American utilities. The committee warned that "power shortages were a possibility in the new Millennium, not only because of utilities' lack of preparedness but the fact that few had any idea whether their supply chain partners were compliant either." This pessimistic appraisal prevailed in spite of the fact that, as the committee acknowledged, "All of the utilities contacted or testifying said they would be ready in time."[22]

At the same Senate hearing just mentioned, Shirley Jackson, chairwoman of the U.S. Government Nuclear Power Commission, testified that "nuclear power stations would be required to report their progress in August [1998]" and she "did not expect the Year 2000 code problem to impact on their safe operation."[23] Nevertheless, in the face of such assurances and the vast amount of information on the Internet, the predictions of disastrous interruptions in the nation's power supply continue to pour forth from the supposed experts.

The speaker already referred to at the ministerial association meeting in Oregon claimed to have a Christian "deep throat" contact right next to the Y2K manager for a major electric utility, who told him that he was personally "heading for the hills" before January 1, 2000. This author checked with the person responsible for implementing Y2K preparations in that large utility and the replies he received on the record to specific questions contradicted "deep throat."

Jared Wermiel, chief of the controls branch at the Nuclear Regulatory Commission, states that "most nuclear reactors aren't even operated by computer."[24] Pacific Gas & Electric, one of California's largest utilities, has been working on Y2K for three years. John Greer, manager of computer systems for PG&E, declared that it would finish its preparations by the end of 1998. That is not what the alarmists want to hear. Said Greer:

> We had a magazine call us, and they were milking us to tell them that everything would turn black. But it's not going to happen. Our automated systems tell power plants to come on or off to meet demand. All of that is based on monitoring physical conditions— current, voltage and frequency. They're not looking at what day of the year it is.[25]

Searching for the Truth

The disastrous consequences of Y2K have always been and continue to be overstated. Let us logically and factually consider the multibillions of embedded chips out there. The vast majority of them are in toasters, watches, VCRs, TVs, ovens, air conditioning units, elevators, automobiles, trucks, and other similar places where, even if they all did something weird or froze on January 1, 2000, it would not be the end of the world. Yes, there are millions of them in strategic places, but think about that for a moment.

The warnings of what *could* or possibly *might* happen are everywhere. But as one computer expert who designs complex military systems and writes the software for them remarked, "I have yet to see or hear a specific example of any Y2K computer glitch that would cause a major breakdown in any system."[26]

The fact that the large international banks and multinational corporations are spending millions, and collectively billions, of dollars on Y2K is often cited as proof that they will never make it. We find such reasoning fallacious. These corporations and their senior officers didn't get where they are today by incompetence. The very fact that they are spending these vast sums can be taken as evidence that they intend to complete the job and remain in business.

The latest budget approved by Congress in October 1998 includes $1.1 billion earmarked for the Department of Defense's Y2K compliance efforts. One may be certain that not all of that vast sum will be spent on repairs to existing systems. It will also purchase new software and hardware to replace noncompliant systems. Furthermore, most of what is being fixed or replaced would not have caused a critical problem had it been left untouched.

The fact is that almost no embedded systems are going to care what year it is. The year and century matters primarily for those involved in processes by banks, mortgage companies, insurance companies, the Social Security Administration, or anywhere else where time is measured from a fixed date on the calendar. Even in these cases, however, the sudden appearance of 00 which is either unrecognized or mistakenly taken to mean 1900 is not going to shut the system down. It may confuse the system and alert operators that something is wrong, but it isn't going to freeze up in most cases. This, then, is a problem to be solved on the spot at the time by those operating the computers. It will be an inconvenience because of down time, but it will not be insurmountable or persist indefinitely, as we are being told by alarmists.

Remember, whatever reaction there is to 00, it must have been programmed into the software, either intentionally or by error. In speaking with those involved in designing sophisticated systems and writing and installing their own software, this author has encountered incredulity at the very thought that some programmer would have designed a system that would shut down and refuse to function because it didn't recognize two zeros. "That's incredibly bad engineering," we've been told repeatedly! In fact, one top designer and programmer said in frustration,

> The very idea of this problem being called Y2K elevates it to a place of special importance which it doesn't deserve. It really has nothing to do with the arrival of the year 2000. It is really just a case of inept software design—and of a level of incompetence which no competent engineer would ever allow.
>
> There is an unbelievable amount of intense scrutiny at every level of the design process, You don't build a shutdown into a system unless there is a very good reason, and two zeros showing up just don't qualify for something that drastic.
>
> The alarmists offer vague descriptions in slightly off-the-mark terminology, leading any knowledgeable person to conclude that they don't know what they're talking about. They never give you the specifics. This is physical hardware running and there has to be an explanation for what it does.
>
> In all examples I've heard, they speak in general terms of what might happen *if.* But I have heard almost nothing in the way of a specific example of why power plants should shut down and airplanes fall out of the sky because two zeros show up. I'd love to hear an explicit rundown from start to finish in a particular instance.

As for the Alaska pipeline, for example, it should be a simple thing to go to the construction company and find out what they have in the pipes. It won't do any good to run along the pipeline and look at what's out there, you wouldn't be able to tell anything. It is all on the engineering drawings filed away—they would tell you what, if anything, needs to be done, and then you could send out crews to do it, if necessary.

Most of these people sounding the alarm sound as though they've never been involved in the design process and don't understand anything about it.[27]

A Grossly Overstated Problem

After spending years searching for and correcting Y2K problems, many companies have yet to encounter a Y2K-related situation which, had it not been corrected, would have shut them down on January 1, 2000. For all the general talk about computers crashing, one is hard pressed to find anyone who can give a specific example of a Y2K-related problem that would cause more than a minor irritation. Furthermore, while solid evidence for specific causes of future catastrophe can scarcely be found, evidence is increasingly coming to light that points in the other direction.

The man in charge of implementing Y2K at one of the largest suppliers of electric power in North America personally explained the situation as follows in answer to specific questions from this author:

> 1. Y2K is a huge economic issue. No commercial enterprise can afford to be shut down and thereby interrupt its business and miss essential income, let down customers, etc. It just won't happen!
>
> 2. It is also a huge legal issue around the world. No company of any substance is going to play around with it. The liability for failure to deliver power [or other services, in the case of banks, etc.] to customers could put a company

out of business. Most insurance companies will not insure for Y2K.

3. All power companies are working together among themselves as well as with their suppliers and customers to be certain that everyone will be compliant. This is expected to be completed by March 31, 1999.

4. They have been working on this for years, testing and searching for anything that could possibly go wrong.

5. So far they have found a few minor Y2K problems, but *nothing* that could have shut the system down had they not found it.

6. No one can guarantee that all possible problems have been uncovered; but nothing that may be overlooked could shut the system down. The system is designed to survive random failures. In fact, failures periodically occur, causing short-term disruptions, such as from lightning.

7. The power companies continually make tests to be certain they can operate in any eventuality. They have sophisticated backup and contingency plans for anything, including whatever failures may occur through Y2K computer problems, if any, that haven't been discovered and corrected by 1/1/2000.[28]

Other misinformation is being passed along. Jack Anderson told his audience:

> The last part of the problem, of course, is the connectivity. Because although you may spend a lot of time and money getting your own computers and your business completely Y2K compliant, the fact that you're connected to a whole lot of other folks may result in somebody else having an embedded chip or bad software and having information get into your computer that would shut you down. Or maybe it's worse than that; maybe it wouldn't shut it down, maybe it would just keep feeding you erroneous data and you have no way of knowing it's erroneous data.[29]

Again, while his trusting audience believed that statement because he was the specially invited expert who knew what they didn't, the principal simply isn't true. Data coming into a computer isn't going to shut it down. Data is data. An essential part of Y2K compliancy includes a program for checking all incoming data to make certain it is also compliant, and if not, to reject it. No properly designed program is going to accept false data.

And why would noncompliant software produce corrupt data? Embedded systems are not run by magic, but by software telling the chip what to do. Who would instruct the software to have a chip shut down the system it is monitoring, or start producing wrong data? And *why?* Because of date? That would be unbelievably bad engineering! Consider the following assurance from Boeing:

> Boeing has surveyed its commercial airplane fleet and identified some nuisance flight deck effects that could occur for a few airborne systems. Upgrade programs are now in place to replace the affected systems and ensure operators uninterrupted service both during and after the date change.
>
> As part of its preparations for the date rollover to Y2K, Boeing conducted an assessment of the airborne systems on its commercial airplane fleet. Though all computing systems in use throughout the world are susceptible to problems because of incompatibility between existing and future date functions, the Boeing assessment showed that only a few of the airborne systems on its airplanes use the date function. In addition, no safety-of-flight issues related to Y2K for airborne systems exist for an airplane in flight. [i.e., a glitch isn't going to shut the system down!]
>
> Certain airborne systems on some Boeing models (727, 737, 757, 767, 747, and DC-10) will have erroneous flight deck effects following rollover to Y2K. Although most of these systems will continue to function as designed, Boeing recommends that operators upgrade such affected systems. For the MD-80 and MD-90, no upgrade is considered necessary, but if a change is implemented for other reasons, it will include a Y2K upgrade and will be made available to those operators who request it.[30]

How interesting! So for all of the billions of embedded chips out there, many of which one would think are in aircraft and would be critical to staying airborne, after years of working on Y2K, Boeing found very little that would be disruptive when the clock rolls over to January 1, 2000. Moreover, it views the problem as no more than a possible nuisance in the cockpit. It has upgraded software to cover Y2K, but doesn't say it *must* be installed or the equipment won't fly. It *recommends* that operators acquire the upgrade, but apparently it is not essential for operational safety.

Remember, Boeing is not responsible if a pilot makes an error, but it is responsible for the operational safety of its planes in every respect related to design. Boeing must be very sure of itself to make the above statements. Yet it seems to treat possible Y2K problems casually, as though they can be lived with or compensated for at the time they occur. Either the Boeing engineers have lost their minds, or those who are warning of chaos and disaster because of the change of the clock to the new millennium are speaking from ignorance and are greatly overstating the possible consequences.

The same attitude toward Y2K is increasingly being found among those one would have thought would be the most concerned. Consider Texas Instruments (TI), for example, the leader in the field of DSP (Digital Signal Processors) solutions. A DSP is an example of a rather complex and expensive embedded chip. TI issued its "first detailed 'Year 2000 Ready' product status charts on [its] Year 2000 Internet (www.ti.com/year2000) on August 31, 1998."[31] Is TI worried about the effect that might be created by some of its embedded chips which have not been brought up to date and made Y2K compliant? Apparently not, according to the following notice it has given customers:

> While TI believes most of its products are either
> "Year 2000 Ready" or contain no date logic, ongoing

product assessments have identified minor date-display related issues associated with the Ada Linker and certain C runtime library functions on some TI DSP and microcontroller development tools. The company believes that these issues are unlikely to cause a significant problem in that they only affect the display of date information under specific circumstances and not calculations or comparison of dates.

Free corrective patches are scheduled to be available from September 30 through December 31, 1998 and can be downloaded from TI's Internet site. TI recommends that TI customers...take the following actions:

Review the "Year 2000 Ready" status of products you use. Monitor TI's Internet site periodically for updates...,download corrective patches from TI's Internet site, as they become available.[32]

Here again, like Boeing, Texas Instruments is not overly concerned that any of its products, even though not Y2K compliant, will cause problems when the new millennium dawns. It seems to know exactly which ones need repairs and has already provided "corrective patches" for all of such cases. In other words, Texas Instruments is on top of the Y2K problem and has been for some time. Moreover, TI doesn't consider a lack of full Y2K compliance to pose a serious threat. It *recommends* that customers use the corrective patches, but does not predict disaster if any of them fail to do so. Such a relaxed attitude toward Y2K almost seems like a rebuke of the alarmists.

Has the disaster potential from the billions of embedded chips out there been grossly overstated? From all of the investigating we have been able to do, we think it has been. "Better safe than sorry," of course—but safe from *what*? That is the part that has been exaggerated and has caused unnecessary anxiety and could yet cause panic before this thing is over.

Will It Be Safe to Fly January 1, 2000 and After?

The Boeing Company began working "on the Year 2000 challenge in 1993....[It] estimated that approximately 165 million lines of code might be directly affected....With [the] merger with McDonnell Douglas and Boeing North America, that estimate rose to approximately 250 million lines of code."[33] What has been the result? Boeing is very frank about the situation and it is absurd to suggest that they are lying. Willie Aikens, Boeing's Y2K program manager, declares:

> We can't have any secrets when it comes to Y2K readiness. The FAA, the military, the airlines, our competitors even—this is a global community and all of us need to be prepared....
>
> Boeing plans to be Y2K ready by the end of this calendar year [1998]. The one-year-early completion schedule affords time to remedy any "unknown unknowns" that might crop up....
>
> When the calendar flips to January 1, 2000, we will be ready.[34]

We have asked pilots in cockpits of commercial jets and the mechanics who service them if they anticipate any Y2K problems and have yet to find anyone who was concerned. We have spoken with military men and with scientists and engineers at various corporations supplying sophisticated military systems, and the answer is always that they are compliant already or will be early in 1999 at the latest, and that Y2K is no great concern.

Jack Van Impe warns his viewers not to fly after December 31, 1999. Jack Anderson of the Larry Burkett ministry likewise says that "GM [General Motors] has said there will be no flights for any senior executive after December 15, 1999, period."

"That's very comforting, too," he added sarcastically.

Whether anyone will fly depends upon three major factors: the ability of the aircraft to fly after January 1, 2000; whether the FAA is compliant and the air traffic control system is functioning properly; and whether the insurance companies are convinced and keep their coverage intact, or cancel it. Early in November 1998, it was pointed out that "the insurance industry effectively holds the veto over whether airlines operate on January 1, 2000, not arguments about whether their computer systems are immune to infection by the year 2000 bug."[35]

Global Positioning Satellites (GPS)

Of course, one other factor plays a role in aircraft navigation as well as for ships, missiles and military systems: Global Positioning Satellites (GPS) from which navigational data is received constantly. Here is a brief explanation of Y2K-related problems involving the GPS system:

> The much-discussed Y2K bug caused by two-digit representation of the year in computer calendars could, at best, cause a GPS receiver to output an erroneous date. At worst, the date error could significantly degrade the accuracy of the position data that the receiver calculates. Moreover, GPS receivers have a second date-based problem that will precede the Y2K event. Called the "end-of-week" (EOW) or "week-number rollover" (WNRO), the problem is that GPS satellites will reset the calendar back to time 0 at midnight on August 21, 1999....
>
> The problem isn't inherent in the way GPS operates; rather, some equipment is not designed to fully meet the GPS spec. The GPS calendar started at time 0 at midnight on January 5, 1980. The satellites transmit an offset from that date rather [than] transmitting an absolute date. The GPS week field increments using a modulo 1024 count, so, slightly less than 20 years after it began operation, the week count will go to 0. Properly designed receivers will record the end of the first epoch on August 21, 1999, and will start

updating the date based on an offset of epochs plus weeks. In other words, a similar event will occur every 1024 weeks....

You probably needn't worry about new GPS designs, because the ICs and modules that vendors sell now are largely prepared for both events. However, installed receivers—in applications from navigation to surveying to custom embedded systems—merit an evaluation. More than likely, you'll need to contact the manufacturer of the receiver, module, or chip set in question to find out whether the date-based events will cause errors....

The U.S. Coast Guard site[www.navcen.uscg.mil/gps/geninfo/y2k] details potential problems and solutions for civil receivers and provides a contact list for manufacturers of GPS receivers.[36]

In other words, there is nothing wrong with the Global Positioning Satellites. The only problems that could arise would be in those cases where receivers were not in conformity with GPS standards. Obviously, all military and government receivers would meet GPS specifications. Some older civil receivers may not. The U.S. Coast Guard says it all quite simply:

> The GPS Joint Program Office [JPO] has determined that all generations of GPS satellites are unaffected by the Year 2000 (Y2K) and GPS End of Week (EOW) Rollover issues. However, the Civil GPS users may need to verify that their receivers and applications will work properly through these events.[37]

Aircraft are not going to fall from the sky because their GPS receivers are not set to work properly after August 21, 1999, when the next rollover occurs. They could suffer wrong information for navigation and would have to resort to other methods. In fact, there are several navigational systems at work simultaneously on commercial aircraft, checking against one another.

So the GPS system has been erroneously associated with Y2K when, in fact, it has nothing to do with the year 2000. And for outdated receivers on earth, the result is not an end-of-the-world consequence, but an inconvenience. Of course, all commercial and military aircraft will have their GPS receivers in proper working order well ahead of schedule. There is no reason, other than gross negligence, why they would not.

Should We Stock Up on Food *Now?*

Amidst the hurricane of cries of alarm and predictions of a 1929-like stockmarket crash, worldwide financial disasters, social chaos, and the complete disintegration of civilization as we have known it, it is not easy to lean into the wind and make a calm appraisal. Let us think for a moment about the dire prediction that shelves in grocery stores will be bare and we ought, therefore, to stock up right now. Surely such warnings, if heeded by very many, would in themselves trigger panic and hoarding that could bring about the very disaster such cautions were intended to prevent.

Taking another deep breath and pondering the situation calmly, one immediately realizes that computers have little if anything to do with growing wheat or apples or carrots or chicken or beef or anything else. Yes, on today's modern farms computers monitor or govern many of the mechanized functions. Computer-related failures of air conditioning or ventilation systems probably kill thousands of poultry every year. Feed lots rely upon computers, which have costly failures from time to time. But these computer failures have nothing to do with Y2K. The failure is not expected and does its damage before being discovered. In the case of Y2K, however, the operator will be watching for failure and, if it occurs, should be able to make manual adjustments, repairs, or other adaptations. Crops and poultry and cattle grew quite well before computers were invented. And who would have programmed date dependency into such computers?

It is true also that computers are involved in getting the food or livestock from the farm to processors and distributors and then to markets. Computers monitor and control temperature and humidity in storage facilities. But again, why would these functions depend upon what year or century it is? If they do, it was a mistake. Certainly the manufacturer can tell the operators whether they will have any date-related problems, and they can be repaired. That question should be investigated and settled long before January 1, 2000.

Most railroads are operated by computers from central locations, including switching and routing and location of cars. It is, however, no more likely that the year has anything to do with the function railroad computers fulfill than it does for aircraft (as Boeing demonstrated); or that date-related problems could not be corrected on the spot or bypassed if Y2K glitches develop, again, as Boeing exemplifies. The 28-year solution (explained in Chapter 3) would effectively rescue those operators who were unable to complete Y2K compliance in time.

We are not saying there could not be problems and even serious ones. What we are saying is that it is not the end of the world; the situation is not as hopeless as it is being portrayed.

Considering once again that failure (due to negligence in becoming Y2K compliant) to provide the service customers expect and are relying upon would open the railroads to astronomical losses from lawsuits, it is very unlikely that any railroad will *not* complete all necessary work long before the year 2000, particularly in view of the many new techniques now available for speeding up the Y2K compliancy process. Take Union Pacific Railroad as an example. It has been working on the problem since 1994. Its Y2K task force involves about 100 people, is scheduled to cost nearly

$50 million, and is expected to finish the task long before the deadline.

As for getting food and supplies from trains to stores, it is unimaginable that supermarket chains will allow their trucks to stop running because of computer problems and thereby leave shelves bare, giving competitors a chance to steal customers. The availability of electricity and fuel would be the main concern, but we have assurance that those systems will be running and have dealt with that already. The Y2K problem, as we have repeatedly been reminded, is understood and solvable by a variety of means now available. Perhaps the smaller store will not be ready and will have to hustle to do far more manually, but the larger grocery chains will surely be all set to keep food on their shelves on January 1, 2000, and thereafter.

Yes, undoubtedly there will be problems arising January 1, 2000, and for some time thereafter, but nothing of the magnitude so many are suggesting as possible and even inevitable. Christians must beware of becoming victims of fear, "for God hath not given us the spirit of fear, but of power, and of love, and of a sound mind" (2 Timothy 1:7). A sound mind recognizes the contradictions and exaggerations of well-intentioned warnings and refuses to panic.

Making a Calm Appraisal

The author asked a computer expert to listen to some tapes by one of the most highly qualified Christians sounding the Y2K alarm, and consulted him on some of the statements in various books written on the subject. This man, currently working at the highest security clearance level, designs complex equipment and systems, including some of the most sophisticated weapons systems, for which he writes his own software. Here is a summary of his reactions:

Most of what is said is vague. Some of the problems they point out may be true in the final analysis, but we need convincing explanations of *why* this is the case, and we need some specific *examples*—and I haven't heard any yet from those sounding these warnings. As to the general consequences they are warning about, they use such qualifying phrases as, "it would not surprise me" and "who knows" and "it very well could be," but nothing definite. I find it difficult to imagine any legitimate programmer making a function dependent upon the year, though some may have.

They talk about the billions of embedded chips, but most of them are in toasters, microwave ovens, wrist watches, thermostats, television sets, VCRs, etc. And why should any piece of equipment care what year it is? Why would something go awry because of a date problem? I can't imagine a heart monitor, an EKG, or a respirator in a hospital going bonkers because of a date change. If 00 comes up, it must have been programmed in there with some provision for what it means.

Yes, there are billions of lines of code, but most of them have nothing to do with dates, and most of those which do aren't going to shut down or do something strange because of a date. Again, I can't imagine a programmer worth his salt not accounting for all possibilities.

I don't deny there is a real problem, but in everything I've listened to or read I have yet to be given a specific example that would be cause for the current alarm. I've heard much speculation and sensationalism, but no hard examples, so apparently there couldn't be very many or we would be hearing of them.

In fact, a common denominator in much of this stuff is conspiracy. What it seems to boil down to, at least for many of the alarmists—especially the Christians writing and speaking on this subject—is that the Y2K problem opens the possibility of government abuse. It is not just the irksome problems we have to be concerned about, but what really can happen is the president puts us under martial law, takes over as a dictator, and abuses our privileges and rights.

As for banks or Social Security Administration or one's insurance carrier losing records, that is an exaggerated possibility. They all have backup systems. Obviously you should keep your own hard copy, whether the year 2000 is coming up or not. The large defense company I work for lost all of its E-mail and all E-mail addresses because the hard drive on that computer (and we're all tied into it) flew into pieces. But over the weekend technicians managed to recover everything, and Monday morning when I went into my office there was all of my E-mail back again.

Yes, there are some serious problems. The big problem is code, and it is true that some programmers have been notorious for not documenting what they have done. It will be difficult to find and take care of everything that needs to be corrected. But I still can't imagine specific problems due to date. There seem to be a lot of vague suggestions, exaggeration, and no specific examples that cause me to be concerned.[38]

We have provided many reasons, rooted in facts and logic, for rejecting the disaster scenario in general and Y2K in particular. On the other hand, alarmists would have us believe that the business and banking world and the U.S. military are sitting around helplessly wringing their hands because there is no way they can possibly get ready for the dawning of January 1, 2000. We have cited and quoted those who are already Y2K compliant and are helping others.

Earlier we referred to the fact that Hewlett-Packard is already Y2K compliant and is making certain that all of its suppliers and customers are as well. This is the largest manufacturer of test instruments on this planet, one of the largest manufacturers of personal computers, and it leads the world in the most sophisticated medical equipment. Consider the following news released November 23, 1998, and the implications it has for the entire Y2K problem:

After testing over 18,500 different instrument products in its catalog for Y2K compliance, Hewlett-Packard Co. has concluded that about 1,250 models, or roughly 8 percent, require some form of updating.

The other models do not perform any date-related processing, and so will be unaffected by any year 2000 difficulties.

To address the models that need correcting, HP has launched a four-prong program to help customers navigate through the issues. The program includes: a new website; customer care and update programs; and compliance for all new test products.

"We want to make Y2K a non-event for our customers, and if that requires us to go down oil wells, we'll do it," said Scott Conrad, a Y2K program manager for HP....

In reality, that step probably will not be necessary, although HP said its sales force is contacting worldwide customers to encourage assessment of the Y2K situation. Or customers can use an 800 number to have a rep walk them through updating routines.

Conrad said that small and medium-sized customers were not responding to Y2K as much as the large users. "We need to raise their awareness," he stated, "so that they don't panic at the zero hour, take extreme actions, or change their behavior. That will create a crisis, rather than the actual problem."

Customers visiting the newly established website are able to enter a particular product name or number and learn whether the product is Y2K compliant, how it uses date information, and specifically what needs to be done to make it compliant. The site provides testing protocols, FAQS, links to support centers and service notes, and other information.

HP said its TMO operation would respond to questions via e-mail or by phone if it is provided with a phone number. The company also said it would commit to no-charge updating if a product is covered under a current applicable support contract, is under warranty, or was delivered after January 1, 1997.

Software downloads or front-panel date resets will take care of most necessary updating, which can be done during a calibration cycle in order not to upset production schedules, said Conrad. "But there's no point in pulling an instrument out of production if the user doesn't care about the date-processing features," he said....

Because of the large-scale interconnection making up much of the test and electronics worlds, Conrad offered some advice to those companies being attentive to possible Y2K trouble. "Put in a contingency plan, assume the worst, and have a SWAT team standing by to ensure your customers are not affected," he said.[39]

Clearly, very few embedded chips or software features will even be affected by Y2K, and those that are will not bring down the system except in rare instances. And even for those problems one is not aware of, it is possible to have a contingency plan and to handle the crises if and when they occur. In the meantime, not only Hewlett-Packard but other manufacturers as well offer full service to bring those using their products into Y2K compliance, even walking them through the necessary remediation over an 800 number!

What Virus?

As we have already pointed out, much hype and disinformation surrounds the Y2K scenario as it has been laid out for us. The Y2K problem is often called a "computer virus." It is not a virus. Author and editor Julian Gregori, for example, uses that term even though he says of himself, "I make my living with computers and have learned enough about programming to know how some of America's most important computer programs were written and revised to perform complex tasks for the 20th century."[40] A few pages later he says: "This y2k computer virus holds lots of surprises. Even if some computers seem to be totally fixed, other computers might mess up the work of the very best programmers in the world. The fixed computers could possibly become unfixed in the blink of an eye."[41]

That is pure misinformation. The Y2K problem is not a virus, and though it may properly be called a bug, it doesn't leap or creep from one computer to another. The speaker at the Oregon ministerial association meeting told assembled pastors (and no one disputed this misleading idea) that even if some banks were to get their computers fixed, if the banking system couldn't "guarantee 100-percent compliance in the whole network, they must shut down because they would be corrupted from outside."[42]

Not true. Y2K is a programming problem, not a virus. The computers which must be fixed have not been invaded and corrupted by a virus but have been improperly programmed, and that is what must be fixed. There are solutions. One of the most obvious is simply to purchase new equipment or new software, which is the approach many managers have taken, using Y2K to justify replacing old equipment that they had wanted to upgrade for years.

Another piece of misinformation that has been passed along (one author quoting another who supposedly quoted an expert) is that even after the problem has supposedly been "fixed," it would take many more months to test and find out whether it actually would work properly when January 1, 2000, rolls around. Gregori says, "Since most testing procedures take 18–24 months, many y2k repair projects entered the 'hopeless' category in June of 1998."[43] Again, not true. That length of time would be appropriate for full *development* of a guided missile—not *testing* it. Most testing procedures can be completed in a matter of a few days or weeks at the most. Someone replies, "Windows 95 has been around for several years and they are still finding new problems." That's true, but none of the problems has voided the system—it has worked well for millions of people all of these years.

As early as March 1998, *Business Week* acknowledged that "the securities industry, big banks, and the Federal Reserve have been taking Year 2000 seriously for years. Chase

Manhattan Corp. is spending $250 million on the problem, while Wells Fargo & Co. will ultimately deploy 400 people to fix Y2K. Later this year and next year, Wall Street firms will run an industry-wide test simulating the rollover to Jan. 1, 2000."[44] Actually, they ran it successfully in July 1998, and it took a few days, not 18–24 months.[45]

What About the "Silver Bullet"?

We referred earlier to "windowing" as a possible solution. While that technique can only be used in the absence of birth or contract dates or other dates in the system going back earlier than 1950, there are other methods of delaying the solution. There is, for example, the "28-year solution" previously mentioned. This entails simply turning the computer clocks back 28 years, the period of time for a full leap-year cycle, so that the dates would be correct for the days of the week in each month. Only the year would be wrong, but unless some special meaning had been programmed in, the computer wouldn't care what year it was.

While the "28-year solution" has its limitations, it is viable for the military (the U.S. Navy has proposed using it) and for public utilities. Of course, it would only be used in affected parts of a system and only to the extent to which a full solution had not been achieved. Certainly, this technique alone eliminates the scenario of lengthy power outages, which is the main concern.

One statement repeated by most of those trying to alert us to the grave dangers posed by the coming of January 1, 2000, goes something like this: "Don't imagine that someone is going to come up with some shortcut solution. *There is no silver bullet!*" In fact, a *number* of shortcuts that have been developed are now in use, and we have mentioned several of them. There will no doubt be more.

The newest has recently been granted worldwide patents. Called Hybrid-Radix, it is offered by StepWise

Solutions of Watermill, New York (cited previously). This special program searches for, identifies, and repairs anything in a system that is not Y2K compliant—it does it speedily and economically, and the result is guaranteed: "The resulting code including Y2K modifications from our pre-compiler are guaranteed to successfully compile. The resulting code is *fully compatible* with *existing* files, databases, screens and reports. Again, there is no need to modify existing files... *existing data is not touched.*"[46]

These "silver bullets" that supposedly could never be invented are arriving on the scene one after another. They effectively eliminate the major problem that is so often cited as proof that Y2K problems cannot be solved: not enough time before the deadline of January 1, 2000. In fact, there now is plenty of time.

One thing is clear: the disastrous scenario that has aroused such alarm and has been the basis for so many news-letters, websites, books, and the sale of so much emergency food and supplies will have to be surrendered to the reality of solutions now available. These time-saving solutions effectively sound the death-knell of the Y2K bug, turning it into a bugaboo that can frighten only the superstitious and uninformed.

Advice that Very Few Can Take

For the vast majority of people, much of what is cited as urgent action which *must* be taken "while there is still time" is simply impossible. For example, we are being told to move out of cities into select locations complete with acreage, a private water well, diesel engine for alternate power, wood stove, and safe space to store extra food, water, wood, and other supplies. Again, chaos and panic would indeed be created if millions of people all tried to do that by mid-1999. Furthermore, who can afford it? Even among those who may have sufficient funds, how many families are able to leave jobs, to suddenly pack up and move to a "safe" location? McAlvany admits some of these problems, yet continues to urge his readers to do what for the vast majority would be impossible:

> MIA [McAlvany Intelligence Advisor] continues to believe that every American family should have a half-year supply of dehydrated/freeze-dried food reserves. *These supplies are very thin at this writing, as thousands of Americans are moving to purchase same in preparation for Y2K and the coming financial crisis.* Deliveries are now running very slow (*up to three months*) and supplies could dry up completely over the next 6–12 months.
>
> *If just 5,000 people tried to purchase a one-year supply of reserves, the entire (very small) industry in a nation of 270 million people would be thrown into gridlock....*One large supplier of packaged food now has *nine-month delays* in deliveries and is taking *no new customers.* If you have not purchased a one- or two-year supply of food reserves, we would strongly encourage you to develop a sense of urgency regarding same.
>
> Study the enclosed flyer on food reserves and call International Collectors Associates at 1-800-525-9556 and order same today.[47]

How can "every American family" purchase the recommended one- or two-year supply of food when a mere 5,000 attempting to do so would completely overwhelm available sources? Such warnings, if heeded by very many, would indeed create the panic-driven runs on grocery stores and banks which these advisors predict! Suppose that millions of people who couldn't afford freeze-dried foods began denuding grocery shelves of such items as canned meats and vegetables, rice and beans, and dried fruits. It would be as impossible to satisfy very many in this manner as it would be for all to stock up on freeze-dried food. Production and distribution to grocery stores is set up to meet a steady demand based upon ordinary customer requirements, not a sudden, unanticipated stockpiling of months or even weeks of emergency supplies.

If and when the Y2K computer problem should turn out to be a bothersome mouse instead of a devouring lion, these same prophets of doom may salvage their respectability by claiming that it was, after all, their sounding the alarm that aroused the effort that saved the day!

We believe that evidence and sound reason indicate that Y2K is not going to create the total disaster which so many are predicting. There is evidence and reason to believe that the power grid is not going to go down. Major banks will continue to operate, airlines to fly, and most businesses to continue. There will be some problems, but most will amount to little more than a bothersome nuisance that will be dealt with as each arises, though in some cases with considerable distress—which could have been avoided by commonsense preparation.

At the stroke of midnight, December 31, 1999, our world will be faced with the greatest challenge that modern society has ever had to experience....We must ask ourselves, "Will we be ready?"

> —Jerry Falwell in a sermon at
> Thomas Road Baptist Church[1]

I'm not a Y2K expert, but I play one on TV....There is no such thing as a Y2K expert...because [of] the information blackout around this issue, crisis, problem.

> —Drew Parkhill, Y2K editor for CBN News,
> Virginia Beach, VA[2]

We're going...to see some things that people before us have longed to see; and I think that it's going to bring a form of revival in the church. Don't know how it's going to come about, but I just feel like it's going to happen....It is not a time to be fearful and anxious, but rather a time to anticipate and to see what God is going to do. And that's going to be exciting.

> —Jack Anderson of Larry Burkett's CFC[3]

One of the main speakers at the [Christian Y2K] conference..., Jim Lord, who speaks all over the country...said during a special luncheon for leaders of Y2K preparation...that all over the country it's the Bible-believing Christians who are responding to this....God is raising up His people to address this issue and that is a great encouragement.

> —Dan Dillard, Chairman, Y2K Preparedness
> Committee, Bend, Oregon, Ministerial Association[4]

There is little doubt that some Christians are in full panic. Many others are on the verge. Christians are selling their homes, liquidating their assets and purchasing guns. Is the panic justified? NO. I think [Y2K] will cause us little more than a bump in the road. What should you do...? Probably nothing....We should each be prepared for common, ordinary disasters that can befall us (earthquakes, tornadoes, hurricanes). I don't see the need to do anything else.

> —Steve Hewitt, founder and editor-in-chief of
> *Christian Computing*[5]

Chapter Five

The Church's Finest Hour? or Greatest Folly?

As we have seen in previous chapters, although there has been much concern expressed in the secular media and by secular business and government leaders, Christians have to a large extent been the most persistent in sounding the warning concerning Y2K and the disaster they believe it will produce. There are several reasons for this unfortunate fact.

First of all, most Christians have at least some idea of Bible prophecy, and though their eschatological views differ, in general they expect some kind of apocalypse, possibly Antichrist taking power with some kind of end-of-the-world scenario developing. There is a natural temptation for Christians to suspect that the apocalyptic predictions involving Y2K must have some connection to what the Bible foretells for the last days. They tend, therefore, to be more interested in, and pay more attention to, news of coming disaster. Y2K seems made to order for the church—too much so, as we have already noted.

Second, most of the Christian speakers and authors dealing with this subject suggest that Y2K could be the church's finest hour, offering the greatest opportunity in history to show needy neighbors and friends the love of Christ by meeting their needs and presenting the gospel. What could be of more interest to Christians than that?

Indeed, during the last ten years a number of AD 2000 organizations have sprung up—from Campus Crusade for

Christ's to the Roman Catholic Church's and much in be-tween—which have adopted the seemingly admirable goal of evangelizing the world by the end of the year 2000. Why that year should mark the culmination of the evangelization of the world, however, no one has been able to say. But now, suddenly, it all seems to make sense: Y2K is going to frighten multitudes into the kingdom!

The Hottest Topic in the Church

Several popular Christian leaders have been prominent in trying to awaken America, and especially Christians, to the seriousness of the crisis which they believe the entire world now faces. Chief among them are authors and radio, television, and conference speakers Larry Burkett, Grant Jeffrey, Donald S. McAlvany, Chuck Missler, and Gary North. Each edits his own widely circulated newsletter and website: Burkett, his *Money Matters: A Christian Economics Newsletter* as well as his Weekly E-mail; Jeffrey, his *Intelligence Reports;* Missler, his *Personal Update;* McAlvany, his *McAlvany Intelligence Advisor;* and North, *The Remnant Review.*

These well-known authors have influenced many others, who in turn echo the same level of concern to those in their congregations and on their mailing lists. And, as already noted, James Dobson has also joined in sounding the alarm, as have Pat Robertson, Jack Van Impe, and Hal Lindsey on their television programs.

Larry Burkett is to Christian financial planning what James Dobson is to Christian psychology, and the two of them sometimes work together. Burkett warns that the Y2K problem will occur in "the dead of winter"; therefore, everyone needs to buy a generator and "they'll need to get their orders in soon...[because] most manufacturers are backlogged."[6] Chuck Missler draws large crowds when he speaks on any topic, and during 1998 he was alerting audiences all over the country concerning the awesome consequences of the Y2K problem. Pat Robertson's Christian Broadcasting Network (CBN) is sponsoring Y2K seminars nationwide, such as the three-day conference held in Virginia Beach in mid-October 1998.

Grant Jeffrey's *Millennium Meltdown* has been a bestseller, as has been Michael Hyatt's book *The Millennium Bug*. Shaunti Feldhahn's *Y2K, The Millennium Bug: A Balanced Christian Response*, which just came off the press in late November 1998, began selling out of Christian bookstores as fast as they could stock it. There can be no doubt that as a result of the warning that has been sounded by these Christian leaders, many Christians are being aroused to concern and action.

Y2K is the hottest topic going now, especially in the church. Sadly enough, Y2K is taking time and effort that used to be given to prayer, study of God's Word, and evangelizing the lost. Religion News Service recently commented:

> In Christian circles, conversion is often a topic of conversation as believers seek to bring more people into their fold. But lately, leaders of Christian groups— like many others—are preaching about a different kind of conversion—adapting computer systems to avert problems with what's known as the Y2K computer bug.
>
> Ministries used to disseminating books, videos and correspondence about the Holy Trinity now are also distributing materials about how to deal with computers and other technology that could read dates ending with "00" as 1900 instead of 2000 at the turn of the century, prompting possible computer malfunctions.[7]

Mobilizing the Church

What has happened in one small Oregon town (population about 35,000) is probably typical of much of the rest of the country. That town is certainly less vulnerable to Y2K disaster than larger cities. A large percentage of the people living there have wood stoves for heating, and there are plenty of trees to cut for firewood. A large river runs through the town from which numerous irrigation canals feed out in all directions, making fresh water no problem, even if there was no electricity.

Food, of course, is something else. The Christians there have taken the lead in alerting the community and in preparing to help themselves and those in need. The small ministerial association, under evangelical leadership, has its own Y2K committee which meets weekly.

Early in October 1998, the local ministerial association had a special speaker from another Oregon town 125 miles away to address the subject of Y2K. He painted a scenario of disaster: computers crashing, no power, no water, no food on the market shelves. Pastors were urged to alert their members to buy wood stoves and generators, to stock up on wood, food, water and to have enough to share it all with unsaved neighbors who would be caught unprepared. Christians, like Joseph in Egypt, would thereby be able to rescue those around them and as a result win them to Christ. Pastors must get together to plan for the rescue of their town; and, by the way, since the Mormons already had their food and water storage perfected, pastors should work with and learn from them—a seemingly plausible idea bearing the seeds of a deadly ecumenism.

The suggestion was preposterous. They could never do it. A moment of calm and rational thought would have indicated that the logistics of such an operation would completely overwhelm the tiny Christian minority. That fact, once considered, should have raised questions about much of the other information being given. But there was little hope for rational thought because it all sounded so urgent. They were assured that rescuing a town would bring unprecedented opportunities to win the lost to Christ.

On the Dobson program to which we have earlier referred, Chuck Missler mentioned a church in Michigan that is planning to feed the entire community. Pat Robertson ran a CBN TV special commending that church as a positive example. It has stored ten tons of food. That sounds impressive. However, Gary North comments:

> That [ten tons] sounds like a lot. It isn't. One adult eats about 40 pounds of grain a month, or 500 pounds a year. A ton of food will feed a family of four adults for one year, and feed them minimally. The church can feed 20 families in the community for six months....
>
> What if every family in the church has not stored enough food for its members for a year? (Count on it.) The church will barely be able to feed its own members, let alone members of the community, if y2k turns out to be a full-scale disaster.[8]

Like the Michigan church, the ministerial association in this Oregon town is serious about Y2K. Its Y2K committee meets weekly "to figure out ways churches can help the community respond to problems such as widespread power outages and a global recession." The committee chairman says, "We've read enough to convince us this could be a serious problem, so our focus now is on solutions." The ministers are working on establishing neighborhood groups to assist neighbors during a disaster and are putting together "a handbook to guide people," convinced that by helping others Christians can have a powerful witness for Christ.[9] As some are saying, "The Lord is counting on us to turn this opportunity into a victory for the Kingdom of God."[10] The chairman of the Y2K Preparedness Committee explained:

> We're going to try to understand the problem...
> and also that there's an opportunity involved....
> Always when there's a crisis or some big disaster

people are more open to the gospel. Not that we want to use this because people are vulnerable.

Isn't it just like God to look at this little problem that was created a number of years ago and know at that time that the fruition of this problem was going to be the year 2000 and the possible havoc that it could wreak....Nothing catches Him by surprise... and we ought to be able to take comfort from that fact and it ought to make each one of us more settled in our view of how this whole thing is going to come about....[11]

Later in October this small ministerial association was pleased to obtain as its special speaker Jack Anderson, an expert with an international reputation who has been associated with Larry Burkett's Christian Financial Concepts for more than 20 years. This was a conference of church leaders (to which we have earlier referred a number of times), but the meeting was open to the public and was well attended, even by those from neighboring towns.

The Best-Informed People on Earth?

Addressing that conference in Central Oregon, Jack Anderson gave Christians credit for being more aware of the problem than their secular friends and neighbors and suggested that the "general public is largely unaware or unconcerned." A major idea at that meeting (as at so many others like it) was that Christians, when the crunch came, would be better informed and better prepared than the world around them and would thereby be able to help others and use the opportunity presented by the Y2K disaster to preach the gospel to those who otherwise might turn a deaf ear.

Whether Christians as a whole are better informed about Y2K than non-Christians would be debatable. It also would depend upon the accuracy of the information which Christians have been given in books, tapes, and seminars. There is little doubt, however, that as of late 1998 the Christian community was far more active than the secular world in seeking to arouse awareness and make preparations. Unfortunately, as we have documented, much of what has been and is still being presented by Christian Y2K experts is not based on fact and sound reason.

Anderson explained that it was important for Christians to begin their food storage and accumulation of emergency equipment and necessities immediately because non-Christians would not remain heedless of Y2K forever. In fact, some concern was expressed that when the secular world eventually awakened to the problem, there would be a run on food and supplies, leaving little for latecomers. Christians needed to stock up quickly not only for their own sakes but to have a supply to share with others. Anderson warned that, in fact, the run on scarce items had already begun:

> What I think will happen is, somewhere around February or March of next year [1999] the press, the media, will all of a sudden decide this is a big story. And so there won't be little bitty snippets in the paper anymore, there will be a large article done and it will be carried in all of the syndicated newspapers...you'll find that things that were available before aren't. And so I think this is a very timely conference.
>
> I know that in my own case I decided that one of the ways that I would store some food was, I'd get some of the military packets rations....So I bought three cases....Then I got thinking that maybe a few more cases wouldn't be a bad idea. So I called my supplier and he said, "You know, funny thing on that, I had 4,000 cases of those last week and now I don't have any, and I don't know if I'm going to get any more."[12]

Increasingly, pastors across the country are addressing Y2K in sermons intended to inform and arouse their churches to action. To his congregation and television audience, Phil Arms presented an informative two-part series, taking an even more frightening angle than most, even suggesting that Y2K had been deliberately created for some insidious purpose by those in power, and that as early as April 1999 our military would be paralyzed and our country defenseless against Russian missiles.[13] Jerry Falwell preached a three-part series on Y2K. Commented Falwell, "I would say the response of the Y2K message exceeds any response we remember in recent years. I think we do have a major problem coming, but I think it's wrong to be too strident about that because it can become a self-fulfilling prophecy."[14] What is "too strident" becomes a question of judgment, depending upon one's convictions concerning what Y2K will bring upon us.

Falwell's *National Liberty Journal* for October 1998 may have sounded too strident for some: "Furthermore, many technology experts believe that computers could begin to show signs of breakdown as early as January 1, 1999.... It behooves all Americans to prepare now for what appears to be an inevitable problem." The *Journal* article continues:

> If you live in downtown New York [or other large city], you should probably make plans not to be there January 1, 2000....The nation's inner cities could face major looting and violence....Be sure to put away enough food and provisions to include neighbors, Christian brothers and sisters and the poor around your family dinner table....
>
> Pastors, begin to educate your flock now on the Y2K computer problem so each family can prepare individually...and be prepared to help those in your community who face problems caused by Y2K. The church [with]...a large... food supply can use Y2K to share God's love and act as servants.[15]

There Are No Y2K Experts

Three weeks after Anderson spoke to the pastors, the ministerial association sponsored a follow-up Y2K conference on November 14, 1998. The special speaker on this occasion was Drew Parkhill. He was introduced as being "from Pat Robertson's CBNC ministry...the Y2K editor for CBN News, a division of the Christian Broadcasting Network in Virginia Beach...[who has] appeared numerous times on 'The 700 Club' with Pat Robertson to discuss the potential impact of Y2K."[16] As a result of these TV specials, CBN has received more than 120,000 requests for free materials.

Parkhill reassuringly told the audience that he was not a Y2K expert but just pretended to be one when he addressed this topic on TV. He explained that the picture was too uncertain and would change too rapidly for there to be any experts. Nevertheless, he was brought all the way from Virginia to Oregon to share his expertise on the subject. Indeed, he travels all over the country giving lengthy talks about Y2K. Jack Anderson had already made the same point clear:

> I'm not sure there's anybody out there who fully understands this problem. We understand where it came from...and some of the ramifications of it..., but I don't believe anybody's got a full, complete comprehension of the whole thing, and there's a lot of people out there studying. The problem is that we keep uncovering more things; every time we turn over a rock another worm crawls out.[17]

Like most of those attempting to inform the church about Y2K, Parkhill could only deal in vague generalities about what *might* happen or *could possibly* happen *if* computers and software were not fixed in time—and he didn't hold out much hope that they would be. Like so many others (they seem to echo one another and all the same alarming reports), Parkhill stressed the point that, for many companies and government departments, there was simply not enough time left to make the necessary corrections. That statement was lacking specifics, and missing from it completely was any mention of the new methods which have cut compliancy time to a fraction of what it once was. He emphasized that no one could possibly know what would happen January 1, 2000, yet he had a great deal to say about what he thought *could* very well happen.

Parkhill echoed much of what Jack Anderson had already presented, including patting attendees on the back for being better informed than the ungodly. He told his excited and concerned Christian audience, "You just happen to be in the top 1 percent of 1 percent....Public awareness in the United States is very low."[18] Christians, presumably, are generally just a whole lot better informed than non-Christians.

Like Anderson, Parkhill predicted that the lack of awareness on the part of the general populace wouldn't last forever. He told the audience not to imagine that people would suddenly wake up January 1, 2000, and wonder why nothing worked: no electricity, no phone. "That won't happen," Parkhill said. Instead, "awareness of Y2K is going to be 110 percent in the United States. Absolutely!"[19] So whatever food, emergency equipment, and supplies they intended to purchase should be acquired quickly.

Christians Lead the Y2K Parade

On the Dobson program, Shaunti Feldhahn spoke highly of Jim Lord and favorably quoted him as saying, "It's all over the country that Christians are responding to this [Y2K]."[20] Steve Hewitt agreed that Christians are responding everywhere, but he did not view that fact favorably. This contrary opinion separated him from the other panelists. He expressed concern that the Christian response to this potential problem may be "too strong." "My cry," he said, "is for some balanced reporting on this."[21] Hewitt bluntly blames Christians for fearmongering:

> Where is the fear coming from? It is coming as a result of reporting that is poorly researched, emotionally presented and sensationalized for effect. While Christian leadership is not solely responsible for spreading the Y2K fear, they are the leaders.
>
> Christianity now has a host of national leaders, preachers without a church, as a result of radio, television and print. They have an audience of thousands and even millions, scattered across the church in all denominations and in all areas of our nation.
>
> While in the past many of these leaders have held differing ministries and even different theology, they all seem to have recently united around the belief that Y2K poses as the most devastating disaster to hit our nation (and the world) in our lifetime. They present their case using many facts and figures that are either out of date or not properly researched.[22]

Dr. Dobson said to Steve Hewitt,

> I heard your interview with Jim Warren on Moody's Prime Time Live...and you leaned real heavily on the fact that Christians are the ones who are upset about this and that other people are not terribly upset about it, and almost drew the conclusion that for some churches it's self-serving....I mean, their motives were questioned. This does not seem to me like a Christian issue. It seems like something that everybody is concerned about.[23]

"It isn't [just a Christian issue]," responded Steve.

> But my concern is,...I was reading everything about Y2K that came across from CNET and *Wired* and *USA Today*, and all of a sudden I started getting e-mail...from people who were not listening to

CNET and USA and the the Gartner Report and the Merrill Lynch Report..., [but] they were listening to Christian evangelists on TV and the tape series they got and someone was trying to sell them a $275 Christian Survival Kit, four VCR tapes on how to sharpen a knife....So I started to see where they were getting this from, and I looked at what the Christians were saying..., and the Christians are saying store up three years of food and bury gas cans....If you over-react, if people who are not familiar with guns are arming themselves and churches are firing their pastors and putting bars on their windows....[24]

Shaunti Feldhahn stepped in to say that she had developed some of the same concerns:

I saw something on the Internet where a pastor was, for example, teaching members of his congregation how to make their house look like it had already been looted...: put a burnt car in the driveway, and break some windows and put some boards up...so when the roving gangs come looking for your food they'll think you've already been looted and pass by. I've seen so much of this sort of fear and obviously there are some cases where the Lord has called us to protect ourselves, but...the biblical model and what I see in Jesus is exactly the opposite.[25]

One viewer of TBN's "International Intelligence" program, hosted by Hal Lindsey and Cliff Ford, wrote to this author to share his concern about the Y2K Special the night of November 29, 1998. These comments come from a very knowledgeable Christian leader:

The overwhelming weight of the information they presented could only bring one to the reasonable yet frightening conclusion that the computer problem will bring life as we know it to a devastating end. In one of the multitude of examples given, they claimed that our military is so dependent upon computers and the GPS guidance systems that we will be rendered completely vulnerable to less sophisticated World War II equipped military powers. In fact, we'll be left with less than 30,000 ground troops to defend our country.

At the close of the show, both hosts thanked TBN for being courageous enough to allow them to help prepare the church for the very difficult times ahead. They also mentioned the book they are writing to further help the body of Christ prepare itself.[26]

The *Anchorage Daily News* ran a feature story in late November 1998 about how Christians in Alaska are preparing for Y2K. The article was titled "Preparing for the Unknown: Churches, Governments and Individuals Make Plans for 2000." It said in part:

> The next century may begin with a few computer glitches or a complete meltdown, but the congregation at Aurora Heights Assembly of God isn't taking any chances. In a cubbyhole beneath a staircase under construction at the church, sacks of rice, bags of beans and military meals ready to eat are being squirreled away.
>
> The Rev. Rufus Tallent wants to be ready to feed his community for three months should the U.S. food distribution system crumble into chaos in a computer-generated chain reaction of biblical proportions.
>
> "I pray God that doesn't happen," Tallent said. "If we're overprepared, we're still going to give the stuff away."
>
> Tallent isn't alone in his fears. People across the Kenai Peninsula, and the world for that matter, are being whipped into a survivalist frenzy as rumors fly about what the millennium bug will unleash as the clocks tick from Dec. 31, 1999 to Jan. 1, 2000....
>
> Will power failures ripple across the country? What about the money supply? And will transportation snafus unleash food shortages? Questions like that have led state

and local governments across Alaska to create year 2000 task forces, charged with figuring out if utilities, banks and hospitals will work right [27]

InterVarsity Christian Fellowship, convinced of the seriousness of Y2K, is taking no chances. It "announced in October [1998] that it would postpone Urbana, its usually triennial conference in Illinois, from December 27-31, 1999, to the same dates in 2000." The conference attracts about 20,000 participants. Said Melody Hanson, InterVarsity's associate communications director, "We're watching how the Christian...community is responding to it. The concern was that the perception would be that it would be...an unfavorable thing to do to either send your child to Urbana during those dates or to go yourself." A major reason behind the cancellation was "the decision by the person coordinating travel to the event to pull out of her contract because she couldn't assure quality service."[28]

"Don't Be Scared—Be Prepared"

To his credit, Drew Parkhill stressed a number of times that Christians should not panic but trust in the Lord. On the other hand, with his next breath he painted a picture that was more than enough to create deep concern about the future in anyone really listening to what he was saying. Telling audiences not to panic, he encourages them like this, "Let's be calm about it....You just need to get over it." He tells us that the "worst case scenario" won't happen.[29] That sounds reassuring.

A moment later, however, he likens Y2K to the sinking of the Titanic! Next on this roller-coaster ride comes the comforting assurance, "We're going to get through this. We got through the Depression, we got through the Civil War, we got through World War II, we got through the Revolutionary War, we got through all of them, we'll get through this."[30]

In fact, few if any in his audience "got through" any of those horrors—and those who actually lived through the Revolutionary or any other war at the cost of great suffering and loss of family and friends would have been shocked to hear how casually he refers to what they suffered. But most of his audience doesn't know any better; they've only read of these events or seen pictures and haven't the least idea of what it was like. His assurance is empty at best and misleading at worst.

Throwing in a bit of wisdom that seemed more applicable to Y2K, Parkhill adds: "By the way, a lot of men lived through the Titanic by jumping off early. They were what I call the smart money....They jumped off the ship while the lifeboats were still close enough and they swam to the lifeboats and got in."[31] The audience gets the message; they'd better act quickly.

It is amazing how easily one can convince a Christian audience that the Civil War, 1930s Depression, World War II, and the sinking of the Titanic are all "nothing to be afraid of." Yet the calm assurance that we'll make it seems a bit shallow if Y2K is going to live up to the predictions so many have made. So what if 1.5 billion will die in the process, as Gary North assures us? Just keep calm, we'll get through it!

Interestingly, Jack Anderson had previously warned his audience at the same large church that "there are fearmongers out there making money out of stirring people up."[32] Yet that comment came after his listeners had been stirred to near panic by the gloomy outlook he had presented. How do we tell the difference between fearmongering and inciting people to legitimate concern and action?

There is nothing wrong with being afraid. After all, there are things which any intelligent person should fear. That kind of fear is healthy because it causes us to take action. David admitted that "the floods of ungodly men made me afraid" (Psalm 18:4). In his fear, however, he turned to the Lord: "What time I am afraid, I will trust in thee" (Psalm 56:3).

Therefore, though *naturally* afraid, he could say, "The Lord is the strength of my life; of whom shall I be afraid?" (Psalm 27:1). Paul, too, admitted to fear: "We were troubled on every side; without were fightings, within were fears" (2 Corinthians 7:5). But his fear did not rule him and become panic, because his trust was in God.

The CBN (Christian Broadcasting Network) website says, "Remember the key point: don't be scared, be prepared."[33] Yet the information that is given is very scary, and much of it is outdated. Current, encouraging developments are conspicuous by their absence.

Why No Mention of Recent Positive Developments?

The most "encouraging" article on the CBN website as of December 2, 1998, dated back 11 months. It was by Roleigh Martin, who refers to himself as the Paul Revere of Y2K, called to warn the church. Martin calls his ministry the "Community Alert Campaign on the Y2K Threat to Core Infrastructures." He advocates using every available means to arouse everyone to the danger of Y2K, and he wants to enlist as many people as possible across the country to awaken their friends, neighbors, and community leaders to the threat we all face.[34] He cheers us on with these words:

> Take an inventory of what you regularly use and need. Then begin building up your supplies of those items. It's impossible to know with certainty how long the crisis will last. As time goes by [how much time?], the various Y2K shortages will lessen, and products will become available.
>
> Remember, too, that even for items you store up, you may have to ration your own supplies to get through the hardest period, because it could stretch on longer than we can see at this point. Among the things you need, keep in mind the possibility that you might have to do without power, heat, usable

water or other utilities for at least some period of
time. [How long?][35]

A review of the CBN website as of December 2, 1998,
revealed nothing but gloom-and-doom articles. Nothing
from the vast amount of recent encouraging news was cited.
Furthermore, some of the articles were more than a year
old; one, written by Rick Cowles, telling how hopeless the situation was for electric utilities, was dated August 15, 1997,
which could hardly offer factual information on that subject
in December of 1998! There was plenty of current information available about power utilities and the national
power grid to show that the Cowles' concerns expressed 17
months ago were unfounded—but that was news which CBN
News somehow overlooked.

What a pity that when CBN's Drew Parkhill spoke in
Oregon on November 14, 1998, he failed to refer to the
November 1998 *Bulletin* of the Northwest Public Power
Association containing the latest factual information his
audience needed to know about their own region. (After all,
electric power is the key factor.) Much of what Drew said
about potential disaster would have had to be revised, and
much of the concern aroused in his audience that day would
have evaporated had he quoted merely the following
excerpts:

> If you were looking forward to a cataclysmic event on
> the power system at midnight December 31, 1999, don't
> hold your breath. The North American Electric Reliability
> Council (NERC) recently found that while much work
> remains, the nation's electric utility industry has a handle
> on the Y2K problem, and a look around the Northwest
> would appear to bear that out. From the Oregon coast to
> the desert of eastern Washington, utilities report they have
> Y2K programs in place and are intent on making the tran-
> sition to the new millennium a seamless event.

"We're right on target," according to Brian Furumasu, one of three Y2K managers at BPA [Bonneville Power Administration, with jurisdiction over 70-80 percent of the Northwest's transmission]. On average, the Northwest is neck-in-neck with the rest of the country on Y2K readiness, he said....

Furumasu is overseeing readiness on BPA's transmission system and is working with the interconnected customer systems. The goal for Y2K at BPA is "to make the transition into and through the year 2000 a non-event for continuation of power services and business operations," he said. ...BPA's remediation activities are scheduled to be done by March 1999....The industry predicted a lot of problems with embedded chips, but they have not materialized, he said....

"One of our primary concerns is to assure that everything is in alignment with our business partners," he stated. "In the end, we have to make sure things operate across the region, and we are working with a lot of entities, in concert with the Western Systems Coordinating Council and NERC....An important part of contingency planning will be to have enough staff at hand when the date change actually occurs...."

Jeff Brune, Y2K project manager at Washington Water Power (soon to be Avista Corporation), said his utility is well on the way to becoming Y2K ready. Over 90 employees have participated in the project....We looked at over 550,000 items and fewer than 3,000 were date-sensitive; of those, only 300 required remediation, Brune said. "None of these would have caused a disruption in service," he added....

We've been aware of Y2K for several years, according to Dan Reeves, director of administration and finance at Peninsula Light Company. He said Peninsula had postponed until recently the purchase of new billing software because it wanted something that was Y2K compliant. ...We've managed Y2K in our normal equipment-replacement cycle, Reeves said. We have all of our equipment and software compliant, he reported, and have come up with nothing Y2K related that "is of a critical nature."

Reeves said that in addition to obtaining statements from vendors about Y2K compliance, Peninsula will do a live test on each of its business systems by the end of the year [1998] to make sure they will accommodate the change from 1999 to 2000. "We don't want to get surprised," he said, "and this will give us all of next year to take corrective action so things are working properly....Any business that is going to be around has to validate its activities and corrective actions."[36]

The report above confirms our own findings. We have yet to hear of anything the power utilities have found in their search through hardware, software, and embedded chips that would have caused an interruption in service had it not been found. The facts are, there will not be any serious interruption of electrical service across the country as a result of any Y2K-related glitches in computers. But somehow alarmists don't seem to come across that information—and it was totally lacking from Parkhill's presentation that day. Had he known and given it, there wouldn't have been much else to say.

Exhortation and Organization to Action

A recent Barna poll of senior pastors, commissioned by CBN, found that "78 percent of them were familiar with the Y2K problem, but only 21 percent had taken any steps to evaluate its potential effect on their church. Even fewer (13 percent) said they had taken steps to alert their congregations about potential ministry opportunities or social consequences related to the issue."[37] Gary North, always the pessimist, warns:

> The church of Jesus Christ will not be ready in 2000. It will not be able to say, "We sounded the

alarm early. Our members are ready. We're here to help."

The church will say, "What happened? You mean that God brings sanctions in history? You mean that God holds society responsible for public evil?"[38]

Obviously, if one is to take seriously what is being said on this subject, it is not enough merely to be aware of Y2K, but action must be taken to prepare for it. That is where the local Y2K committees being formed by churches across the country come in. Activists are recruiting pastors to help one another and their flocks to seriously and diligently prepare for the possible Y2K chaos and calamity being predicted.

Ministerial associations in many towns and cities around the country have already formed Y2K committees similar to the one mentioned above. In that Oregon town the ministers have organized a Y2K Preparedness Committee, described by its chairman as

> a group of volunteers...who want to help prepare our community for possible problems due to the Y2K computer bug; and also for any other kind of natural disaster...that could occur....While any number of [disasters] could happen...God knows when those would be, they're all part of His plan....But we're focusing on Y2K because this is one *we* know about. The date is very definite, it's immovable, can't be postponed....We don't know what exactly will happen in Y2K, but we know enough to know that we should prepare.[39]

One of the major parts of this program was the establishment of a comprehensive "Y2K Neighborhood Watch Plan" to cover the entire town with subcommittees. These subcommittees meet frequently to plan strategies for getting the churches prepared not only to take care of their own people but of unsaved friends and neighbors as well. It seems that Christians are far more concerned and involved with Y2K than is the secular world.

In fact, in at least some instances the secular world is looking to churches for help. That is the case in St. Paul, Minnesota. On December 2, 1998, St. Paul's mayor, Norm Coleman,

> ...called on the city's churches and synagogues... to provide temporary refuge for residents forced out of their homes by potential computer snafus beginning January 1, 2000.
>
> That's when the millennium bug, Y2K for short, will kick in, possibly jeopardizing electrical service, food distribution and public safety," [Coleman] said at a news conference updating city efforts to combat the bug....Coleman acknowledged that "no one knows for sure what will happen when the calendar turns." But he warned that despite the city's best efforts, officials probably will be unable to reprogram all of the computer-run operations in time.[40]

In view of the concern being expressed by city officials not only in St. Paul but elsewhere, we can hardly fault sincere Christians for their concern and willingness to assist their communities. And to their credit, while Christians involved in Y2K preparedness recognize the importance of the physical side, they put even greater emphasis upon spiritual preparedness. After Jack Anderson had finished his speech to the Y2K Preparedness Committee in that Oregon town, the chairman exhorted the audience:

> What is going on in your heart and your mind and your emotions is going to determine how you act..., how you evaluate the situation, what kind of principles guide your action and your response....
>
> The most important spiritual preparation is a faithful Christian life....

> Most of the history of God's covenant is a record
> of people in crisis. And that's oftentimes when God
> does His most powerful work....Many of the Psalms
> are written in the crucible of crises and frequently
> the Psalmist is crying, "O God, the waters are over-
> whelming me, help me."[41]

Many of the Y2K Christian groups forming around the
country have taken their cue from the "Joseph Project 2000,"
an interdenominational ministry founded by Shaunti
Feldhahn in May 1998, and directed by her. It is sponsoring
or inspiring seminars and conferences across America. Says
Shaunti, "Suddenly we started to get phone calls and e-mails
from Christians all over the country, asking how they could
do what we were doing." The first conference brought
together nearly 3,000 people on September 12, 1998, at the
New Birth Missionary Baptist Church in Atlanta, Georgia,
"for the Atlanta Y2K Community Awareness Event...and at
the end of the day, 100 people volunteered to carry forward
the work of the Joseph Project in Atlanta."[42]

"The Joseph Project 2000"

Shaunti Feldhahn introduced her ministry on the James
Dobson program: "Storing some of the necessities...that's
one of the reasons why we named the project the 'Joseph
Project 2000,' just because of the biblical story of Joseph
where he saw the famine coming and prepared for it and
then was able to open the storehouses and bless others."
Dobson interjected, "Now what is the Joseph Project, essen-
tially?" Shaunti responded:

> Well, what we're doing is to try to generate Chris-
> tian leadership in communities...to try to address this
> issue of getting pastors on board so that they're com-
> fortable leading, so that it's not necessarily just being
> done by people who are under no accountability or
> authority. [To see] that there is a movement in every

city, every community in the country and internationally so that the church is perceived to be the
answer on Y2K, which it is, so that this is an opportunity to not go overboard[43]

At that point, for lack of time, Dobson changed the subject to banking and The Joseph Project was not further
explained. However, Dobson is strongly backing and promoting "The Joseph Project 2000." The packet of information sent by Focus on the Family to those requesting information about Y2K contains a Joseph Project 2000 brochure with
a quote on it from Larry Burkett, "I support the work the
Joseph Project 2000 is doing nationally to generate Christian
community awareness on Y2K. I would encourage you to
work together with the local Joseph Project director and
his/her leadership team to begin preparing to minister to
your area in the changing days ahead."[44] As to how this may
work, Burkett goes into more detail in a quote provided by
Shaunti Feldhahn in Chapter 10 of her book *Y2K: The
Millennium Bug—A Balanced Christian Response*:

> Do the same thing with the church, as you would storing
> individually. Put in enough food so that you could feed half
> of your church families and half of the other families in the
> community. [He doesn't say for how long.] You could do
> that...to buy a 50kw generator for a church is a doable thing
> for 200 people....Granted, it will cost you some money.
> Granted, you may be ridiculed if you cleared out two rooms
> of your church to store food in and then you didn't need
> the food. But, you know what, there are always hungry
> people, you can get rid of that food, no problem....
>
> For example, there's a church here in Georgia that...
> erected a tower...on 5 acres on the crest of a mountain...,
> bought a generator..., they all bought cell phones that also
> work like walkie-talkies, so they can communicate with each
> other, no matter what..., they bought soy beans, wheat,
> etc....They've got their [diesel] tanks and their generators...,

they believe they're going to be the only people who are ready with lights, food, and communication.[45]

It is rather naive to imagine that Christians are the only ones who know about Y2K and have been gathering food and supplies and preparing with diesel generators and other commodities. Whether that is the case or not, however, the Joseph Project 2000 insists that it is the responsibility of Christians to take the lead in uniting and providing for the unsaved community around them. As for giving away the food to the poor and hungry if it isn't needed, if these churches succeed in storing enough food for their entire community for six months or a year, it would take a community of homeless people the same size to consume it. And even those who frequent skid row missions may not want freeze-dried food when fresh is available.

Obviously, providing for the entire community is a herculean task which requires that all churches work together. Preparing for Y2K will prove to be one of the most powerful ecumenical forces imaginable if The Joseph Project—which is off to an impressive start nationally and plans to be international—is successful. Shaunti Feldhahn writes:

> First and foremost, all the churches in a given geographic area should come together to discuss working as a team to prepare and respond. The power of the body of Christ working in unity will be so much more effective than that of "lone rangers" going it alone.
>
> Furthermore, after the year 2000 hits, it is very likely that a given church will *have* to depend on other area churches for something anyway; it is only prudent to set up those networks now....Thankfully, some communities already have a formal or informal infrastructure for inter-denominational cooperation....
>
> More likely, however, if your area doesn't have a usable network, you need to start one. All it takes is a few pastors or Christian leaders to gather together in agreement that

> Y2K is a serious issue, one that needs to be addressed in unity by the Christian community....
>
> A group of churches in a given city or town can easily organize a "Y2K Community Awareness Seminar" for the entire area, offering it free or at a low cost simply as a service to the community. This event should bring in a Y2K expert or play an informational video...bring in local municipal officials...try to do this on as large a scale as you can, to reach your whole city or regional area....
>
> Community working groups and task forces in each geographic location should be set up....Help your local neighborhood organization to think through ways to impact your own small area, and draw neighbors together....
>
> While church members may be most comfortable helping their own mercy ministries, evangelism programs, and education centers prepare for Y2K, it is important that we as Christians reach out to the charities run by secular organizations and people of other faiths.[46]

So concern about Y2K, rather than about Jesus Christ, the Bible, and sound doctrine, becomes the unifying factor bringing everyone together regardless of their differing and sometimes false doctrines. A new and unbiblical ecumenical unity is being created by this alleged crisis. At the same time, we are being told by the most vocal "experts" that Y2K could usher in the church's finest hour. Anderson told his Oregon audience, "We're going to see some things that people before us have longed to see, and I think it's going to bring a form of revival....It is not a time to be fearful and anxious, but to anticipate and see what God is going to do."[47]

Exactly who in the past may have longed to see Y2K, and what God will supposedly do through His people as a result of Y2K, wasn't made clear.

Joseph *Who?*

Whether getting churches together to store food for feeding the community is biblical and rational is an important conclusion upon which each person and church must individually decide. Certainly those involved in doing so are earnest and sincere, but much of their planning is based upon misinformation. Obviously, before becoming caught up in the emotion of rescuing communities (an appealing and exhilarating idea), we need to think it through biblically and logically. The Joseph Project 2000 brochure sent out by Focus on the Family states:

> The Year 2000 computer problem is looming larger and larger on the horizon....How should Christians respond...? How can we prepare our community? We believe the Lord is powerfully stirring His people for action....
>
> As with Joseph in Egypt, God may be calling Christians to prepare not just for themselves, but for others as well. The Joseph Project 2000 facilitates Christian leadership in readying homes, churches, businesses and communities for Y2K. As JP2000 "chapters" spring up in response to this urgent need, we want to serve those with a heart for this action in their community....
>
> The work of the Church on Y2K is truly a "God-sized work" and we are watching for His guidance as we move forward. We hope you will join us.[48]

In fact, if the truth is faced, instead of Y2K "looming larger and larger," it actually wanes smaller and smaller. It is being increasingly admitted, even by those who only a few months ago were so certain of major disruptions and shortages, that Y2K's results will probably not be so bad after all. Is God really "stirring His people to action" through the misinformation and emotion surrounding this subject? Or have a few zealous Christians (who admit they don't know for sure what is going to happen) come up with an exciting idea on their own? We know for certain that their use of Scripture to support this action is faulty.

Those behind this interdenominational movement may call it what they will, but it shouldn't be called the *Joseph* project. To do so is a travesty upon Scripture and logic. There is neither relationship nor resemblance to what occurred in Joseph's day. To imply that today's humanly devised Joseph Project 2000 is anything like what Joseph accomplished is extremely misleading and potentially dangerous to the Christian witness.

The original Joseph project in Egypt was not an idea of, nor was it run by, the people of God. It was a project of the godless Egyptian government overseen by Joseph. It came about by a specific revelation from God, not even to Joseph, but by means of a dream which He gave to pagan Pharaoh. In his interpretation of the dream Joseph said, "God hath shewed Pharaoh what he is about to do...the thing is established by God, and God will shortly bring it to pass" (Genesis 41:25,32).

A Misnamed Misconception

The situation in Joseph's day—how God called Joseph, what He called him to do, and the purpose behind that call—bears absolutely no resemblance to Y2K and the ambition of feeding the world, to which the church is so mistakenly aspiring in our day. God very clearly showed Pharaoh what would happen; God has shown no one what will happen regarding Y2K. In fact (except for a few extremists), all those warning about Y2K admit that it could turn out to be nothing.

It was not the people of God in Joseph's day to whom God revealed what would happen so that they could prepare food for Egypt and the rest of the world. It was the world, the ungodly heathen, whom God blessed with superabundant harvests for seven years so that they could set aside enough to feed themselves during the seven years of famine.

Practically speaking, there is no way everyone in America could possess six months' or a year's supply of food without months of preparation on the part of those who provide it. It would have to be specially grown, prepared, processed, and distributed to markets in addition to the normal amount— and there is no provision for doing so. It took the Egyptians seven years to accumulate their supply; there is no such accumulation in the normal food supply chain. Therefore, for Christians to acquire their stocks of food to help people in the future would actually deprive multitudes in the present of the normal supply which would thereby be depleted.

Nor was the food in Joseph's day stored in the homes of God's people (much less in churches); it was all placed in central storehouses under the control of the Egyptian government. Then, instead of giving back to the Egyptians the food they had gathered from their fields, Joseph *charged* them for it, and when they had no more money with which to pay, he took their possessions and lands for Pharaoh, eventually charging them rent as tenants over what had been their own land (Genesis 47:13-26). Is that the secret intent of those behind today's Joseph Project? Surely not. Then, please, don't use that name!

We are not trying to be critical. As we have emphasized, no doubt those who are leading this movement have the best of intentions. However, they tread on dangerous ground when they claim to be following the example of Joseph. They are not by any means following either the example of Joseph or any other example one could glean from Scripture.

It is amazing how Shaunti Feldhahn, founder and director of The Joseph Project, manages to find a spiritual lesson even in the Egyptians' eventual loss of their property and slavery of themselves to Pharaoh. She writes:

> The biblical story of Joseph tells us more than
> just to bless those around us, it tells us what happens
> when we do. Year by year, as the famine worsened

and the surrounding peoples [Egyptians] became increasingly desperate, they had less and less to trade in return for the food Joseph had stored. First their money ran out, then their livestock. Eventually, all they had to trade were themselves and their land. "Buy us and our land in exchange for food; we will then become servants to Pharaoh," they said. "So Joseph bought all the land of Egypt for Pharaoh.... Thus, all the people of Egypt became servants to Pharaoh" (Genesis 47:19-21).

While at first we may be offended by this story and consider it the worst case of loan-sharking ever seen, we must look deeper. Instead, this account conveys a fundamental truth about what happens when desperate people are provided for: in exchange for having their needs met, they freely and willingly give themselves to the provider.[49]

The Egyptians "freely and willingly" gave themselves to Pharaoh? Hardly! It was turn themselves and their lands over to Pharaoh or die from starvation. Does Shaunti expect the unsaved whom the Christians feed (if it all turns out as she foresees) to give themselves to the Christians who feed them? Of course not, but to give themselves to God. It doesn't work that way, nor is this the gospel. Instead, it could arouse resentment if the recipients suspect this to be the motive.

Furthermore, we can't attribute to Joseph the process of taking the Egyptians' land and making them slaves. Joseph was only administering what Pharaoh decreed. But there is not a word about Christians today submitting themselves to government oversight of their Y2K preparedness. *Joseph Project*, indeed.

Is the Church Called to Feed the World?

On the Dobson program, without any correction from the other panelists, Feldhahn declared that the church is called to be "the answer on Y2K." To the contrary, any call upon

Christians must be found in the Bible—and this "call" is absent from its pages. Nowhere in Scripture are Christians called upon to feed the world, nor did they ever attempt to do it.

On the program, Shaunti added,

> We have a model throughout history of Christians who were willing to sacrifice on behalf of those around them, to really, truly love their neighbors as themselves…: in some of the great plagues in the Roman Empire, and in England when the Puritans were willing to stay in the city and minister when everyone else fled. And we have to decide, I think, with Y2K; if there are problems, we have to decide what we really believe. Do we really believe this world is not our home, are we really willing to believe our own theology and be willing to sacrifice and prepare to serve and witness? I think this could be one of the most exciting opportunities that God is presenting to us.[50]

It sounds appealing, but it isn't biblical. There are many fine examples of self-sacrifice for the good of others in history, but nothing that fits Y2K and the unrealistic ambition for a small Christian minority to feed entire communities which the Joseph Project is inspiring across this country. Nor is there *anything* in the Bible that would even remotely justify such a project. Indeed, we have an example to the contrary in the early church which lays this subject to rest:

> And in those days came *prophets* from Jerusalem unto Antioch. And there stood up one of them named Agabus, and signified by the Spirit that there should be great dearth throughout all the world: which came to pass in the days of Claudius Caesar.
> Then the disciples, every man according to his ability, determined to send relief unto the *brethren* which dwelt in Judaea: Which also they did, and sent it to the *elders* by the hands of Barnabas and Saul. (Acts 11:27-30, emphasis added).

Here, instead of the uncertainty of Y2K, was a direct word by the Spirit of God through a prophet of God that a great famine was coming upon all the earth. Yet there is not a whisper that the church began to gather stores of food or money or other supplies in order to *feed their communities*. If they did not do it then, by what authority can we say that we are to do it today?

Remember, the church of that day was under the direct leadership of Peter, James, and Paul, and the other apostles who were still alive. Therefore we must accept what that church did or did not do as our example. To engage ourselves in activities which the early church under the apostles' direction never engaged in is to waste the Lord's time and money and to run the risk of being led off into greater error. Humanitarian activities, commendable though they may seem from a humanistic perspective, should not be promoted as *Christian* and as the special obligation of Christians and the church.

The Greatest Opportunity in History for Witnessing?

Another misconception associated with Y2K which has bewitched the Christian community is the belief that Y2K will bring about the greatest opportunity in history to tell the lost the gospel of Jesus Christ. Jack Anderson said, "We're going to have an opportunity to witness to an awful lot of people. They're going to look at you and say, 'Why aren't you worried sick?' Well, let me tell you about that. There is a way that you can be assured that no matter what happens you're still going to be...right in the palm of God's hand, and He's sovereign."[51]

We hear this same idea repeatedly as the reason why Christians ought to be in the forefront of Y2K preparedness. Christians have used a variety of gimmicks for supposedly witnessing for Christ; is this just the latest and most elaborate? The following ad was in Jerry Falwell's *National Liberty Journal:*[52]

Y2K
THIS IS DEFINITELY ONE OF THE GREATEST OPPORTUNITIES PERHAPS EVER TO WITNESS FOR JESUS CHRIST

What better way to witness than with a Y2K T-shirt that is guaranteed to start a conversation....

We will offer for a limited time this top quality 100% pre-shrunk cotton t-shirt, silk screened in Gold Metallic ink...

ATTENTION FUND-RAISERS, THIS IS A GOLDEN OPPORTUNITY TO MEET YOUR FINANCIAL GOALS. DISCOUNTS ARE AVAILABLE.

With Christians supposedly the only ones prepared to feed not only themselves but the rest of the community, the unsaved will presumably beat a path to the doors of Christian churches and homes begging for help. And in the process of providing that help, like a mission on skid row, the gospel will be given out and eagerly believed. But anyone who has preached and worked in such missions can testify that of the large numbers of men and women who have reached the bottom and desperately need help, relatively few respond to the gospel when it is presented along with food and shelter night after night.

Christians have used all sorts of unbiblical and unfruitful motivators to induce people to "make a decision for Christ." And now we have a new one: "Believe in Christ because His followers went to the trouble to protect you from the Y2K crisis. Christians are way ahead of this problem, better informed and prepared than the world, and they will take care of you." It sounds dangerously like the prosperity gospel which probably has the largest following among Christians today (it certainly commands much if not most of the radio and television time), yet it is a false gospel that may very well be sending multitudes to hell.

Perhaps We *Need* Y2K for a Great Spiritual Harvest!

One hears it repeated frequently in connection with Y2K preparedness that people who find themselves in the midst of disaster are more tender to the gospel. (Tell that to Moses or Jeremiah!) Therefore, Y2K is supposedly going to soften millions of hearts for the greatest spiritual harvest in history. One almost gets the impression that we *need* Y2K to see the world converted, and one wonders why God hasn't allowed more of these crises. Larry Burkett waxes enthusiastic on this subject as he tells us of the ultimate purpose behind the preparation for Y2K by the church in Georgia mentioned earlier:

> But most importantly, they are holding classes to train everybody in the church on how to witness, and renewing them on the scriptures, because they believe they're going to be the only people who are ready with lights, food, and communication. They said, "People are going to come knocking on your door when you've got lights, and no one else does."
>
> They think that people are going to come to them for help, and ask, "How did you know this?" And they're going to have an opportunity to witness like they've never had in their life.[53]

If there was ever an opportunity for witnessing by the means Y2K is expected to bring about, it was handed to the early church in the example we referred to from Acts. They had a clear prophecy from God informing them ahead of time. In that case, they certainly knew what the world did not. They could have told their friends and neighbors and unsaved relatives exactly what was going to happen; and when it did happen as foretold, surely that would have convinced the unsaved that this was the true church in touch with God. Then when the church fed the hungry all about them, by today's reasoning, this would have been the church's finest hour and the greatest opportunity for the gospel, an opportunity which God had specifically given to them and told them about ahead of time so they could prepare. *Yet they did none of this.* The apostles apparently had a different leading from God than so many are claiming for themselves and the church today.

The situation today doesn't even come close to the opportunity the early church had for what by today's unbiblical and ill-advised definitions would have been called its finest hour. Moreover, no prophet has "signified by the Spirit" exactly what is going to happen as a result of Y2K. No one knows.

Remember, too, that no one faced greater difficulty for maintenance of daily living than did the children of Israel in the wilderness, and no one saw so many miracles from God in providing for their needs. Yet no one was so disobedient and rebellious and faithless as that generation! We see the same thing in the days of Christ, who fed and healed all in need, yet of whom the Bible says, "But though he had done so many miracles before them, yet they believed not on him" (John 12:37). Indeed, many whom Christ had previously fed and healed were later in the mob that screamed for His crucifixion.

The Gospel Blimp Revisited

Much time and money and effort is being put into preparing for Y2K *future* witnessing that ought to be spent more wisely in the propagation of the gospel *right now.* Is it possible that the elusive hope that Y2K is *going to be* the church's finest hour, providing the greatest opportunity *in the future* for proclaiming the gospel in church history, is taking time and energy that could otherwise be spent in winning the lost *now*? Feeding communities that will supposedly be starving for lack of preparation, and then giving them the gospel as a result of this kindness, is a well-intentioned ambition, but it is the height of folly.

We are convinced that Y2K is not going to turn out to be the disaster that so many predict and which now, apparently, we ought to hope for because it will bring multitudes to Christ. Who could be so hardhearted as to wish Y2K *not* to be a disaster, when apparently the greater the crisis, the greater the number of lost delivered from hell! If that is true, shouldn't we forget our own comfort and pray that Y2K, no matter how much we may suffer as a result, will be everything the extremists predict and more! And then prepare with all our might to win the world to Christ as a result of our stores of food and provisions!

Even if Y2K does turn out to be the means of bringing desperate, hungry sinners to church doors, we still must face the question: how many "conversions" or "decisions for Christ" made under the pressure of getting out from under the Y2K problem would be genuine? Would such "converts" truly be coming to Christ as repentant sinners believing He died for their sins and rose again? Or would they be making a "decision for Christ" only in the hope of escaping starvation and destruction? All of this costly and time-consuming preparation to witness *in the future* when supposedly the unsaved will beat a path to Christians' doors for food and shelter when computers crash on January 1, 2000 cannot be justified on the basis of one verse in the Bible.

One is reminded of the book of some years ago titled *The Gospel Blimp*. It was the story of well-meaning Christians who, instead of witnessing to their neighbors and those with whom they had personal contact, used a blimp to fly over the city trailing a biblical text and from which gospel tracts were thrown, fluttering down into swimming pools and other inconvenient places and arousing resentment rather than salvation.

As the world begins to back off and to recognize that Y2K will be no more than a minor inconvenience, the church is being whipped into ever greater effort to prepare for the worst-case scenario. And if one is really going to be prepared for Y2K, shouldn't it be for the worst possibility? Sadly, the emphasis within the church upon Y2K disaster preparedness is rampant with speculation that is causing many Christians to take extreme measures for fear of being left without the basic essentials of life for weeks and perhaps months or years. And the idea that they can use all of this to win the lost only increases the misconception.

If that were not bad enough, Christians run the risk of holding the name of God and Bible prophecy up to ridicule when this all turns out to be a huge mistake and when the warnings Christians have passed along to their unsaved friends and their promise of helping them during the coming disaster are exposed as foolishness after January 1, 2000. It could turn out to be the church's greatest folly if Christians continue on this path.

There is a danger here in justifying Y2K preparedness and plans on the basis of historic examples of self-sacrifice, such as Feldhahn offers, to rationalize the Joseph Project 2000. Those times of crisis came without warning; this one is presumably known. This introduces a new problem: when Christians, on the basis of their belief that Y2K will culminate in worldwide calamity, warn of a danger that doesn't materialize, they thereby discredit the Bible and our Lord.

This is especially true if they have connected Y2K with Bible prophecy and God's judgment—and that is exactly what many Christians are doing.

The so-called "millennium bug" could scramble the electronic minds of computers worldwide in the year 2000...and the universal panic inspired could be the catalyst for the rise of the Antichrist, the mark of the beast "666" system for buying and selling, and the advent of the great tribulation!

> —Jack Van Impe[1]

[Y2K is a message from God] to bring us to the...understanding that all that we have lived for on this earth, all that we have invented, improved, struggled for and built is worthless.

> —Fred Moody,
> http://www.biblecode.com[2]

It's hard to say that the Bible does not say anything about the Y2K problem...because of the many prophetic signs that have appeared in the last fifty, or so, years....The confusion created by the Millennium Bug will create a hunger for "religion," and the religion of the future will offer it....Will it be the universal adoration and worship as is predicted for the Antichrist?

> —N. W. Hutchings and Larry Spargimino of
> Southwest Radio Church[3]

We cannot lose sight of the fact that we are not dealing with a clear prophetic word from God here. We are dealing with predictions of fallible men.

> —Albert James Dager, Founder-Director, *Media Spotlight*[4]

Y2K has forced my marriage to grow and strengthen. Y2K has forced my relationship with God to grow and strengthen....For all this I am thankful.

> —The Y2K Weatherman[5]

[Y2K] is too large an issue to ignore for someone who has very specific millennial or apocalyptic beliefs. They can point to Y2K and say, "Look at this impending, horrible crash. We are obviously in the end times."

> —David Kessler, executive administrator, Center for
> Millennial Studies, Boston University[6]

CHAPTER SIX

A Biblical Rejection
of Y2K Disaster

As happened with the Gulf War, the Y2K threat to computers is being tied in with Bible prophecy by many Bible teachers and some Christian leaders. Several prominent prophecy teachers were convinced that the Gulf War would lead into Armageddon, and even that the United States would be defeated by Saddam Hussein's forces. This author was not among them. It was quite obvious that such speculation had no basis in Scripture. It is equally clear that Y2K is not and cannot be a fulfillment of Bible prophecy.

There are skeptics and critics who reject the very idea of trying to correlate current events with Bible prophecy. They are afraid of what they call "newspaper eschatology" because it seems that each time it is attempted it proves eventually to be wrong. Some of us are old enough to remember when Hitler was identified as the Antichrist and some of President Franklin D. Roosevelt's innovative ideas during the 1930s depression were identified with great conviction as the mark of the beast. Unfortunately, such mistakes have caused Bible prophecy to be neglected by Christians and ridiculed by the world.

Although newspaper eschatology can lead to error, it does not discredit biblical prophecy. It cannot be relegated to allegory or spiritualized away. Prophecy does refer to real events, many of which have already occurred, and others which are yet to occur on this earth in the last days. Certainly, all of the following events have happened exactly as God foretold, have been witnessed by the world, and are part of world history: the scattering of Israel to every nation; the rampant anti-Semitism worldwide against God's chosen people; their preservation as an identifiable, ethnic people for 1,900 years, though without a land of their own; the return of Israel to the very land that God had originally given her 3,500 years ago; and God's protection upon that tiny nation in spite of its being surrounded with enemies which outnumber her many times over in troops and tanks and warplanes, enemies which have sought her annihilation since her rebirth in 1948. These events must be acknowledged as the fulfillment of many specific prophecies in the Old Testament, among them the following:

> In the same day the LORD made a covenant with Abram, saying, Unto thy seed have I given this land, from the river of Egypt unto the great river, the river Euphrates....And I will give unto thee, and to thy seed after thee...all the land of Canaan, for an everlasting possession (Genesis 15:18; 17:8).

> The land whereon thou [Jacob] liest, to thee will I give it, and to thy seed (Genesis 28:13).

> The land shall not be sold [or exchanged] for ever: for the land is mine (Leviticus 25:23).

> If thou wilt not hearken unto the voice of the LORD thy God, to observe to do all his commandments and his statutes...ye shall be plucked from off the land....And the LORD shall scatter thee among all people, from one end of the earth even unto the other;....And thou shalt become an astonishment, a proverb, and a byword, among all nations (Deuteronomy 28:15,63-64;37).

> And I will...deliver them [Israel] to be removed to all the kingdoms of the earth, to be a curse, and an astonishment, and an hissing, and a reproach, among all the nations whither I have driven them (Jeremiah 29:18).

Though I make a full end of all nations whither I have scattered thee, yet will I not make a full end of thee: but I will correct thee....Behold, I will bring them [the scattered Jews] from the north country, and gather them from the coasts of the earth....He that scattered Israel will gather him, and keep him, as a shepherd doth his flock...; it [Jerusalem] shall not be plucked up, nor thrown down any more for ever" (Jeremiah 30:11; 31:8,10,40).

Signs of the Nearness of Christ's Return?

In spite of the fulfillment of many specific prophecies, it is becoming increasingly accepted among Christians, even in evangelical seminaries, to reject the very idea of looking for any signs that we are in the last days prior to Christ's return. Obviously, that attitude is antibiblical and even anti-Christ, because it was Christ who gave us the signs.

The disciples earnestly asked our Lord, "Tell us...what shall be the sign of thy coming, and of the end of the world?" (Matthew 24:3). They had heard Jesus rebuke the Pharisees for not recognizing the signs that their own prophets had given, which, had they heeded them, would have told them that it was time for the Messiah to appear and that indeed He was that promised One: "Ye hypocrites, ye can discern the face of the sky and of the earth; but how is it that ye do not discern this time?" (Luke 12:56). The disciples knew there had to be signs. This was the way God had worked from the beginning through His prophets: "Therefore, the LORD himself shall give you a sign" (Isaiah 7:14).

In response to their question, Jesus did not reply, "There won't be any signs." Nor did He say, "It will be wrong to look for signs," or "It would be dangerous to look for signs because you wouldn't be able to recognize them anyway." When the disciples asked Jesus for the signs that would herald the nearness of His return, He gave them many—real events that could be recognized and their significance understood.

Therefore, it is biblical to be eagerly anticipating and watching for the very signs which Jesus foretold.

There are, however, several problems confronting anyone attempting to recognize the signs as they appear.

Words of Caution

First of all, it is only logical that at least some of the signs would be described in a way that would make them difficult to recognize. Obviously, this would be necessary in order to prevent Satan and his followers from deliberately trying to prevent fulfillment. Second, we must overcome the temptation to make Bible prophecy fit current events rather than to evaluate current events strictly on the basis of what Scripture says. That error is most apparent when one attempts to fit too much detail into prophecy, where the Bible generally presents a broad picture.

Y2K is such a detail. Even if it lives up to the worst-case scenario, one can never say that it was prophesied because it can't be found in Scripture. Even if Y2K produces effects similar to world conditions prophesied in Revelation to be present during the Great Tribulation and the reign of Antichrist, we cannot say that it was the God-ordained means of fulfilling those prophecies. In fact, we can say with certainty that Y2K will *not* be the means of ushering in the Great Tribulation, and it will *not* live up to the doomsayers' expectations because to do so would actually be a contradiction of Scripture, as we shall see.

We must be extremely careful in correlating current events with prophecy. And we must beware of violating Scripture in our zeal to "prove" the Bible from the daily news. For example, one of the fondest ambitions of many prophecy teachers has been to identify the Antichrist. Sermons are preached and books are written telling us who Antichrist is. High on the list of recent favorites have been King Juan Carlos of Spain and Prince Charles of England.

Such speculation is vain and unbiblical. It should never be engaged in by any Christian. Why? Because Paul tells us in 2 Thessalonians 2:6-8 that Antichrist can only be revealed "in his time," and until then his identity must remain a secret. Chuck Missler cautions:

> In the book of Daniel it talks about the Antichrist..., the coming world leader. He's going to be a very, very dramatic guy. He's going to rise in financial terms..., he becomes militarily strong subsequently....
>
> But here's the phrase that's interesting: "And he shall think to change the times and the laws." Does this have anything to do with the year 2000? I don't know. But...there will be prophecy buffs publishing newsletters that link the Y2K problem to the year 2000 to the Antichrist making his appearance....To me it's a little aggressive.
>
> At the same time...I do believe...that you and I are being propelled into a period of time about which the Bible says more than it does about any other period of time in history.[7]

Gordon McDonald, of Chuck Missler's Koinonia House, points to a number of developments that seem to set the stage for the final apocalypse, such as "the proliferation of biological weapons; the spread of Islam...; the possession of nuclear weapons by at least 17 mutually hostile nations." McDonald then adds,

> Suddenly we have Y2K, an issue that could cause literal worldwide economic collapse. There is no known technology that will fix it. And if inner cities are hard-hit, if there are no more entitlement programs, if there is global chaos and an absence of law and order, the stage could be set...for the man the Bible says will deceive many with signs and wonders, to rise up and present a one-world solution.

McDonald's timing, however, is faulty. The Antichrist (as McDonald himself believes) cannot take power until the Rapture removes the church. And, as we shall see, Christ comes for the church during prosperity and ease and partying, not during social upheaval, an international banking collapse, and worldwide chaos such as so many are predicting Y2K will bring upon us on January 1, 2000.

There has been much speculation concerning exactly what will set the stage for Antichrist to take charge. Logically, it is the Rapture itself which alone could produce the worldwide chaos and *terror* necessary to catapult the Antichrist into power. Indeed, nothing else could. Even the greatest problems forecast by the most pessimistic prognosticators resulting from Y2K pale into insignificance in contrast to the sudden and *terrifying* disappearance of perhaps 100 million or more from the face of the earth. *That* is a real crisis that calls for a superman to take charge!

Discrediting the Bible

Sadly, each time a correspondence has been attempted between a current event and a specific biblical prophecy and the event failed to live up to that expectation (as in the case of the Gulf War), Bible prophecy was discredited, even though the fault was not with the Bible but with those who misinterpreted it. There is a great danger of the same disillusionment occurring again when Bible teachers link Y2K with Bible prophecy. While there is usually considerable hedging (*could it be that*, etc.) rather than dogmatic declarations, nevertheless, the suggestions are often strong enough to leave little doubt concerning what is meant.

Ron Reese of Maranatha Ministries published a tract in mid-1998 which quoted Gary North extensively and linked the anticipated Y2K chaos with specific Bible prophecies. Along with considerable misinformation, Reese mixes in the Bible:

The Bible prophesies *several major military conflicts* the final seven years of Tribulation before the Second Coming of Christ. *More than half of the population of the world will die during this cataclysmic time!!!* Could this computer Y2K crisis play a *major* role in bringing about these horrible wars, where the Bible strongly implies the use of weapons of mass destruction...?!!

The data corruption problem is like a *virus* or a *cancer.* Even the computers that *do* become Y2K compliant will quickly be infiltrated with false data and the *virus will corrupt all computers across the globe in a very short space of time and an economic earthquake will erupt almost overnight!*

Dr. Gary North states, "*Today*, we face the mother of all bank runs....The simple truth is this: If you cannot fix all the computers, there is no use in fixing any of them because of the data corruption problem. *The banking system is doomed...!*"

The word is slowly leaking out...that there *is no way to stop this from happening...!* When the public catches on to the full implications and magnitude of this crisis, the result will be *sheer panic...!*

Dr. Gary North states, "It will take only 72 hours for frightened consumers to strip supermarket shelves bare. Bank depositors will rush in droves to withdraw their savings. Jittery investors will pull completely out of the stockmarket...panic will spill over to every industrialized country on earth."

In short...you do not have much time to prepare for what will *soon* be known as *the greatest social, political, and financial crisis mankind has faced,* at least since the great plagues of the 14th century that wiped out one-third of Europe. Only instead of a deadly bacteria, we face a *devastating...computer virus that is likely to lay low the governments and economies of the whole world!!!*[8]

That the Bible contains so many prophecies which lend themselves to association with Y2K may explain why so many individual Christians and the churches they attend have given it such close attention. Jack and Rexella Van Impe are a husband-and-wife team seen weekly on TBN. The back cover of their video "2000 Time Bomb" suggests that the video reveals vital information which is somehow being withheld from general circulation (though the only sources they quote are available to anyone):

> The time bomb is about to go off—and the enormity of potential disaster awaiting the American people and the world in the year 2000 has been hidden from you and your family! [Not if one reads papers, magazines, logs onto the Internet, or watches TV.]
> See how the effects of this predicted computer catastrophe coincide with Bible prophecy regarding the coming of the Lord and the latter days of time on this earth![9]

Y2K Prophetic Absurdities

No hedging there. Y2K actually coincides with Bible prophecy for the last days! That statement has viewers on the edge of their seats. Unfortunately, some of the connections being made between Y2K and alleged Bible prophecy border on the ridiculous. For example, Van Impe says: "The reason I believe that this [Y2K] could be the prelude of the final sign before the return of Christ is because they're talking about aviation, planes....Robert Bennett of Utah said, 'I won't get anywhere near a plane December 31, 1999.'" How Bennett's fear of flying at the turn of the new millennium relates to last-days prophecies remains a mystery. Van Impe's explanation fails to unravel the mystery:

> It's going to be dangerous to fly....The reason I believe that this computer situation where they're warning us not to fly has to do with the times preceding the coming of the Lord is because we've only had airplanes since the turn of the century and the Bible speaks about Christ coming at a time when

men fly like clouds, Isaiah 60:8. You couldn't have
that 3[00] or 400 years ago, only in our time.[10]

Isaiah 60:8 asks, "Who are these that fly as a cloud, and
as the doves to their windows?" We don't know who they are;
Isaiah doesn't tell us. They could be angels. But at least they
are *flying*, not grounded by Y2K. It is true that the Wright
brothers flew the first powered airplane in December 1903.
We've had airplanes for 95 years. Why a sudden correlation
with that verse now? How does the possibility that planes will
be grounded due to computer failures in 2000 relate to a
verse about flying like clouds? And how does the Y2K computer crash grounding planes become a sign of the nearness of Christ's return? Concerns about Y2K seem to have a
way of inspiring strange ideas.

Y2K: A Prelude to World Government?

In the excellent three-part Y2K series James Dobson ran
on his radio program in October 1998, he asked his panel of
experts, "Is it possible that we are sliding into the end-time
events that I have read about and heard about in my childhood,
in my family, and in my reading of the book of Revelation...*all
my life?* In fact, the Lord told us to watch for His coming. Do you
see any possibility in this?" [Emphasis added.][11]

Chuck Missler was the first to respond:

I'll step up to that, because I think one of the things that
could happen—this is an extreme view, but it could
happen—there could be anarchy, and strong leaders always
rise on the heels of anarchy. And so if this is as global as
Yardeni seems to emphasize, then it's not just a national
problem....But refocusing on our own nation's system...
there are people in Washington who have the fear that we
won't have elections in the year 2000...because the administration presently in power will not overlook the opportunity to exploit this politically. We've talked about the Y2K
technically..., the implications broadly, economically. The

ones that worry me the most personally are the opportunities for political exploitation....What worries me are the executive orders, the powers that are available to the Chief Executive of the United States are absolutely staggering to read through...and all that's required to invoke those is a stroke of his pen.[12]

Steve Hewitt was the next to tackle the question:

Is it part of the end times? When I was a pastor...and first got the little computers on my desk, I had people come into my office very uncomfortable with me as a pastor with a computer back in the '70s and '80s. That's supposed to be the "mark of the Beast...."And I've seen the cover of a book, *Y2K = 666?* You almost can't have your cake and eat it too. A lot of people see technology as one of the signs of us getting closer to the Second Coming, because some way we're all marked...debit cards, cashless society, and so if we see *technology* moving us toward this end time, the *breakdown* of technology with Y2K moving us back to the beginning of the 19th century...would be hard to make that analogy. [Emphasis added.][13]

Ron Blue jumped in to voice his agreement with Steve:

I often get asked on the radio if this is the prelude to a one-world government. Well, every premise for one-world government that I've heard of envisions a one-world computer system. And if there was ever a blow to a one-world computer system, it's going to be Y2K. So, I think when you face a disruption like we face, I guess it's natural for us to think of the endtimes, and it may very well be, because God can do whatever He wants to do....I think we have to be very cautious about thinking that just because we're going to have our creature comforts interrupted and be inconvenienced—or maybe worse—that that's got to be the end and Jesus is going to come and rescue us.[14]

The point they made is a good one. How could Y2K be resolved by a totalitarian regime taking control? It couldn't, because without computers working the means of control is lacking. Y2K is a computer problem that can only be repaired through a lot of hard work on the part of thousands of computer programmers (not by command of a world ruler), and that is exactly what is happening and (with few exceptions) will be carried to a successful conclusion before January 1, 2000.

Y2K, as it is being hyped, will not and cannot be the means of Antichrist seizing power. Antichrist will be able to do "signs and lying wonders" (2 Thessalonians 2:9), but he can't wave a wand and correct the world's billions of computers. Without computers, how can he take over the world, control all banking and commerce and make everyone take his mark and worship his image? He can't.

So anyone who believes that Antichrist is going to take over the world, as the Bible clearly says, would be suspicious about the possibility that Y2K will be the undoing of our computerized world. Indeed, it would seem to require computers for the biblical prophecies in Revelation 13 regarding Antichrist to be fulfilled; that fact makes those prophecies from 1,900 years ago all the more remarkable—and pretty much eliminates the possibility of any real disaster resulting from Y2K.

Y2K as a "Last Days'" Sign?

Apparently without realizing it (at least they didn't make that point) the Dobson panel presented a powerful and obvious argument against Y2K causing any great disruption: Antichrist *needs* computers. Yes, *Antichrist* is a person, although there is a *spirit* of antichrist as well (1 John 4:3). The Bible tells us (as Missler pointed out) that someone called Antichrist is going to take over the world, that he will be so powerful that no one can withstand him, that he will literally be worshiped as God and that he will control all banking and commerce worldwide so that no one can buy or sell without his mark (whatever that may be and mean). He can apparently keep track of where everyone is and what everyone does. At least these conclusions seem reasonable in light of the following scriptures:

> Little children…ye have heard that antichrist shall come (1 John 2:18)

> Then shall that Wicked [one] be revealed,…him, whose coming is after the working of Satan with all power and signs and lying wonders. And with all deceivableness of unrighteousness in them that perish; because they received not the love of the truth, that they might be saved (2 Thessalonians 2:8-10).

> And they worshipped the dragon [Satan] which gave power unto the beast [Antichrist]: and they worshipped the beast, saying,…Who is able to make war with him?…And it was given unto him to make war with the saints [those who believe in Christ during the Great Tribulation after the church has been removed in the Rapture], and to overcome them: and power was given him over all kindreds, and tongues, and nations. And all that dwell upon the earth shall worship him.…
> And I beheld another beast [the false prophet]…saying to them that dwell on the earth, that they should make an image to the [first] beast…and cause that as many as would not worship the image of the beast [Antichrist] should be killed.
> And he causeth all [upon earth]…to receive a mark in their right hand, or in their foreheads: and that no man might buy or sell, save he that had the mark (Revelation 13:4, 7-8,11,14-17).

These prophecies have been in the Bible for some 1,900 years. Through the centuries many Bible scholars considered them to be figurative, spiritual allegories, because there was no known way that one man could control the entire world even to the extent of preventing anyone from buying or selling unless they had his mark. Some still spiritualize these prophecies away, or insist that they were all fulfilled in the days of Nero, who they claim was the Antichrist. When interpreting the Bible, however, one simple rule must govern: if what is said *can* be taken literally, it *must* be taken literally.

Our generation is the first one able to understand how these prophecies could be literally fulfilled: obviously, through computers—and *only* through computers. Antichrist *must* have a worldwide network of powerful computers to accomplish his biblically defined role. Satan's man cannot run the world, control all buying and selling, and keep track of everyone without an international network of computers and the satellites functioning with them. It hardly seems reasonable, then, that we would come this far in history to the development of the very technology that the Antichrist needs, only to have it all fall apart. Why? Just to be built again years later so Antichrist can at that time take over? It doesn't make sense.

Confirmation from God?

Throughout this book we provide sufficient documentation to show that there will not be a general failure of computers on January 1, 2000. Yet a surprising number of Christians say that God has been confirming the worst Y2K disaster scenario to them by revelation and dreams. According to Mark Andrews, founder of Prep 2000, many Christians are convinced that God is telling them to move out of the cities and stock up.

Through radio interviews, videos and a busy national speaking schedule, Andrews "is broadcasting his Y2K preparedness message....He has set up a self-sustaining home site in a rural area...a couple of modest, three-bedroom manufactured homes...[with] enough food stores to last a couple of years." And Andrews claims he's been told by numerous Christians "that they've 'sensed God preparing them for endtimes and leading them to be a source of help and refuge for people God brings their way' as millennial events unfold...retreating to rural areas out of what they believe to be obedience [to God]."[15] What will they say when what they believed was "God's guidance" proves to be false?

Unquestionably, some of those who are sounding the alarm are men and women of God. They must have heard from Him as well. Jerry Falwell would not allow his *National Liberty Journal* to suggest getting out of the cities and stocking up on food and supplies unless he believed this was the will of God for at least some Christians. Jack Van Impe seems so urgent in his warnings. We cannot fault these men for their genuine concern, but it is misleading for anyone to claim that Y2K is a fulfillment of Bible prophecy.

The End of This Present World?

Dave Wilkerson reminds us that "43 million Americans are deeply invested in the [stock] market, with $1.5 to $2 trillion committed by individual investors. Thousands of these investors have actually quit their jobs so they can stay at home and play the market on their computers." He is convinced that God's judgment is about to fall on America:

> I tell you, the stockmarket has become America's golden calf! People see it as a financial savior, and they worship it daily—trusting in it, depending on it, giving it all their energy and attention. But it's going to fall suddenly—and none of the small, individual investors will be spared. They'll suffer the most, losing their homes, their cars—everything!...
>
> The masses who were driven by money and success won't be able to endure the failure and poverty they face. Many will opt for suicide—including corporate leaders....It will...[be] a severe humbling of our nation, through a long, terrifying period of

chaotic conditions—including rioting, looting and burning in our major cities.[16]

The stockmarket happened to be down from its earlier highs when Dave wrote this article. That fact may have been at least partially responsible for what he said. Wilkerson has been making similar predictions of disaster for at least two decades. Eventually he will be right. So will Gary North. God's judgment will indeed fall with horrible vengeance upon America and the world. Their timing, however, does not fit Bible prophecy.

The judgment Wilkerson has so often described (and which Gary North and many others are now saying Y2K will bring upon us) would be appropriate during the Great Tribulation, but not prior to that time. The Bible doesn't support some earlier catastrophic judgment coming upon the world. In fact, it supports just the opposite, as we shall see.

The question as to whether Y2K might be God's judgment upon America and possibly the world was raised on the Dobson program, and we have previously quoted the remarks of some of the participants. Shaunti Feldhahn commented,

> I had the privilege of interviewing several Christian leaders for this book, and I interviewed Dr. Henry Blackaby who wrote the *Experiencing God* series. One thing he said that I thought was so on target about Y2K was that we talk about whether this is the judgment of God on the world...and as he pointed out, it's more likely to be a judgment of God on the people of God, because if you look throughout Scripture, more often the judgment of God was upon the people of God..., and the people of God really need to get their hearts back in touch with the Lord and be prepared to minister spiritually no matter what happens.[17]

Yes, the Bible does say that judgment begins first with the house of God and, that being the case, raises the question, "what shall the end be of them that obey not the gospel of God?" (1 Peter 4:17). Obviously, God's judgment upon an ungodly world will be far worse than His discipline of the church, but in the case of Y2K the same fate comes upon all. Furthermore, the Bible doesn't even hint at any judgment from God that could be tied into Y2K. Even those most concerned can't say with any certainty exactly what will happen, so how could it be related to Bible prophecy? It couldn't, at least not at this point in time.

Don't Forget the Rapture

Increasing numbers of Christians today are too absorbed in Y2K preparedness to give any thought to prophecy. In fact, to some it seems irrelevant. On the Dobson program, Shaunti Feldhahn said,

> It's easy to talk about the endtimes, and I agree it would be great if the Lord came back with His trumpet sounding. But quite frankly, I guess what I'm doing in the book and what we're saying around the country is, I'm more concerned about the state of our hearts right now—about *our hearts*, not *their* hearts, not the government, not the people we rightly have problems with the way they conduct themselves, not the immoral society that we live in— *our* hearts.[18]

Indeed, the condition of our hearts is paramount. But the measure of that condition involves more than a concern for those who may suffer from a Y2K computer crash. Above all should be the Christian's love for Christ and longing to be with Him and like Him in the Father's house: "The Spirit and the bride [Church] say, Come....Even so, come, Lord Jesus" (Revelation 22:17,20).

Yet not many of those who claim to belong to Christ give any indication today that they long for His return. So much else, much of it good, has our attention. It would be "great," says Shaunti, *but*....One often gets the impression that the Rapture, should it occur in our day, would be a terrible inconvenience that would interrupt many important plans and activities!

Mark Andrews, founder of Prep 2000, a grass-roots Y2K awareness coalition, says, "The Bible paints clearly for us a picture of what the world will look like in the last days. The scenario that's unfolding as we approach the new millennium matches perfectly with Scripture's prophecy of global economic collapse and a one-world government."[19] Andrews makes it clear that he is talking of conditions during the Great Tribulation under Antichrist. And those conditions cannot occur until after the Rapture of the church from this earth to heaven.

Not Longing to Escape Trials, but to Be with Christ!

This is not to say that the Rapture is intended to help Christians to escape all trials and persecution. Down through the ages, Christians have suffered terribly and such is the case today, especially in Muslim and Catholic countries. In Chiapas, Mexico, evangelicals have been under attack by Roman Catholics for 30 years, with many killed and thousands having to flee their homes and land.[20] On a lesser scale, similar persecution is being experienced by evangelicals in Acapulco and other parts of Mexico as well as in Ecuador and other South American countries where Catholics are in control. Protestants and their churches have been physically attacked by the Orthodox in Ethiopia, Romania, and elsewhere; Turkmenistan has relegated all Protestant churches to illegal status; in China, Christians are once again being imprisoned and killed for their faith; in Sudan, Christians are being kidnapped and killed by the thousands, with some literally being crucified—and on and on it goes. It has been estimated that more Christians have been martyred in this century than during the entire prior history of the church.

Let it be clear, then, that we do not view the Rapture as an escape from the persecution which, according to the Bible, is to be the experience of all true Christians: "We must through much tribulation enter into the kingdom of God" (Acts 14:22); "Yea, and all that will live godly in Christ Jesus shall suffer persecution" (2 Timothy 3:12). We believe, however, that the Rapture will indeed deliver the church composed of all true Christians, Christ's bride, from the wrath of God which will be poured out upon this earth in the Great Tribulation:

> Ye turned to God from idols to serve the living and true God; and to wait for his Son from heaven, whom he raised from the dead, even Jesus, which delivered us from the wrath to come (1 Thessalonians 1:9-10).

> Because thou hast kept the word of my patience, I also will keep thee from the hour of temptation, which shall come upon all the world, to try [test] them that dwell upon the earth (Revelation 3:10).

Christ does not say that He will keep His own *through* the hour of testing that will come upon all the world, but that He will keep them *from* the very hour. His own are not sheltered by Christ during the Great Tribulation but are subject to the Antichrist's destruction. If the church were here it would be destroyed because Antichrist has power "to make war with the saints, and to overcome them" (Revelation 13:7)—a further reason for the church's removal to heaven before Antichrist is revealed. Christ's promise is to keep His own from the very hour of temptation itself: in plain words, they will not be here at all during that time.

Great Tribulation and the Second Coming

It should be very clear that we are not in that prophesied period which Jesus described as "great tribulation, such as was not since the beginning of the world...no, nor ever shall be" (Matthew 24:21). Indeed, he goes on to say that unless that time were cut short by His intervention, "there should no flesh be saved" (Matthew 24:22). Even the most pessimistic Y2K alarmists have not predicted anything like a potential destruction of all mankind through the crashing of computers on January 1, 2000. Therefore, Y2K could hardly bring about the Great Tribulation to which Scripture refers. As we shall see, it is contrary to the Bible to imagine that a Y2K breakdown could be the prelude to the reign of Antichrist and the Great Tribulation. There is no relationship.

This intervention at Armageddon by Christ's personal return to earth to stop destruction that would otherwise wipe out "all flesh" is called the Second Coming. There is no question that it occurs *after* the Great Tribulation; but it is equally clear that this is not the Rapture of the church to heaven, but the rescue of Israel here on earth. Indeed, when Christ's feet touch the mount of Olives at that time He brings *all the saints* from heaven with Him (Zechariah 14:4-5). Obviously He must have already taken them to heaven in the Rapture or they could not accompany Him to earth.

John refers to the Second Coming in these words: "Behold, he cometh with clouds [the saints in resurrected, glorified bodies as the armies of heaven]; and every eye shall see him, and they also which pierced him: and all kindreds of the earth shall wail because of him" (Revelation 1:7). In referring to this same event, Jesus said:

> Immediately after the tribulation of those days shall the sun be darkened, and the moon shall not give her light...the powers of the heavens shall be shaken; and then shall appear the sign of the Son of man in heaven: and then shall all the tribes of the

earth mourn, and they shall see the Son of man coming in the clouds of heaven with power and great glory (Matthew 24:29,30).

The conditions on earth at the time of the Second Coming are terrible beyond description, threatening, as Jesus said, to wipe out not only the entire human race but *all flesh*—and that includes cockroaches, mosquitoes, and even microbes. Our generation is the first having the capability of fulfilling that prophecy. Obviously, the threat to destroy "all flesh" is not caused by some Y2K problem that has crashed the computers so they can't run the modern weapons necessary to wipe out all flesh.

Contrasting Conditions

It is precisely here, in relation to the Second Coming, that we encounter an apparent contradiction which has stumbled many. Consider these words of Jesus: "But as the days of Noe [Noah] were, so shall also the coming of the Son of man be....They were eating and drinking, marrying,...until the day that Noe entered into the ark" (Matthew 24:37,38). How can He say that the world will be, as in Noah's day, at ease, prosperous, and partying at His coming, when the conditions at His Second Coming in the midst of Armageddon are without question the very antithesis of Noah's day?

Either Christ is contradicting Himself and much clear prophecy concerning Armageddon, or He is not referring to His Second Coming to rescue Israel at all but to an earlier coming to take the church to heaven—an event called the Rapture.

There is no denying the fact that conditions at the time of Christ's Second Coming, portrayed in Revelation 19, will be the exact opposite of those in the day of Noah. Already in Revelation 6, more than one billion people have died within a short period of time from famine, pestilence, rioting, and earthquakes that displace mountains and islands and destroy entire cities. All that has nothing to do with computer failure; *that* cannot produce *earthquakes*.

There is a further contrast between the Second Coming and Noah's day. Just before the flood, no one expected God's judgment to fall. God had left man alone since the creation and had not intervened globally to chastise the wicked. The flood took earth's inhabitants completely by surprise (though unnecessarily so). But at the Second Coming, the entire world is aware that God is in the process of pouring out His wrath upon earth and that the worst is yet to come: "And the kings of the earth, and the great men,...and every bondman, and every free man...said to the mountains and rocks, fall on us, and hide us from the...wrath of the Lamb: for the great day of his wrath is come" (Revelation 6:15-17). Isaiah prophesied the same:

> For the day of the LORD of hosts shall be upon every one that is proud and lofty....And the loftiness of man shall be bowed down,...the LORD alone shall be exalted in that day....And they shall go into the holes of the rocks, and into the caves of the earth, for fear of the LORD, and for the glory of his majesty, when he ariseth to shake terribly the earth (Isaiah 2:12,17,19).

These are the conditions already in place at the end of Revelation, Chapter 6. Thirteen chapters later this earth is in a state of utter destruction as a result of having suffered God's uninterrupted wrath for more than three years. The time for the great battle of Armageddon has come, with the armies of the world attacking Israel. This scenario bears no resemblance to Noah's day, yet it is the time of the Second Coming. Many passages in the Bible make that clear. For example:

> Behold, the day of the LORD cometh....I will gather all nations against Jerusalem to battle;... Then shall the LORD go forth, and fight against those

nations,...his feet shall stand in that day upon the
mount of Olives (Zechariah 14:1-4).

In that day shall the LORD defend the inhabitants
of Jerusalem....And I will pour upon the house of
David, and upon the inhabitants of Jerusalem, the
spirit of grace and of supplications: and they shall
look upon me whom they have pierced, and they
shall mourn for him, as one mourneth for his only
son, and shall be in bitterness for him....

And one shall say unto him, What are these
wounds in thine hands? Then he shall answer, Those
with which I was wounded in the house of my
friends (Zechariah 12:8,10; 13:6).

Jesus Revealed as God at Armageddon

Jesus was taken up into heaven from the Mount of Olives
40 days after His resurrection. "And while they looked stead-
fastly toward heaven as he went up, behold, two men
[angels] stood by them in white apparel; which also said,
...this same Jesus, which is taken up from you into heaven,
shall so come in like manner as ye have seen him go into
heaven" (Acts 1:10,11). Clearly, the One who comes to rescue
Israel in the midst of Armageddon and whose feet "stand in
that day upon the mount of Olives" is Jesus Christ at His
Second Coming, exactly as the angels promised to the disciples.

Yet the prophet Zechariah declares that it is God Himself, Yahweh/Jehovah, who comes to fight against all the
nations of the world which *He has gathered against Israel* to
execute judgment upon them (Ezekiel 38:16-23). Israel is
astonished to see that her God, Yahweh, is a resurrected man
who was "wounded in the house of my friends" (Zechariah
13:6) and pierced to the death by His own people, the very
people He has nevertheless, in love and mercy, come to
rescue. Says Yahweh, "They shall look upon *me* whom they
have pierced." But then Yahweh says "they will mourn

because of *him.*" Yahweh was pierced, but *He* was pierced; Yahweh comes to fight against Israel's enemies and *His* feet touch the Mount of Olives; but Christ returns to the Mount of Olives to rescue Israel and *His* feet stand upon it. It seems clear that Zechariah is stating exactly what Jesus said: "I and my Father are one" (John 10:30); and, again, "he that hath seen me hath seen the Father" (John 14:9).

So, clearly, there are two comings of Christ which yet lie ahead: one, at a time of the greatest distress this world has ever seen and in the midst of the greatest war in history; the other, during a time of peace, prosperity, and ease, when judgment is the last thing the world could imagine coming upon it. Without this understanding, Christ's seemingly contradictory statements concerning conditions upon earth at His coming have confused many Bible students.

Prosperity Precedes the Rapture, Which Precedes the Second Coming

Those most concerned about Y2K think that the destruction which they imagine it will bring fits in neatly with Bible prophecy for the last days. They seem to forget, however, that Jesus not only prophesied judgment and destruction for the last days, but also foretold a time of great prosperity, ease, and worldly success—and He said that these conditions would be upon the earth at the time of His coming.

Obviously, the prosperity must precede the judgment portrayed in Revelation, because the latter culminates in Armageddon. There is no recovery from the destruction that comes upon all the earth under Antichrist except by Christ's intervention from heaven to destroy Antichrist and to set up His kingdom on David's throne in Jerusalem, as the Scriptures promise. A previous destruction brought about by Y2K doesn't fit the Bible—unless, of course, we imagine that after many years of difficult recovery the world finally gets back to where it is now. Why not let Jesus rapture His bride now, or in the very near future?

It is tempting for those who believe in a prewrath or post-tribulation Rapture—or in no Rapture at all (a position growing in popularity)—to imagine that every new catastrophe confronting us is leading to the biblical apocalypse. But the huge disasters come during the Great Tribulation, not just before the Rapture. Indeed, many clear statements of Christ and the apostles and prophets which foretell this time of peace and prosperity would have to be set aside in order to sustain the utter Y2K gloom and doom now being forecast.

If, as Jesus says, the world will be enjoying ease and plenty with no thought of judgment at the time of His return, we can only conclude that He is referring to His return to take the church to heaven, because such conditions will be impossible at the time of His return to rescue Israel. The Rapture of the church, then, must be the next great prophetic event, and it must precede the Great Tribulation and Antichrist's reign. Thus we can only conclude that world events will be moving us toward the peace, prosperity, pleasure, and self-confident rejection of any thought of God's judgment which the Bible foretells—*not* toward a computer collapse and chaos.

Y2K and the Rapture Don't Mix

That being the case, we have a biblical reason for knowing that the incredible Y2K disaster being trumpeted will not occur. Nor can Dave Wilkerson's stockmarket crash and God's righteous judgment being poured out upon America and the world take place until after the Rapture. If disaster on that scale should strike now, it would contradict what Jesus Himself said. Consider His words again, this time from Luke's Gospel:

> And as it was in the days of Noe, so shall it be also in the days of the Son of man. They did eat, they drank, they married wives, they were given in marriage,

until the day that Noe entered into the ark, and the
flood came, and destroyed them all.

Likewise also as it was in the days of Lot; they did
eat, they drank, they bought, they sold, they planted,
they builded; but the same day that Lot went out of
Sodom it rained fire and brimstone from heaven,
and destroyed them all.

Even thus shall it be in the day when the Son of
man is revealed....I tell you, in that night there shall
be two men in one bed; the one shall be taken, and
the other shall be left. Two women shall be grinding
together; the one shall be taken, and the other left.
Two men shall be in the field; the one shall be taken,
and the other left (Luke 17:26-30,34-36).

This idyllic peace and prosperity, according to Jesus, will
characterize conditions on earth at the time of His coming.
We have, then, a biblical reason for knowing that the incredible Y2K disaster being foretold will not occur. Obviously, to
make the point once again that we have been emphasizing,
the verses above do not refer to Christ's Second Coming in
the midst of Armageddon to rescue Israel. Why not? Because
the world at that time will be the utter antithesis of the world
in Noah's day. Just before the flood there was pleasure and
ease and prosperity. Judgment had never fallen upon the
earth, disaster had never struck in any form, and that is why
Noah's warning about God judging the world by a flood was
ridiculed.

Christ's declaration here, that at His coming some will
be in bed, others grinding meal or working in the field, indicates that this event will occur worldwide in all time zones.
It is often suggested that those who are taken away are taken
to judgment after Armageddon, but we have seen that the
world conditions Christ describes at this time are the very
opposite from Armageddon. Furthermore, there is no teaching in Scripture of the wicked being snatched out of beds
and fields to be taken to *judgment*. It certainly sounds like the

Rapture—the believers being "caught up to meet the Lord in the air." And that would fit with Noah entering the ark and Lot being taken out of Sodom.

We know the days of Noah and Lot were characterized by great evil—evil so pervasive and perverse that it caused God to destroy all flesh in Noah's day and the cities of Sodom and Gomorrah in Lot's day. And so it is in our day. It is not the *evil* of that time, however, to which Christ calls our attention, but the pleasure and ease and prosperity. Judgment had never before fallen upon the earth nor had disaster ever struck in any form; therefore, that was the last thing anyone expected.

Furthermore, Christ specifically states that these conditions of peace and prosperity held true until the very day that Noah was safely in the ark and until Lot and his family likewise had departed Sodom. Therefore, the Rapture will not occur in the midst of World War III, as some have suggested, nor when the world is reeling from an international banking collapse and is in the midst of deep financial depression, with millions starving to death from a Y2K computer collapse. It will occur when the world is prospering and feeling secure, when an apostate church has joined with the ungodly to make a new world (for the new millennium?) and all are rejoicing in that prospect.

A Prosperous Church at the Rapture

If Y2K should indeed turn out to be as bad as the doomsayers predict, Christians, having lost their worldly goods and their hope in this world, would be longing for and expecting the return of Christ. Rather than hastening His return, that would delay it. Not only would world conditions be wrong, but the Rapture comes when very few expect it: "Therefore be ye also ready: for in such an hour as ye think not the Son of man cometh" (Matthew 24:44).

Many Bible scholars believe that the seven churches in Asia, to whom Christ writes the letters through John (Revelation 2–3), present a picture of the condition of the church down through the ages from its inception to the time when Christ removes it at the Rapture. While this author is not an advocate of that view, those who are can make a fairly good case by comparing the conditions in these seven churches with history. It is at least worth considering that the church at Laodicea (mentioned last) sounds precisely like the church of today: "rich, and increased with goods, and [in] need of nothing" (Revelation 3:17).

Once again, that is hardly the description of a church which is in the midst of or has recently gone through a Y2K collapse of the world's financial markets and the rest of the disasters being predicted. A Y2K meltdown would bring about the very antithesis of conditions in the days of Noah and Lot. Steve Hewitt writes:

> One article on the net, entitled, "The State of the Church in the last months of the twentieth century," states that "credible experts are now predicting widespread disruptions, including a bank collapse that will demolish the present economies in North America, Japan and Europe....I believe pastors must face the reality that society as we know it could cease to exist."
>
> His message is that the church should be ready to step in and take over after the utilities stop, the police quit, and everything falls apart.
>
> While the church should always have a disaster relief plan, his statements are extreme, and in my opinion dangerous. They are also not based upon fact, but the speculative statements of questionable sources.[21]

In contrast to such gloomy expectations, *The Wall Street Journal* recently reported, "A strong economy and renewed spirituality have spawned a building boom in new religious construction. Last year [1997] it reached its highest level in three decades, 41 billion square feet. Americans spent $6 billion in 1997 on houses of worship, up from $4 billion in 1994."[22] Those statistics could be supported with many other examples.

Under the heading, "Liberty University Prepares for the Third Millennium," Jerry Falwell's *National Liberty Journal* offers a picture of a building under construction with this explanation: "$100 Million Capital Gifts Campaign Underway: The new six-story dormitory nears completion on the campus of Liberty University. The dorm will house 425 female students." Jerry Falwell adds: "As I face the Third Millennium, having reached the age of 65 on August 11, I find myself dreaming as never before. At this moment, we are now planning to implement the first stage of the relocation of a new 12,000-seat Thomas Road Baptist Church to Liberty Mountain, an ultimate $200 million futuristic project."[23]

A Y2K computer crash would put an end to such plans, not only at Liberty University and Thomas Road Baptist Church, but all across the country. On the contrary, the Bible seems to indicate that the church will be "rich and increased with goods" at the time of the Rapture. Either the Y2K disaster won't materialize, or the Rapture cannot be expected for many years. But that very thought does away with imminency, the hope of the church down through the ages that Christ could take His own out of this world at any moment.

Biblical Prophecy, Y2K, the Rapture, and Reason

In his new book *January 1, 2000: The Day the World Shuts Down,* evangelist Morris Cerullo relates Y2K to Bible prophecy. "Simply put," he writes, "the government and business leaders are terrified that they will not get the Year 2000 problem fixed in time and the world will be thrown into utter chaos....The world may very well be headed into the worst tribulation it has ever known."[24] He doesn't come right out and call this "worst tribulation" the "great tribulation" that Jesus foretold, but the implication seems to be there.

Jack Van Impe voices more clearly what Cerullo implies: "I believe judgment is coming and this [Y2K crisis] could be the prelude—not the tribulation hour but the prelude leading to it described in Revelation (16–18), when 21 judgments fall upon the earth."[25]

In fact, we could not, as a result of Y2K, "be headed into" the Great Tribulation, as Cerullo suggests, nor could a Y2K computer collapse be "the prelude" to the Great Tribulation, as Van Impe believes. We reach this conclusion for the reasons given above and further reasons which we will document more thoroughly in the next chapter. Both the present anticipation and fear and the actual crashing of computers and resultant chaos (if they occur) are the antithesis of the biblical prelude to the Great Tribulation. Paul states unequivocally: "For yourselves know perfectly that the day of the Lord so cometh as a thief in the night. For when they shall say, Peace and safety; then sudden destruction cometh upon them, as travail upon a woman with child; and they shall not escape" (1 Thessalonians 5:2,3).

With the threat of a Y2K computer collapse hanging over our heads, no one is saying "peace and safety" right now. The general expectation is disaster. As we have already noted, there are suggestions that nuclear missiles will fire accidentally because of computer glitches. There are also suggestions that due to the Y2K computer collapse the United States, without its high-tech weapons systems, will be vulnerable to enemy attack, a sitting duck for some power like China or Russia with massive numbers of ground troops. If that were not enough, there are also predictions of power blackouts, collapse of the banking system, food shortages, social upheaval, riots, and death. Neither the present fearful anticipation nor the predicted Y2K apocalypse fit the conditions that the Bible states will be present on earth at the time of the Rapture to usher in the day of the Lord.

Biblical Reasons Why Y2K Won't Be a Disaster

The truth is that both the world and the church are presently (apart from Y2K) in exactly the condition Christ declared would characterize this earth just prior to the Rapture. We have great prosperity; Y2K would destroy that for some time to come and thereby delay the Rapture far into the future. The church is "rich and increased with goods." Some megachurches are larger and of richer construction than many shopping malls. Y2K would destroy that wealth. The present church is so busy with its building plans for "the next millennium" that instead of eagerly awaiting the Rapture, it is sleeping, exactly as Christ foretold in Matthew 25: "While the bridegroom tarried, they all slumbered and slept" (verse 5). A Y2K disaster of anything near the proportions which many predict would shake a sleeping church into wakefulness and repentance and make it eager for Christ's return. But Christ said He would come when very few, if any, were expecting Him.

There are, then, a number of solid biblical reasons for rejecting the Y2K disaster scenario. Certainly it can be argued that Christ may not come for many years yet, so Y2K could occur and present civilization go down in flames, then after many years build itself back up to the present or an even higher level of prosperity. That is an outside possibility. However, *all* of the requisite conditions are *now* present for the first time in history: Israel back in her land and a "cup of trembling," "a burdensome stone" to the world and a devouring fire to "all the people round about" (Zechariah 12:1-6);[26] growing apostasy in the church and a preoccupation with worldly success and prosperity (we even have a *prosperity gospel* being taught by Kenneth Hagin, Kenneth Copeland, Frederick Price, and others, and being promoted by TBN, the largest Christian television network in history); and a rejection of sound doctrine, especially the doctrine of the Rapture by many, and a lack of interest by those who profess to believe in this hope. Why not now?

There is still another possibility: Christ will indeed rapture His church out of the world before the year 2000, and Y2K, as so many think, will set the stage and help to bring about the chaos and disaster foretold in Revelation for the Great Tribulation. We can think of no good biblical arguments against that scenario—but Y2K won't fulfill those expectations, as we have documented and will continue to do in Chapter 7.

No one knows the day nor the hour, and we are not making any predictions. However, looking at conditions in the world and the church and comparing them with Scripture, we suspect that the Lord will delay His coming until after the year 2000. If so, the failure of the doomsday predictions to materialize will likely create a reaction against Bible prophecy. Increasing prosperity will make the world all the more proud and boastful, and certain that it does not need God. Even many of those who have believed in the Rapture will conclude that if it didn't occur within 2,000 years after Christ's birth, then it could be another 1,000 or 2,000, and that perhaps it is a false doctrine. The failure of Y2K predictions of great calamity could add great impetus to the spiritual delusion which is already building to a climax worldwide.

It is likely that after the year 2000 very few will continue to believe in Christ's return to take His own out of this world, much less look with eager anticipation for it to happen at any moment.

If this should occur as a result of the failure of Y2K doomsday forecasts, then the final piece in the puzzle will have been put in place. Surely at that time, Christ's warning will apply more than ever before, with very few taking heed: "Therefore, be ye also ready: for in such an hour as ye think not the Son of man cometh" (Matthew 24:44).

I'm more positive than I was six months ago.

> —Senator Robert Bennett, chairman of Senate Special
> Committee Year 2000[1]

[Y2K] will be a nonevent. I'm not planning to take my money out.

> —Cheryl Kane, Bank of America executive vice presi-
> dent of technology[2]

It's going to be a dud...we're going to wake up and nothing will have
happened.

> —David Starr, former technology officer at General
> Motors, ITT, and Citicorp[3]

We are confident...we will finish....The year 2000 computer problem
will be a nonevent.

> —Sally Katzen, administrator of U.S. Office of
> Management and Budget[4]

The...infrastructure of the country will hold. The banking system is in
very good shape.

> —John Koskinen, chairman of the President's Council
> on Year 2000 Conversion[5]

Year 2000. In 60 days Oracle can solve a problem that took 2,000 years
to create.

> —Oracle Corporation[6]

The NRC [U.S. Nuclear Regulatory Commission] has no indication
[after audits] that significant Y2K problems exist with safety-related
systems in nuclear power plants for those systems that directly affect the
ability to safely operate and shut down....Most nuclear plant safety systems...[use] analog equipment which is not...susceptible to the Y2K
problem.

> —NRC Testimony Before Congress[7]

CHAPTER SEVEN

A Contrary Scenario

Computers are so incredibly helpful—and, yes, *necessary* in today's world. What could we do without them? Are we about to find out to our sorrow? We don't think so. The stockmarkets around the world are an example of what instant computerized calculations and communication can produce. Without computers we could not have the wealth reflected in these markets and the means to trade stocks instantly anywhere in the world and to know exactly what trades are being made that produce the markets. And without electricity we have no computers and almost nothing else in our modern world—including no stockmarket.

The alarmists are still predicting a power grid failure, but we have documented that there is no factual reason why the power grid would not be intact after January 1, 2000. The greatest fear has been triggered by the possibility of nuclear power plant failure. The quote opposite, from the U.S. Nuclear Regulatory Commission which oversees nuclear power plants in this country, ought to provide at least some reassurance: "Most nuclear power plant safety systems [involved in operation and shut-down] are operated and controlled by analog [noncomputerized] equipment which is not date-dependent and is not susceptible to the Y2K problem."[8] The following excerpt from an NRC report to Congress offers helpful and reassuring information:

Since 1996, the NRC has been working with nuclear power plant licensees and the Nuclear Energy Institute, an industry organization—to assure plant systems are "Y2K compliant" before the year 2000. In May 1998, the NRC notified all utilities operating nuclear plants (Generic Letter 98-01) that they are required to inform NRC of steps they are taking to see that computer systems will function properly by the Year 2000. All licensees responded to that Generic Letter, stating that they have adopted an NRC-endorsed industry program that is designed to make them Y2K ready by July 1, 1999....

Y2K problems have been found in non-safety, but nevertheless important, computer-based applications, such as security computers, control room display systems, engineering programs, control systems, radiation monitoring and emergency response.

In September, 1998, the NRC started conducting Year 2000 audits at 12 nuclear power plants. These audits are to evaluate the effectiveness of measures licensees are taking to identify and correct Y2K problems at their facilities. ...Several observations can be drawn from the first few audits of nuclear power plants:

- —There is limited use of computers in systems essential to plant safety and continued operation.
- —Industry's guidance has yielded effective Y2K readiness programs....
- —Sharing information among plants has helped plants deal with the Y2K problem....
- —Nuclear power reactors have two independent sources of offsite power, and are designed to safely shut down if a loss of all offsite power were to occur. In the event of a loss of offsite power, onsite electric power systems provide adequate electrical power to safely shut down and cool down the reactors.

Conclusions

The NRC and the nuclear power industry are addressing the Year 2000 computer problem in a thorough and deliberate manner. To date we have not identified or received notification from licensees or vendors that a Year 2000 problem exists with safety-related initiation and actuation systems. Further, we believe that we have, through Generic Letter 98-01 and the planned follow-up inspections, established a framework that appropriately assures us that the Year 2000 problem will not have an adverse impact on the ability of a nuclear power plant to safely operate or safely shut down. We recognize the importance of maintaining a reliable electrical grid, and we will continue to work with the President's Council on Year 2000 Conversion Energy Working Group, the Federal Energy Regulatory Commission, and the Department of Energy to give assistance and share information regarding potential problems associated with the coming of the Year 2000.[9]

An Overstated Problem

On February 4, 1998, President Clinton "created a White House council [Year 2000 Conversion Council]…to coordinate efforts to head off computer problems that threaten critical federal services when the calendar year changes to 2000….'The American people…deserve the confidence that critical government functions dependent on electronic systems will be performed accurately and in a timely manner,' Clinton said."[10] On July 2, Vice President Al Gore declared, "We have set a deadline of March 31, 1999 for the Federal Government to be in full compliance, and we are hopeful that we will meet it."[11]

At the time, such statements from Clinton and Gore were scorned by the skeptics as a smoke screen to cover government inefficiency and incompetence. However, we have shown that even government agencies can handle the necessary repairs for timely compliance. Only a very small percentage of computerized systems, government or civilian, care what year it is, and of those, only the tiniest fraction would shut down on January 1, 2000, without modification.

As Dallas Semiconductor Corp., one of the world's largest makers of timekeeping chips for embedded applications, says, "For products that have no calendar or date functionality there is no issue of Year 2000."[12] Furthermore, even many devices which keep real time can continue to operate into the next millennium with only two digits for the year. While not technically Y2K *compliant*, many if not most of them are Y2K *compatible*, as Dallas Semiconductor explained in a letter to its customers:

> Dallas Semiconductor defines a Y2K compliant RTC [Real Time Clock] as one which calculates and stores a true 4-digit year in hardware. In addition, it will treat 2000 as a leap year. Most of Dallas Semiconductor's microcontrollers with RTC capability are Y2K *compatible*, in that they do not have a century counter (as they only store the year as a two digit value) but know that the year 00 should be calculated as a leap year...and will continue to work correctly through the year 2099. [Emphasis added.][13]

Most devices involved in the power grid or military defense and security don't care what year it is. For those that do, as Dallas Semiconductor declares, not every system needs to be changed over to the use of four digits for the year in order to continue to function properly into the next century. The Y2K problem, though a serious one, has been exaggerated out of all proportion.

If the Southern Baptist headquarters can do it, so can everyone else. The Southern Baptist Annuity Board, which distributes 28,000 retirement checks a month and handles assets of close to $7 billion, does not anticipate any problem getting benefit payments delivered on time [in 2000], officials say. Board staff completed an assessment of computer systems in the second quarter of 1998 and modifications and testing of software are supposed to be completed this fall

[1998]. Monitoring will continue after the testing is completed.[14]

According to the alarmists, the Baptists, like everyone else who says it isn't such a big problem after all, simply don't understand the real problem; or they, too, are part of a vast conspiracy to willfully deceive the rest of us.

By late 1998, it was becoming quite clear that the Y2K problem had been overstated. Some of those who had led the way in warning of the coming year 2000 catastrophe and who had been the most pessimistic only a few months earlier had already changed their tune. The Gartner Group, a highly respected Y2K research organization, had originally been pessimistic and was often quoted to that effect by alarmists. Yet in October 1998, Jim Cassell authored a "Gartner Group research study that advised Americans not to go overboard [re Y2K]."[15] We have quoted other experts, in a previous chapter, who since have tempered their original pessimism with considerable optimism concerning Y2K.

The end of July 1998, White House Y2K czar John Koskinen, chairman of the federal commission dedicated to fixing the Y2K computer problem, was convinced that "not everything will be fixed" and that his goal was "to keep disruptions down to a manageable level."[16] *Time* magazine described Koskinen as the man "in charge of making sure the U.S. government's computers don't crash come January 1, 2000."[17] The President's executive order signed February 4, 1998, stated specifically that the chairman of the Year 2000 Conversion Council was to "oversee the activities of [federal] agencies to assure that their systems operate smoothly through the year 2000...."[18] *Time* added this biting comment, "Koskinen's task is not just daunting: it's impossible."[19]

At the end of November 1998, however, Koskinen declared that "61 percent of the federal government's 'mission critical systems' are already corrected...[and] that 85–90 percent will meet a March [1999] deadline for compliance."[20] Obviously, the government is speeding up its Y2K rectification effort. Koskinen's task no longer seems impossible but is clearly on course to be accomplished in good time.

Pessimists Will Be Pessimists

Nevertheless, in the face of positive developements, pessimistic Christian leaders were not backing down. Michael S. Hyatt, whose book paints one of the grimmest pictures, had become even more pessimistic as 1998 drew to a close. In a November 30, 1998, article titled "Why I Am More Pessimistic Than Ever," Hyatt had this to say:

> One of the questions I'm asked the most is this: "Since you finished your book, *The Millennium Bug,* have you become more optimistic or less optimistic about the impact of Y2K?
>
> Before I answer that question, you need to understand that I am an optimist by nature. I get up in the morning expecting good things to happen. I typically see the cup half full rather than half empty. I don't like negative people, and I don't like gloomy reports. But try though I may, I can't seem to come to any other conclusion about Y2K than one that is pessimistic. The facts that I am confronted with daily don't warrant any other conclusion.
>
> For example, in just the past two weeks, we have had several bleak reports.
>
> 1. Congressman Stephen Horn's (D-Calif.) Subcommittee on Government, Management, Information, and Technology issues a quarterly report card on the Y2K progress of 24 key federal government agencies. The most recent report was issued on November 23 [1998]. Based on *current rates of progress*, more than a third of agencies (9 out of 24) will not get even their mission-critical systems finished by January 1, 2000. Worse, over one-half of the agencies do not [*yet*] have contingency plans to ensure that their services will continue if their systems fail....
>
> 3. The Defense Department's Inspector General accused the Pentagon of (once again) falsifying Y2K compliance

reports....Pentagon officials were at a loss to explain why
the agency misreported the data....

When it comes to public utilities or businesses, how do
we know that they aren't also overstating their Y2K progress? They certainly have *plenty of reasons for doing so.*

4. The Bank of Japan admitted that 75 percent of the
country's largest banks will miss the deadline they had set
of having their computers repaired and tested by *December
31, 1998....*

5. Major television news coverage is still woefully inadequate....

I would have thought by now that the story would be the
size of the Monica Lewinsky case or the O. J. trial. What
happens when the public finally "gets it"? Will we have widespread panic? It seems to me that the longer we wait, the
more certain this becomes....

You don't have to be a natural skeptic or pessimist to
read the *handwriting on the wall.* Even a natural-born optimist like me can see that we are on a collision course with
reality. Unless something truly extraordinary happens in
the next few months, we're in for a mess. I hope you are
preparing accordingly. [Emphasis added.][21]

While claiming to be a born optimist, Hyatt betrays all
the earmarks of a pessimist. Note the words and phrases we
have italicized. Why would we assume that *current rates of
progress* for government agencies would remain static? Isn't
it more likely that efforts would be redoubled and progress
would increase dramatically in view of the necessity to do
so? Isn't it good to know that someone is checking on
progress and pushing them to readiness? Moreover, we have
named a number of techniques now available which dramatically reduce the time it takes to become compliant. Yet
Hyatt never mentions them.

He argues that businesses have *plenty of reasons* for overstating their Y2K progress. In fact, as we have shown, they
have plenty of reasons for telling the truth, among them

staying in business, customer relations, and legal liabilities that could bankrupt them.

Most Japanese banks are going to miss the arbitrary deadline they set of December 31, 1998. The report doesn't say how far behind they are. Days? Weeks? Months? They still have a year to go and that is plenty of time, with the new techniques that could make them all fully compliant in 60 days or less even starting from scratch. No mention of that, but it is assumed that because they are behind schedule at the end of 1998, they must necessarily fail to be ready by January 1, 2000.

Major television coverage is still woefully inadequate? What does that have to do with Y2K readiness? If any IT manager or CEO still needs television coverage to inform or motivate them, one can only wonder what role TV played in bringing them to their present success and responsibilities. Television coverage is more likely to frighten the public than to enlighten the corporate board room. (Hollywood is reportedly set to produce "Y2K," a frightening major film starring Chris O'Donnell[22]—Robin in the Batman movies—that should add to the growing hysteria.) Could it be that the news media has tired of quoting uncertain speculation about what *might* happen or someone thinks *could* happen *if* computers fail, but *maybe they won't* and really no one *knows* what will actually happen?

Hyatt calls all of this *handwriting on the wall*, i.e., doom is sealed. If that isn't unwarranted pessimism, in light of one year remaining and the new techniques available which make that time more than adequate, then what is it? No credit is given or allowance made for the fact that these government departments, banks, and businesses are going to break their backs to do whatever is necessary to be ready for the new millennium. And the reports he lists are those that make him "more pessimistic than ever"? Amazing!

What's Happening in the Real World?

In contrast to the prognostications of the gloom-and-doomers that very few companies or banks will make it and those who claim they will are lying, let's see what the real world is actually like. The Securities and Exchange Commission (SEC), which sets policies and regulates and enforces its rules, "recently announced that public companies could face fines if they deliberately conceal a lack of preparation [for Y2K]. The year 2000 problem will not be viewed as an 'excuse for failing to protect investor assets.'"[23] Pressure is on to make everyone compliant long before the year 2000 dawns. The SEC is not going to wait until January 1, 2000, to find out how everyone is doing. Progress is being checked, firms are being audited, and a material part of any accounting statement these days is whether or not the company is doing everything possible to become compliant and is in fact going to make it by the deadline.

Nor is the SEC the only one applying pressure. Customers apply the heaviest and most persistent pressure. Common sense tells the management of every company, large or small, that they're out of business if they fail to become compliant—not just meeting the deadline by the skin of their teeth, but well ahead of time in order to assure customers that their product will not be adversely affected by the year 2000 rollover. Otherwise customers will go elsewhere. The world of business is a cutthroat, competitive contest where only the most fit survive and thrive. As a major computer trade magazine reminded its readers in December 1998:

> Clearly, one needs to ensure that his or her own products are Y2K compliant. An original equipment manufacturer (OEM) must have its products free of Y2K problems, and a software company must remove bugs from its programs. Malfunctioning products will mean seriously displeased customers....If a

supplier appears not to be ready, then alternative sources [of supply] need to be established.... If you can't prove that your product is Y2K ready, why would someone want to buy it...?

In speaking with large and small contract manufacturers (CMS), I [author of the article] found that all companies had dealt with it [Y2K] on some level....LeeMAH Electronics, Inc. (San Francisco, CA) [for example] expects to be completely Y2K compliant by the beginning of 1999, which includes identification of compliant vendors and their own internal systems....

"It took us three months to get our company compliant," said SMS Technologies' (San Diego, CA) vice-president of sales and marketing, Elliot Shev....They carried out a methodical inventory, testing and upgrade of all internal systems....

CONCLUSION: IT'S NOT THE END OF THE WORLD

The abundance of thoughtful sources of information on the Internet covering the year 2000 bug and the interviews conducted...are reassuring. In nearly all cases, management is being responsible in addressing the problem with the attention it requires. Running off into the desert with a stockpile of food and supplies...seems extreme.[24]

This is the real world where customers and profits don't come easily, where you scramble for business and do everything you can to keep customers happy. If your product line is not fully Y2K compliant or compatible, you are finished. You don't lie to customers. They will find you out and turn to someone else who is honest and whose product is reliable. If you are a public company, you don't lie to the SEC. Not only fines but prison await top management for fraud, to say nothing of lawsuits that would put your company out of business. The almighty dollar calls, and those who pursue it are not going to bury their heads in the sand.

Alarmists would have us believe that with regulating agencies looking over their shoulders, with customers demanding products that will work in the year 2000 and thereafter, with lawyers looking for any excuse to sue, with reputation and customer goodwill on the line, with the very existence of the business hanging in the balance, with the problem known and techniques for speedily solving it available, managers and owners who got to where they are today by fierce competition and efficiency are going to squander their time, lie about their progress, and come up short on January 1, 2000! That's not the real world. We make no apology for adopting a contrary scenario to such unrealistic pessimism. The predicted disaster is not going to happen.

All the incentive anyone could ask for exists, as well as the means available for anyone to solve the Y2K problem in time. There is therefore no excuse for any company that fails this one! They will go out of business. Some other company will buy them out or competitors will take over their customers.

Nor will it take until the year 2000 for reality to catch up with the laggards. Companies are cracking down on their suppliers. For example, this is what Dallas Semiconductor has done:

> A list of all vendors has been compiled, and vendors were asked to provide proof of their products' Year 2000 compliance....Vendors still found to be non-Year 2000 compliant as of November 1998 will be notified that contracts may be terminated. Alternate sources are being identified and will be put in place as necessary to avoid disruptions in delivery of manufacturing or other needed materials.[25]

In other words, the scoop in the business world is, get your house in order pronto! We're not messing around, folks. Shape up or perish. Your product must be Y2K compliant *now* or we're not going to buy it. Now let's have the facts. You can't fool us! That's the real world of business, and it doesn't fit the picture being painted by alarmists.

What About Banking and Insurance?

Chase Manhattan Bank in New York City is America's largest bank, with $336 billion in assets. It launched its formal Enterprise Year 2000 effort in 1996. But even earlier than that it had already been dealing with dates 2000 and beyond. Says Brian Robbins, vice president of enterprise architecture, standards and Year 2000 program: "A number of systems were updated already for the Year 2000 because they were already booking past the millennium. The loan system and trading systems dealing in long-term bonds all had to deal with this issue years ago."[26]

Chase Manhattan had to deal with 200 million lines of code. That was a lot when they started, but with systems available today that will do 4 million or more lines per hour, that's only a week's work for the computer. While some companies could conceivably resort to manual handling of transactions if their computers didn't work, that isn't possible for major banks because of the huge volume of business. Says Steve Sheinheit, senior vice president, corporate systems and architecture:

> In some cases it might be possible to…[use] short-term manual intervention. But in general, banking has gotten to a point of scale where we're pushing between one and two trillion dollars a night. Millions of transactions go to make that up. You can't handle these things manually anymore. We are completely reliant on technology to make the business work.[27]

"See there!" say the pessimists. "They're completely dependent on computers and they'll never make it! There isn't time!" That is not the attitude we find in the real world. Chase Manhattan isn't going to lose a customer or a competitive edge to its rivals. It didn't get where it is today by giving up in the face of difficulty. Says Sheinheit, "Rather than thinking in terms of contingencies, we think in terms of guaranteeing that it's done early enough that we're sure it's fixed."[28]

Another high volume business that couldn't get by without computers is insurance; at least that is true for the major companies. And, like banks, they are very much date dependent because much depends upon the date of birth of those whom they insure and the expiration dates of contracts, annuities, and mortgages. Let's take Prudential Insurance Company of America for our example in this industry. Prudential is one of America's largest insurance and financial services companies, with statutory assets as of December 31, 1997, in the amount of $194 billion and with $37 billion in revenues that year. It employs nearly 80,000 people and serves nearly 40 million customers worldwide. Its gross information technology (IT) budget for 1997 was about $1 billion.

On May 7, 1998, Irene Dec, Prudential's vice president of corporate information, testified before the Subcommittee on Oversight of the House Committee in Ways and Means for its Hearing on the Year 2000 Computer Problem. What she had to say provides further insights into the real world, which, once again, shows how unreal is the perspective of alarmists:

> Because of Prudential's size and scope, the magnitude of our Year 2000 problem is monumental....Prudential's senior management team sees Year 2000 as a *business* issue— not as a *technology* nuisance. Early on, Prudential realized the potential business risk represented by Year 2000, and sought to manage that risk intelligently. Year 2000 is a risk to all businesses. It is essential for all organizations to run Y2K projects with a sound risk management philosophy....
>
> We began addressing the Y2K issue at Prudential in 1995. While we are confident we'll meet our objectives, we are

not wasting one single day. This is the ultimate information technology deadline.....*Failure is not an option.*

For us at Prudential, and for any organization that plans to succeed into the 21st century, *failure is not an option.* Those were the confident and determined words [in response to the words of Jim Lovell, commander of the ill-fated Apollo 13 mission, "Houston, we have a problem"] of Gene Kranz, Mission Control Chief, who was largely responsible for returning the astronauts safely to Earth.

[Yes], there is a problem. And its name is Year 2000. Yet, I believe that if you are smart and strategic, if you make every second count from now until the clock strikes midnight on December 31, 1999, you will achieve your goals and survive this mission critical assignment.

Because we at Prudential have zero tolerance for Y2K failure within our own organization, we have zero tolerance for Y2K failure within any of our business partners' organizations. We are aggressively working with all our partners in fields as diverse as finance, law, medicine—and government—to ensure that Prudential's customers will not feel so much as a tremor when we collectively blast into the new millennium....

As world leaders, we Americans must take the lead in Y2K compliance. We must set the example for other countries to follow. We must demonstrate with decisive action and bold measures that *failure is not an option.*....Thank you for giving me this opportunity to speak with you today.[29]

Michael S. Hyatt agrees that failure is not an *option*; he says it is a *certainty.* He declares in no uncertain terms that there *will* be a "worldwide computer crash that will happen as a result of the Millennium Bug....The result is going to be a billion times worse than the worst computer crash you have ever experienced—or can imagine."[30] He tells us there is no shortcut and that we simply don't have the time to fix it.

The Confidence of Those Who Know the Most

In contrast to those who know the least but talk the most, the lack of concern regarding this subject among those in the real world who know the most, indeed the absolute silence about Y2K that bespeaks a total confidence in some of the most informed quarters, has lately become almost deafening. Embedded systems have received the most attention by those warning of the coming meltdown. Yet the premier trade magazine on the subject, *Embedded Systems Programming*, in its Tenth Anniversary Issue (November 1998), in contrast to the ever more shrill cries of alarmists, did not contain so much as a whisper about Y2K in its nearly 150 pages!

Of course it's all a cover-up. Or is it just plain stupidity? There must be an explanation as to why the Christian experts who stump the country stirring up the church to action are so concerned, but those who are responsible for implementing compliance in business, industry, the military, and government keep saying it's going to be okay. Or else, they're just lying. That's got to be it. They must be lying about their progress!

Really? These are some of the rationalizations alarmists must resort to in order to explain why their level of concern isn't reflected in the real world. The one thing that doesn't make sense is the view that those responsible are lying. Liars, unless they are hopelessly pathological, must at least have some expectation that their untruthfulness won't be discovered. But here is a supposed lie that will be exposed to the whole world on January 1, 2000, if it is indeed a lie. Few people would be such fools as to play that game. Surely not those at the highest levels of responsibility in government and business with their very survival dependent upon actually meeting the challenge!

This author interviewed one of the top computer experts in the country, Warren S. Perry. He is senior project manager for a division of a large information technology

(IT) company that doesn't accept clients with revenues of less than $500 million per annum. He travels all over the United States as an IT troubleshooter helping customers with high-end tech matters which the salespeople are unable to handle. We asked him the question, "What is your opinion of the Y2K problem we are facing, and what have you found the companies you deal with are doing about it?" He replied:

> I find it interesting that many companies have gone out and bought second mainframes to run their testing on, which I don't think is necessary. The truth is that a lot of IT managers are using the concern over Y2K as an opportunity to upgrade [computer] hardware they have wanted to replace for a long time but haven't been able to get the board of directors to approve. That may be why some of them have gone along with so much of the hype surrounding Y2K.
>
> I deal with 7 to 10 IT managers of major corporations each week and always ask them about Y2K. I have never found even *one* that is still worried. Everyone I deal with feels they have finished, they've done what they needed to do, and Y2K is now history.
>
> What I've found especially interesting, over the last month I've been asking whether there would have been serious problems if they had done nothing about Y2K. The answer I most often get is "No."
>
> Yet there is so much talk and concern about Y2K, especially among Christians. I was watching a program on Christian television the other day. It's amazing how they can go on at great length in generalities, getting the audience aroused, and yet say absolutely nothing of substance.
>
> I've learned over the years to listen very carefully to *what* a person is really saying and *how* they are saying it. It's very interesting—if one applies the very Berean principles you promote, what they say boils down to nothing: "the checkout equipment in the supermarket *might* fail *if*... the banking system *could be* in jeopardy *if*, and so forth." You get nothing but generalities but not a single *how* and *why*.

We are never told that some system will fail because of this particular reason, and why. When they are challenged to provide specifics, they have no answer.

I listen carefully and with great interest when the announcer refers to the coming big disaster in the year 2000. But when the expert comes on, I find it amazing how they can carry on for an hour and say absolutely nothing.

Understand, I am not prejudiced against the thought of a Y2K disaster. I'm more than willing for it all to be true, because anything that has the potentiality of causing computers to fail is a revenue opportunity for me. But I haven't found any factual basis for all the concern.

You may be certain that every mission-critical operation in the world will have the entire staff present when the clock rolls over to January 1, 2000. If anything at all goes wrong, the programmers will be right there to fix it.

What will happen? There could be some minor inconveniences: maybe some teller out there in a tiny midwest town goes off line for 3 hours, or someone up in Maine can't get a dial tone—but whatever the problems are, they will be quickly fixed. All this talk about shortages of food will pull forward revenue and for two weeks in January no one will be buying anything. Grocery stores will have a great December and lousy January.[31]

What Is Actually Happening Where It Counts?

In Chapter 3 we noted that "in July [1998], the Securities Industry Association sponsored a two-week test [it didn't take 18 months!]—the first example of an industry coming together to test for the bug—involving major stock exchanges and 29 brokerage firms, among others. Results are encouraging; no major glitches were uncovered." AT&T, Sprint, and MCI all expect to be ready and in late 1998 the Federal Communications Commission estimated that 98 percent of the nation's 1,400 regional carriers upon which the big three's transmissions depend would be "compliant by mid-1999."

In mid-June, 1998, Michael Powell, FCC commissioner, stated that "telephone equipment manufacturers are already producing software that will function properly in the year 2000, enabling phone carriers to meet their own deadlines."[32] International calls could possibly be a mess for some time, except for those using satellite phones, and especially the expensive Iridium phones tied in with the new Iridium satellite system, from which one can call from *anywhere* in the world to *anywhere* without dependence upon local earthbound systems.

In earlier chapters, we have used Hewlett-Packard (HP), the second-largest information-technology supplier in the world,[33] as an example of a company that has achieved Y2K compliancy for itself and is making certain that its suppliers and customers are compliant as well. This company employs about 120,000 people, 51,000 of them outside the United States. HP is "America's Most Admired Computers/Office Equipment Company"[34] and the third-most admired company in Asia.[35] Its products and services are dispensed in more than 120 countries, giving it a large and important influence internationally.

And right here is a factor that seems to be overlooked in all the declarations about third-world countries being so far behind the West that they'll drag us down with them. The truth is that most of the high-tech equipment in those countries comes from and is maintained by American or European expertise. The multinational companies have united the world as no political machine has ever been able to do. More than 40 percent of Hewlett-Packard's employees are overseas, and their customers are everywhere in the world. HP provides the same service for foreign customers and the same training for foreign employees as it does for those in this country, and it is making certain that its foreign suppliers are also year 2000 compliant, just as it is for its suppliers within the United States.

HP is the world's leading manufacturer of fiber-optic communications transceiver modules, optical encoders, laser printers, color laser printers, desktop and network scanners, communications test equipment, high-frequency computer-aided engineering software, logic analyzers, microprocessor development systems, electronic counters, and overall test and measurement products. And that is only a partial list. It is the world's leading manufacturer of more than a dozen other high-tech computer-related products. HP was itself fully Y2K compliant by mid-1998 and is providing full Y2K service and advice to its customers.

Pity the Patients in Hospitals January 1, 2000?

One of the greatest concerns related to Y2K is the well-being of patients in hospitals and clinics. In this regard it is comforting to know that HP leads the world in medical products. It is the world's largest manufacturer of acute-care patient-monitoring systems, of cardiovascular ultrasound imaging systems, and of clinical-information systems for critical care. Its systems in hospitals are Y2K compliant or compatible, and it provides assistance for its customers to become compliant as well. Hospitals everywhere are taking advantage of this service.

As one would expect, hospitals have been especially diligent in making certain that their equipment functions properly after midnight December 31, 1999. We could give many examples. Consider first of all Catholic Healthcare West, a network of 40 hospitals headquartered in San Francisco. As of the end of October 1998, engineers had tested 92 percent of its 80,000 pieces of medical equipment. Only 3.3 percent involved Y2K problems. And of these, "only nine machines, including a cardiac monitor, a CT scan machine, and a blood analyzer, shut down."[36] That is only .011 percent.

We point this out to show the small percentage of systems actually affected and the even lower incidence of shut-downs.

Of the billions of embedded chips out there only a very small fraction are date sensitive because of the embedded software; and of those, at least judging by this large sample, only a tiny fraction would cause a shut-down of the system. Thus some companies could very well get by rather easily without doing anything about Y2K in advance but simply facing the glitches as they come in the new millennium—but there is no excuse for not checking discrete systems right now by setting the date forward.

For a hospital, however, to take any chances would border on the criminal. As Dr. Kevin Fickenscher, chief medical officer of the Catholic Healthcare West network, says, "We've got to test all of our equipment. We don't think it's acceptable for one patient to have a problem as a result of this [Y2K] issue."[37]

Yet alarmists keep repeating the one example of a respirator that supposedly shut down during a test and offer that as proof that hospital machines will be failing right and left, with patients dying like flies. They say that anyone who questions that scenario is obviously in denial. In fact, the real world bears no relationship to that fantasy.

We have also pointed out that although we have come to take computers for granted and imagine that we cannot get along without them and that the world would come to a halt if they all shut down, that is actually not the case. We have suggested that those who raise crops or poultry or stock, even though they may be fully computerized now, could continue to function without computers by utilizing a great deal of hands-on labor in their place. Hospitals recognize that to be true in their case as well:

> Necessarily, hospitals are brainstorming ways to handle the unexpected once the millennium arrives. Next spring [1999], Hoag Memorial Hospital Presbyterian in Newport Beach [California] will start drills for hospital employees on how to do their jobs, with or without technology.

"Much of patient care can be provided by personnel. Technology allows us to do our job more efficiently or in a more timely way; but care in most instances can be provided without the latest and greatest of technology," says Mary Kay Payne, a vice president in charge of Hoag's millennial project.

Come New Year's Eve 1999, it's clear that many hospital managers...won't be partying. Gordon P. Hosoda, for one, says he'll be patrolling the emergency room and three intensive-care wards at the VA medical center in Loma Linda [California].

Hosoda, the hospital's chief of clinical engineering, will focus on ventilators, heart monitors and other life-support equipment. He plans to test all the equipment in advance. But he'll have doubles for backup, if necessary, because nobody knows what to expect.

"It may be a mouse, it may be a lion," Hosoda says. "We'll hope for the mouse and prepare for the lion."[38]

Quick Cures: Band-Aids that Buy Time

For those who lack the time or funds for a full fix, a number of viable alternative solutions are now being implemented. We have mentioned several emergency techniques that would allow for some years into the new millennium to work out real solutions. At least January 1, 2000, no longer looms as the inflexible deadline by which all must be corrected. The alarmists' mantra, "There just isn't enough time," won't work any more. It no longer applies in most cases. In an October 1998 feature article, *Popular Science* made this observation: "In many cases, it's too late to fix the problem correctly. Instead, programmers are reaching into a bag of tricks and pulling out ways to work around the problem."[39]

We have mentioned the 28-year solution and "windowing." These both allow the continued use into the new millennium of two digits for the year until a full solution can be effected. In the first instance, the clock is turned back 28 years (a full leap-year cycle); and in the second, software is introduced to interpret the last two digits of the date, if 50 or less, as belonging to the twenty-first century; and if 51 or more, as belonging to the twentieth century. That solution covers program-embedded chips as well.

At least chaos is no longer inevitable on January 1, 2000! So what if it does take another five or even ten years to resolve the problem fully (which it shouldn't with the improved methods now available), at least it can then be worked on without a rapidly approaching deadline hanging over one's head. As a result, the collapse of the world economy so direly predicted will not have to occur. Computer programmers will be happy, because at least the first few years of the new millennium will continue to be very profitable for them.

Referring to "windowing," Rich Hoffman of the U.S. Army Materiel Command's Year 2000 team acknowledged, "It buys you time." According to Hoffman, in September 1998 the Army's systems were about 80 percent Y2K compliant and "on schedule to be completely fixed by the end of this year [1998]."[40] Anything left hanging can be "windowed" and taken care of later. That appraisal contrasts sharply with continuing reports that the Department of Defense will never make it, leaving the United States vulnerable to enemy attack.

No Silver Bullet? How About Bullets?

We have mentioned a number of "silver bullets" that supposedly could never be invented but which now provide electronic cures in a fraction of the time required only a few months ago. Some bank had 500 million lines of code to go through and correct, and some government department had 800 million lines—such statistics have been cited as proof that in many cases it is impossible to do the job until years into the next millennium.

Then along came StepWise Solutions with a system that automatically zips through software and hardware at the rate of 4 million lines per hour. So 800 million lines of code would take less than two weeks. Not enough time? That dirge doesn't frighten any more.

Then there was "Y2K Sniff" that Boeing has used and a new technique by Oracle. The latter reminds us: "Never in the history of information technology has one impending milestone influenced so many organizations and their systems at the same time and in the same manner. Year 2000 affects all of us....Date-dependent software and hardware systems need to be able to account for the new century before and after the rollover, and they need to be ready to function when January 1, 2000, rings in." Oracle promises on its website:

> Year 2000: In 60 days Oracle can solve a problem that took 2,000 years to create.
>
> Oracle has a comprehensive internal Year 2000 readiness program designed to ensure that we can continue our business without interruption as we move into the next millennium.[41]

New techniques such as the above for achieving compliancy would surely be known to and utilized by well-financed corporate giants. But what about those smaller companies that couldn't afford major repairs or replacements? We've been told that many of them would simply never get around to doing anything; thus, we could still have major problems due to their importance in the supply chain. So we've heard repeatedly, but once again the real world is considerably different from that which doomsayers have portrayed.

First of all, we're not talking about a huge factor, much less that the world will come to a halt if it isn't taken care of before January 1, 2000. The Gartner Group estimates that only half of the smaller companies will be affected by Y2K at all; and then, on the average, even those will only experience "at least one critical Y2K problem between the fourth quarter of 1999 and 2003."[42] Furthermore, any smaller companies with products that would seriously affect us are more than likely suppliers for large corporations—and the latter are making certain that every supplier of parts needed in manufacturing their products is Y2K compliant. Moreover, solutions which smaller companies could afford and put into effect are also being invented and sold. In fact, the market is literally being flooded with them.

The November 1998 Comdex computer trade extravaganza in Las Vegas included a special Year 2000 Pavilion sponsored by Seattle software maker WRQ Inc. and the U.S. General Services Administration. In the pavilion were at least a dozen companies, small and large, unknown and well known, displaying their Y2K correctives that could be purchased at very affordable prices. Y2K Corp., an organization founded specifically to tap the Y2K-fix market, was offering its Y2K++ for $149. It "plugs into a desktop's serial or parallel ports and instructs the computer's internal systems to read the full four digits in the Year 2000."[43]

Also, Symantec Corp., well-known maker of the Norton Antivirus software, was offering its Norton 2000, "a consumer-oriented version of a corporate Y2K product it released in late summer"[44] which was just entering the retail market in November. Astral Systems Inc. was demonstrating its Astral PC2K, which was expected to be available in stores like Office Max late in December. There were many more similar Y2K solutions being offered, among them: Check 2000, the Millennium Bug Compliance Kit, Y2K PC Pro, Centurion 2000, MFX 2000, and Express 2000.

Some of these new tools automatically identify everything that needs to be fixed. Others not only identify but automatically repair the problem. They retail from as low as $50 up to about $2,000 per computer. To help smaller companies, and individuals as well, know what they need and how to apply it, the federal government is launching "a telephone hotline in January [1999] to help consumers sort through the products and get answers to Y2K problems." The Small Business Administration's website [www.sba.gov] offers similar help, as does the Federal Y2K Commercial Off-the-Shelf Products Database [y2k.policyworks.gov].[45]

It certainly sounds as though no one will have a legitimate excuse for any year 2000-related computer difficulties hanging on as they enter the next century. The truth is, the Y2K computer bug might have caused serious problems had it been able to sneak in and catch us all by surprise when no one was looking. Instead, it was recognized more than 20 years ago, has been the focus of increasing attention, and with the energy and ingenuity of the computer world aiming an arsenal of exterminating products at it, this insect has become an endangered species that will be extinct by January 1, 2000, if not before.

And the Worldwide Banking Crash?

The public should have noted all along that among the authorities in whom one would have some confidence, even those who were most concerned about the Y2K problem, with very few exceptions, used such words as "could" or "might" and "if" in their warnings of disaster. For example, "Elizabeth Moler, acting secretary of energy, said that problems at utility companies *could* be grave. 'Electric power is perhaps the most important part of our infrastructure,' she said. 'And widespread Year 2000-related failures in this area *could* create serious disruptions in services the American people depend upon.'" [Emphasis added.][46] Of course they *could* if not fixed in time.

Such warnings from responsible authorities were intended, it would seem, to arouse to action rather than to create panic. The conditional word "could" was not intended to alarm but to motivate; but the alarmists changed these statements from "could" to "would." Nothing sells books and newsletters like fear. And having once set sail in that direction, it is not easy to turn around and tack into the wind.

At the same time that Moler was making the above statement in early August 1998, Vice President Al Gore was assuring the public that the federal government had been working on the problem for some time, that all of its agencies were being continually monitored and would be A.D. 2000 compliant by early 1999. Such assurances, however, have been viewed with suspicion.

As for the worldwide banking crash, according to a study done by the *Los Angeles Times*, "banks were among the first alerted to the problem. Bank of America has been fixing Year 2000 problems since the 1970s, when 30-year mortgages started triggering errors. The effort is in full steam now, occupying about 1,000 employees a day, and is on schedule to be done by December 1998."[47]

Many people already have credit cards from various banks which have expiration dates in 2000 and beyond and, while there were problems at first, they work very well now. Millions of people owe money to banks for homes and autos and for other reasons. Many of these debts will not be paid off until well into the next millennium, and the computers are not crashing but have already for years been handling dates well into the next century.

Inquirers at any bank that is a member of the Federal Deposit Insurance Corporation (FDIC), which insures all accounts, will be given an FDIC brochure titled "The Year 2000 Date Change: What...[It] Means to You and Your Insured Financial Institution." It says in part:

> There has been a lot of public attention lately concerning the impact that the Year 2000 date change could have on businesses, utilities, and other organizations that rely on computerized systems to help run their operations....Businesses, utilities, and other corporations are

fixing their systems to make sure they will operate properly
when the calendar changes....

From the smallest to the largest, FDIC insured banks and
savings associations are taking steps to make sure their systems will operate smoothly in the Year 2000....

Four federal regulatory agencies...are closely monitoring the progress made by banks and savings associations
in completing critical steps required by their Year 2000
plans....

Banks and savings associations are required to keep
backup records for account transactions so they can recover
this information in case of an emergency....You may want
to start keeping records of banking transactions....These
records will help you to resolve any account errors that
might occur due to the Year 2000 date change.[48]

In spite of the dire warnings of an international banking
collapse by various alarmists, there is no excuse for anyone
to panic. In addition to the FDIC brochure, any bank is prepared to offer to its customers all of the information necessary to lay the rumors to rest. Unfortunately, many people
have been prevented from asking their bank about its Y2K
preparedness by another rumor circulating: that banking
employees have been instructed to lie to cover up their lack
of preparation. We have shown that such a rumor is itself
an unconscionable lie.

Like any other business, banks need the trust and goodwill of their customers in order to make a profit. It would be
suicide to put out false information that would destroy customer goodwill and bring lawsuits and possible prison terms
for officers. But when rumors start, almost anything will be
believed that sustains them. Beginning early in 1998, this
author's small local bank offered the following in a prepared
written statement to all customers who inquired:

[Bank] examiners are serious about getting banks
to address and fix their Year 2000 problems prior to
1/1/2000. We have identified a Y2K team which...

[has] implemented a Y2K plan...approved and adopted by our Board of Directors....They are looking at all hardware and software on our Network and AS400 systems...[and] have contacted every vendor we work with for Y2K hardware and software certification and are tracking vendor response to ensure compliance.

We are initiating software upgrades...[and] will test our ability to process with Y2K dates and make sure that the bank can run successfully in the Year 2000. This will be completed prior to 12/31/98. We will obtain certification that all systems are Y2K compliant....With regard to their banking, our customers do not have to do anything specific for Y2K.[49]

A Word of Caution and Reason

To summarize: we have checked carefully with every source we could contact and have yet to find *any* knowledgeable and responsible person out there in the real world who shares the fears with which we are being bombarded from some quarters. In constantly flying commercially, we have yet to find a pilot in the cockpit who is concerned about Y2K. Most of the older planes still in service, such as 727s and 737s, don't even have computers aboard but are analog operated. The airlines will be flying January 1, 2000. Anyone flying United Airlines in December 1998 found this statement by United's Chairman and CEO, Jerry Greenwald, in the seat pocket in front of them:

> Since 1995 we have had a team of 600 employees working diligently to ensure safe, uninterrupted service when the clock strikes midnight December 31, 1999....We will make sure that you experience the start of the new millennium feeling as safe boarding our aircraft as you do every other day of every year...we will not compromise the trust you have placed in us or the reputation we have worked so hard to earn.[50]

Various scientists and engineers contacted at major defense and research corporations have all said their companies are now or will be compliant long before January 1, 2000. Computer experts, including both designers and builders, have personally told the author there is no cause for alarm. An army officer who is a personal friend and works in the area of global positioning satellites has assured the author that the GPS system is in good shape. The local power company claims it is compliant already, and that its national source of power is on top of the problem and will be 2000 compliant well in advance.

As for the Defense Department being caught short on January 1, 2000, apparently those responsible are confident enough of its ability to be compliant on time that they have energy and personnel left over to help others. U.S. Defense Secretary William Cohen "has offered his Russian counterpart help with solving the Year 2000 problem on Russian military computer systems....The U.S. military is not overly confident Russia is devoting as many resources to solving the problem as [are needed]."[51]

Don't panic. Don't take drastic action. Don't base any action upon the cries of alarm. Act reasonably. We should all be prepared for short-term disasters such as earthquakes, tornadoes, hurricanes, fire, and flood. That will cover you for the worst that could come out of Y2K.

Failed Computers—Failed Predictions

Neither the public utilities nor other commercial companies deny the possibility of some unforeseen problems which may have escaped their best efforts. But computer failures are nothing new. Testifying before the U.S. Senate Subcommittee on Financial Services and Technology July 10, 1997, Jeff Jinnett, president of LeBoeuf Computing Technologies, pointed out that "U.S. securities firms typically suffer 6.9 on-line system failures per year, which collectively resulted in $3.4 billion in productivity losses in 1992."[52]

We have learned to live with these computer problems and to work around them. Undoubtedly, most if not all of the Y2K glitches that may arise on January 1, 2000, will be quickly recognized for what they are and dealt with relatively painlessly. After all the publicity and preparation with carefully laid contingency plans and extra staff on hand watching like hawks for the tiniest glitch, it is difficult to imagine anything taking place that would even come close to present gloomy predictions.

Some of North's prognostications have already proved to be false alarms. For example, he warned:

> For 40 years, programmers have used *99* as a shorthand for a lot of computer operations, including this terrifying one: *end of run*....When a computer so programmed reads 99, it shuts down. Permanently. Warning: fiscal years arrive before calendar years do....Fiscal year 99 rolls over on July 1, *1998* in most state budgets. *If just one state shuts down because its computers are programmed* to read 99 as end of run, *the bank run will begin in that state no later than July 2, 1998.* It will spread to the whole world when depositors realize that the entire payments system—and most governments—will shut down no later than the year 2000. I call this the *Year 1998 Problem.* (We are running out of time!)[53]

July 1998 came and went without even a hint of the problems North predicted. Is there any reason to believe that he won't be just as wrong about 1999 and 2000?

We've Been There Before

In 1983 this author wrote a book titled *Peace, Prosperity and the Coming Holocaust.* The Dow Jones Average, which had been tracing out new lows throughout 1982, was barely

holding around 700 and the stockmarket experts were predicting a crash that would make 1929 look like a Sunday-
school picnic. Interest rates were above 20 percent,
unemployment was very high and rising, we were in a worsening worldwide recession, bankruptcies in the U.S. were at
a record rate rivaling even the 1930s worldwide depression,
and the forecast was for an international financial collapse.

The annual report of the World Bank, released in August
1982, painted a gloomy picture, and the highly regarded
weekly investment advisory service, *International Moneyline*,
warned that America was "on the brink of disaster" and that
the entire world was "headed for an economic abyss and
there's nothing that anyone can do to stop it....There never
has been a more certain scenario."[54] Such a dogmatic pronouncement from that authoritative source should in itself
have been enough to bring its prophecy to pass. And who
would be fool enough, under the horrible conditions of the
time, to dare to contradict the doomsayers?

As for Christian business and financial experts, they
seemed all to be in agreement with one another and with the
world. Some of the most popular books in the Christian
market were bluntly forecasting economic doom for America. Specifically, "the death of the dollar" was written and
spoken of as a foregone conclusion by both Christian and
secular experts.

Prophecy experts, too, in their books, newsletters, audiotapes, and messages to live audiences, were pronouncing
another crisis that would exacerbate the economic woes: War
was on the horizon! With almost one voice, it was being
declared that the prophesied attack upon Israel by the Soviet
Union and its Arab allies was imminent. World War III was
said by many Christian leaders to be a prerequisite for the
Rapture (for those who still believed in this increasingly
unpopular doctrine). Why? It was suggested that a nuclear
holocaust would be the perfect cover for that event because
it would prevent the world from realizing that multimillions

of Christians had disappeared. Furthermore, World War III would supposedly make mankind desperate enough for peace and unity that the world would willingly embrace Antichrist as its leader. (As though war ever willingly united countries!)

A Contrary Scenario

It was in this climate of predicted certain doom that we went against the tide. The first chapter of *Peace, Prosperity and the Coming Holocaust* had the same title as this one: "A Contrary Scenario." We suggested that the doomsayers were wrong, that Reaganomics would work, and that the world would move in the direction of peace and prosperity. There would, of course, be the ethnic clashes around the world which Jesus foretold for the last days: "For nation [*ethnos*, or ethnic group] shall rise against nation [*ethnos*]" (Matthew 24:7). But the Soviets would not attack Israel, and World War III would not come until Armageddon at the end of the Great Tribulation. Instead, prior to the Rapture, there would be a great "peace" offensive accompanied by prosperity, with the world moving in the direction of seemingly solving the age-old conflicts between nations.

That "contrary scenario" has proved to be accurate over the last 15 years. The Dow Jones stockmarket average has broken record after record in what can only be described as an unprecedented and almost meteoric rise. Reaganomics did work. And whether Clinton manages to take some of the credit or not, the fact is that in spite of "famines, and pestilences, and earthquakes, in divers places" (Matthew 24:7) exactly as Jesus foretold, Americans, Europeans and in fact most of the world are better off economically than ever in history.

Again, precisely as Jesus warned, there have been ethnic clashes throughout the world: in Africa, in the former Soviet Union, in Yugoslavia and the Middle East; and religious conflicts in Ireland, the Middle East, and elsewhere. But World War III has not broken out. While neither the "prosperity" nor the "peace" is solidly based, there is no reason to doubt that the trend will continue in the same direction. How long it can last is a most important question bearing upon the future of this world and the timing of the Rapture. If the latter, as Christ declared, must come at a time of prosperity, then a worldwide Y2K crash is highly unlikely on that count alone.

Even as, contrary to expectations, the stockmarket rose and the economy improved, the doomsayers would not give up, turning out such bestsellers as *The Economic Collapse in 1990* and *The Coming Crash in 1994.* As is the case today, some of the most popular Christian speakers at church conferences and seminars were those offering advice on how to survive the "coming crash." Survival tactics took precedence over a study of the Scriptures, and that is, sadly, all too true at the present time.

Trust God's Word

What gave me the courage to contradict the presumed experts, to stand virtually alone in my convictions, and to continue to do so over the intervening years? It was not the belief that I was better able to read economic and political trends than anyone else; I have no such illusions. Forecasting the future did not even enter into the picture. In fact, attempting to do so from the standpoint of human wisdom would actually interfere with the basis of my beliefs about the direction events in our day will take.

My conclusions at that time were based entirely upon my understanding of the Bible, and such must be the case today as well. One must have a firm conviction that the Bible describes the last days in understandable language in order to warn and instruct, and that Scripture also gives us the signs to know whether or not we are living in those days.

We based our conclusions in 1983 upon the absolute confidence that God's Word accurately foretells the climax of the history of this world as we have known it. That confidence remains unshaken.

At this stage no one can accurately predict the consequences of Y2K....In any case, it would be foolish to assume that the problem will be completely fixed in time. There may not be a worst-case scenario to deal with, but there could be some pretty bad-case scenarios to deal with. What must we, as believers in the Lord Jesus Christ, do to prepare...?

> —Albert James Dager, founder-director, *Media Spotlight*[1]

One of the questions that people ask is, "Chuck, where should I flee to...?" The answer is, "Where is the Holy Spirit leading you to minister?"

> —Chuck Missler on the Dobson Panel[2]

Ideally, you want to be located at least 100 miles from any cities greater than 100,000 population, and in as secluded a location as possible. The ideal homestead has rich, fertile soil, a creek or stream, some timber, and is sheltered to the north either by trees (called a windbreak) or hills....Some experts are advising to go north rather than south; hungry vagrants from the cities will likely go south, homelessness being more tolerable in a warmer place....Once a location is established, it is wise to drill a private water well, which is connected to either a hand pump or backup generator power.

> —Julian Gregori, The International Crisis
> Management Center[3]

Our response as Christians...should not be fear or anxiety but rather faith, hope and love—faith in our Lord, hope in His Word and His promises and love toward Him and toward others.

> —Dan Dillard, Bend Ministerial Association Y2K
> Preparedness Committee Chairman[4]

I think the church is going to come together...communities are going to come together."

> —Drew Parkhill, Y2K editor for Pat Robertson's
> CBN News[5]

God is our refuge and strength, a very present help in trouble. Therefore will not we fear, though the earth be removed, and though the mountains be carried into the midst of the sea.

> —Psalm 46:1,2

CHAPTER EIGHT

The Christian Response

As 1998 came to a close, leaving only one year until January 1, 1999, Christians were stepping up their efforts to educate one another concerning Y2K preparedness. Shaunti Feldhahn's book, latest to come off the press (October 1998), painted throughout its pages, through fictional characters and episodes, worst-case, frightening examples of what she believes will probably happen. There were, of course, depictions of informed and prepared Christians rescuing and helping those in dire need. The Joseph Project was at work.

Inspired by such books and the many seminars and conferences, all across the country disaster preparedness committees are being formed and networking with one another. Almost everywhere, Christians (after all, they consider it their godly duty) have been the leaders in organizing neighborhood watches and preparing communities and cities to meet the challenge in case computers crash and the power grid should actually fail January 1, 2000.

Sadly, Christians are not being the Bereans they are supposed to be. The Bereans didn't accept even what the great Apostle Paul told them without checking it out from the Scriptures: they "searched the scriptures daily, whether those things [which Paul preached] were so" (Acts 17:11). In the case of Y2K as well, we need to check the facts. We may have a correct view of the Bible, but if our view of the situation confronting us is warped, that can affect our understanding of what the Scriptures are telling us to do. Thus, a true Berean also checks the facts, as well as the Bible, against what the "experts" are saying. And that is exactly what multitudes of Christians have failed to do as Y2K concerns have built to near hysteria in many circles.

All Christians have a personal responsibility to study the facts for themselves. One cannot blame pastors or leaders or alarmists for what they have said in their sincere concern to pass along information and either warnings or assurances which they themselves believe to be accurate. And right here we see a perennial problem which afflicts too many in the body of Christ. Christians tend to accept whatever the pastor or priest or Bible teacher or televangelist says without checking out what they say from the Bible as the Bereans did Paul's words. Having fallen into that pattern, why should they check out what these same experts are now saying about Y2K? Lack of personal study and accepting personal responsibility to know the truth seems to be congenital in the church today—and it ought not to be!

Thankfully, there are some calming and reasonable voices in the church. According to Steve Hewitt, "Assemblies of God leaders are asking churches and families not to engage in activities such as hoarding food, withdrawing money from banks, believing doomsday scenarios, or expecting the economic, political, and social collapse of Western civilization when the clock strikes January 1, 2000."[6] This advice, too, and what we present as well, must also be checked and not followed blindly.

Unfortunately, as we have documented, most of those seeking to awaken the church and the world to the possible consequences of Y2K have spoken in vague generalities, overstated the danger, and failed to present positive developments which indicate that any problems in entering the new millennium will be rare and of little consequence. As a result, in our opinion, the reaction among multitudes of Christians has been unwarranted and extreme.

We are convinced that the time and effort expended by church leaders to stir up Christians to prepare for a Y2K disaster of "possibly" major proportions has been largely wasted. Furthermore, unnecessary anxiety has been created which could engender disillusionment with the church and Bible prophecy when Y2K doesn't live up to devastating expectations, as we are convinced it won't. We have given more than sufficient reasons from the world of computers, business, banking, the power grid, government, and other areas why the predictions of disaster will turn out to be ill-advised.

We now want to consider further reasons, based upon the Bible, why such predictions will prove to be false, and on that basis to suggest a Christian response to the mass hysteria over Y2K, which is being stirred up in both the secular world and the church.

Trumpeting an Uncertain Sound

In his October 24, 1998, presentation in central Oregon, Larry Burkett's longtime associate, Jack Anderson, cautioned his audience, "You must each carefully and prayerfully consider what is the right action for your family to take."[7] If what he had presented to his audience was not exaggerated but was a reasoned estimate based upon known facts, then there was little to pray about; drastic action had to be taken immediately.

If it is likely that the banks will be unable to provide funds and clear checks because their computers have crashed, the logical thing to do would be to quickly take out everything one has in one's bank before too many other people catch on to the situation and make the same demands, thus closing down the banking system long before January 1, 2000. Nor is there any alternative to stocking up on food and water and wood, getting a wood stove for cooking and heating, and doing it before others exhaust the limited supply, if it is indeed likely that the electric power grid in the United States will suffer major interruptions, possibly for an extended period of time.

Would one tell a family that they are directly in line of an approaching tornado and then suggest that they pray about what to do? The action to take is dictated by the situation. Here we confront again a major problem involving the Y2K warnings: nearly everyone hedges, doesn't give solid information and, after stirring up near-panic, says, "Don't panic. No one really knows what will happen." That is less than helpful.

Christian leaders are giving us the very thing that Paul warned about: "For if the trumpet give an uncertain sound, who shall prepare himself to the battle? So likewise ye, except ye utter by the tongue words easy to be understood, how shall it be known what is spoken? For ye shall speak into the air" (1 Corinthians 14:8,9). Paul wrote that to correct speaking in tongues without an interpreter, but it seems equally applicable to the current Y2K misinformation and doubletalk.

Larry Burkett, who is one of the calmer voices, has also stepped in to provide information and advice concerning Y2K. Nevertheless, in an interview with *World* magazine he recommended gradually stocking up on food, getting "some containers for storing some water...some nonelectric lanterns. And do so soon, because next year at this time, they're not going to be available."[8] That final remark could only help to stir up the very panic which he so wisely warns against. Burkett, however, had already months earlier experienced justification for that remark. He relates:

> I recently called an Amish supply company to order a couple of their coal oil lamps, since they make the best in the world. The person there said,

"I can't give you any delivery time on these....If you
had called me two months ago, I would have shipped
you some; if you had called me a month ago, I would
have told you it would be two weeks late. Today I
must tell you that we are so swamped with orders
that we don't know that we'll ever get to them all."[9]

Typically, Christian leaders dealing with Y2K have seemed
to straddle the fence. We are told not to panic, then given
information which seems to warrant panic. Given the shortages that have already surfaced, how can we all acquire the
emergency equipment, food, and supplies we need? The "Y2K
Position Paper" on Burkett's website as of the end of October
1998 echoed the warnings of possible catastrophe coming
from so many others, but also cautioned against panic. As a
matter of prudence, however, in relation to Proverbs 27:12, it
suggested stocking up on essentials that would be needed in
case of possible breakdowns in public services.[10] Burkett's
Weekly E-mail in mid-November sounded a bit more definite
and urgent:

Store nonperishable canned or dried food in a
cool, dry place. Bear in mind that you may not have
electrical heat with which to prepare food. Buy small
cans, not large—in case there is no refrigeration for
leftovers....Beware that the potential for violence
may increase with sustained periods of power outages or economic problems. Remember that there
is "safety in numbers" [i.e., Christians are to work
together for mutual benefit and safety].[11]

Preparing for...*What?*

Following Jack Anderson's talk, the chairman of the
sponsoring ministerial association's Y2K preparedness committee asked the audience, "How many of you carry fire
insurance?" Nearly everyone's hand went up. He then
chided them, "What's the matter with you? Don't you have

any faith?" They laughed. He then presented what seemed like a bulletproof argument for Y2K preparedness:

> Are you worried that right now your house might be burning down while you're at this conference? Probably not seriously worried. It's not very likely that your house is burning down right now. Well, then, why do you carry fire insurance? Well, because it's prudent wisdom, because if your house burns down and it's uninsured it's going to be very hard to replace that....It's biblical that you have a fire extinguisher in your home that you hope you will never use...a first-aid kit, which you hope you will never use.
>
> I come from South Florida...and every hurricane season we would have our radios on...and we would listen for the hurricane alerts, and when hurricanes began drawing near to the coast of Florida we would make certain preparations... extra groceries, fill up the bathtub with water. ...Sometimes those hurricanes just veered away....Some people didn't prepare and they [suffered the consequences].
>
> It's just prudence [to prepare]. Trust in the Lord and make appropriate preparations, but don't put your faith in your preparations, put your faith in God.[12]

On the one hand, it was wise advice. On the other hand, it left the audience hanging on a rope over a drop of uncertain depth. Fire, hurricane, flood, or other property insurance has a definite limit determined by the value one wants to cover and premium one wants to pay. But Y2K has nothing definite about it, according to those stirring the pot of anxiety. Will it be nothing? some troublesome glitches that interrupt power now and then for a few minutes or hours? total blackout for days, weeks, months, years? people dying from cold and famine?

What will it be? "No one knows for sure" is all those on the Christian Y2K speaking circuit will tell anyone. So what do we prepare for? Good question! Pray about it, and don't trust your preparations, but trust the Lord. Yes, we are trusting God at all times. Anything can happen and we are in His hands, but is there some action we should take and some definite information to determine it?

The verse so often quoted in connection with Y2K says that the "prudent man *foreseeth* the evil, and hideth himself" (Proverbs 27:12). At the same time, however, we are told that no one can accurately *foresee* this evil; no one knows, so what does one hide from?

Shaunti Feldhahn says, "Realistically, we must confront the possibility that Y2K could cause anything from minor personal inconveniences to major global turmoil; again, *no one knows*. We will, however, know the answer soon enough."[13] Not soon enough to know exactly what to prepare for. You could prepare for a month and die of starvation if it went on for six months. What are we to do?

Time, Money, Effort Spent on "Preparedness"

A lot of time and money has been spent by Christians on seminars and detailed planning and in purchasing books, tapes, survival food, supplies, and a host of items which are supposed to be essential inoculation against the deadly bite of the Y2K bug—and which are becoming in short supply. No one disputes the fact that Y2K, as we have already documented, is proving to be very profitable for many who are pushing the disaster scenario. Nicholas Zvegintzov, technical editor of *Software Management Technology Reference Guide*, and co-founder of *Software Maintenance News, Inc.*,[14] is not one to mince words. Here was his insightful, though sarcastic, evaluation of this scene:

> The Year 2000 problem...is the focus of a huge and unique racket. The racket treats the Year 2000 problem as huge, difficult, dangerous, and unique. There are doom-laden articles in the newspapers, expensive conferences..., offerings by consulting groups, special software tools, internet news pages. This is the Year 2000 racket.[15]

By late October 1998 it became apparent that great numbers of Americans and Canadians had already begun to accumulate cash reserves for the Y2K crunch. In anticipation of an acceleration in that trend, The Bank of Canada is preparing to print extra bank notes in 1999 and the U.S. Federal Reserve Board will increase cash in circulation from the usual $150 billion to $200 billion.[16] Will that be enough if panic reigns? No it won't.

In December 1998, the Associated Press reported, "Long-term food is a particularly hot item, sparking a boom in the hitherto small dried food industry. 'In the past three months we've been doubling sales every month,' said Chris Clarke of Emergency Essentials, an 11-year-old Utah-based company that manufactures and distributes dehydrated food." Sales tripled in 1998 for Alpine Aire Gourmet Reserve Foods, a major freeze-dried producer.[17] Has the panic we feared already begun, only to gather momentum until it is out of control? We hope not! And one purpose of this book is to cool that hysteria.

There was little doubt that just as Christians were the major force behind the mushrooming of disaster preparedness committees across the country, so they accounted for the lion's share of buying that had created the boom in freeze-dried foods, diesel and gas generators, oil lanterns, and other emergency equipment and supplies—and the resultant shortages. Y2K sounded too much like a build-up to Antichrist, the Second Coming, and the end of the world for many Christians not to jump in with both feet and unrestrained paranoia. Here is the greatest opportunity ever for Christians to show the world they know what's happening, to demonstrate love and care and win others to Christ—so many sincerely believe, but their action has been based upon misinformation.

The explanation offered by Alpine's Randy White for the sudden explosion in demand for survival foods was most interesting: "A lot of televangelists have kind of picked up on this."[18] Undoubtedly, Christian television was playing a significant role in raising awareness in the church and concern among Christians, and through Christians (thinking this was a great opportunity to "reach others for Christ") reaching non-Christian relatives, friends, and neighbors with the "gospel" of impending Y2K disaster. Christian TV personalities were jumping onto the bandwagon of an exciting topic with great possibilities and, without thoroughly checking the facts, passing along the frightening quotes they had heard from someone else. On the Dobson panel, Steve Hewitt suggested that we ought to

> start becoming informed as Christians. We need not to just look at a televangelist who's listening to some other person who's listening to some other person....[You need to be] going to the sources, looking at the reports, get a balanced view, make your preparations and do some praying. Don't take on the spirit of fear with this. Continue to walk in faith. If it's...a bad winter storm, or if it's the end of Western civilization, it gives us the opportunity to stand like never before.[19]

Major Surplus & Survival, a disaster supplies store in Los Angeles, can't keep up with the demand. One of the more unusual sales it made in 1998 was a seven-year supply of food for one family at a cost of $3,000 per year.[20] The woman who ordered the food didn't explain her reason for buying a seven-year supply, though she must have had a specific reason to order that exact amount. Perhaps she believed Julian Gregori's prediction of a "seven-to-eight-year economic collapse" in America.[21] Or perhaps she had read some of The Joseph Project 2000 material, remembered that Joseph stored up a seven-year supply, and wanted to follow his example.

Al Dager warns against extreme reactions: "Whatever steps we take, we must avoid the hard-core survivalist mentality that says, 'Gold, guns, groceries, and God, and the rest of the world be hanged.'"[22] Chuck Missler told Dobson's radio audience that there are two major mistakes one could make: "The first is not to prepare. That's foolish and not diligent. And the second one is to rely on the preparations. We rely upon Jesus Christ....Individually, in terms of our family, and also by showing some leadership within our church communities to somehow prepare as a community."

Are We in the "Last Days"?

We have provided more than enough documentation and solid reason to remove the uncertainty surrounding Y2K. It is not going to fulfill the alarmists' expectations. There will probably be some glitches here and there, but they will amount to no more than inconveniences. Companies that have not been diligent may go out of business, unable to compete because of customer dissatisfaction with noncompliant products or services. Or they may be cut off from the manufacturers they have been supplying because of their failure to become Y2K compliant on time.

Now we want to turn once again to the Bible to see whether it supports the conclusions we have arrived at on the basis of the facts as we have been able to discover them. Scripture has some definite things to say concerning the way this present world will end—and those specific passages have an important bearing upon how we view the threat of Y2K. That is, of course, provided that we are living in the "last days" as described in Scripture.

The Bible refers repeatedly to the "last days" and gives some very definite signs for us to be able to recognize whether we are living in that time or not. We have mentioned some of these signs in Chapter 6. It is beyond the scope of this book to go into further detail in that regard. Israel has returned to her land as prophesied—a necessity for the last-days events of Armageddon and the Second Coming of Christ to reign over

His chosen people from David's throne in Jerusalem. The apostasy both Christ and His apostles warned of in the last days is surely upon us, as we have documented fully in other books such as *Occult Invasion* and *Global Peace and the Rise of Antichrist*, both available at your local Christian bookstore. Consider, for example, "When the Son of man cometh [Christ asks rhetorically], shall he find faith on the earth?" (Luke 18:8). "Let no man deceive you by any means: for that day [the day of Christ] shall not come, except there come a falling away [apostasy] first" (2 Thessalonians 2:3).

Christ's question and Paul's declaration hardly fit the idea of "last-days revival," which is the majority view among Christians today. Obviously, Christ's words imply a lack of true faith and thus the very apostasy which Paul declares must come before the return of Christ. In addition to apostasy within the church, we have in the world the ethnic clashes Christ foretold; the weapons to exterminate all flesh that could bring a premature end of life on earth which He warned would indeed occur without His direct intervention; and the computerized technology that makes it possible for the Antichrist, the prophesied world ruler, to control all buying and selling and to monitor everyone on earth. As we have already argued, it would be unreasonable that we would come to the point in history when all of these signs were present upon the earth, and yet history would go on indefinitely without experiencing the climax for which these signs have prepared the way.

There are two further reasons for believing that we are very close to the Second Coming. As a corollary to the above, having arrived at the time when these signs are present, and considering how events change rapidly, it seems unlikely that the tenuous peace being established and today's debt-burdened prosperity would remain intact for long. The major reason, however, for our assurance that we are in the last days comes from the lips of Christ Himself. After providing the full list of signs (which we haven't included for lack of space), He said, "when ye shall see all these things, know that it [the Second Coming] is near, even at the doors" (Matthew 24:33). We see almost "all these things" right now. That was not true of any generation before ours. How near is near? "Even at the doors" sounds very near.

The Unique Promise of Christianity

The real hope of Christians is not to live into the next millennium here on earth, having survived Y2K, but to be taken to be with Christ in heaven. And we don't have to die to get there. That is the really good news.

Christianity is absolutely unique in promising heaven without dying! No religion has ever dared to promise that, but Christ promised it and so did the apostles. Jesus gave His solemn word: "In my Father's house [in heaven] are many mansions....I go to prepare a place [there] for you. And if I go..., I will come again, and receive you unto myself [obviously taking us into heaven]; that where I am, there ye may be also" (John 14:2,3).

The transfer of His own to heaven would not only be a gradual process over the centuries, as they died one by one, although we have that promise as well. Paul told the Philippians that he had "a desire to depart, and to be with Christ; which is far better: nevertheless to abide in the flesh [i.e., alive in this body of flesh] is more needful for you" (Philippians 1:23,24). Christ had gone to heaven to be with the Father, and Paul longed to be there too. He knew that would happen through His martyrdom, and He could look forward to it with joy, knowing that it would be his entrance into glory to be with His Lord. He spoke of this departure from this body to be with Christ to the Corinthians as well:

> For we know that if our earthly house of this tabernacle [body] were dissolved [in death], we have...an house...eternal in the heavens....Whilst we are at home in the body [physically alive here on

earth], we are absent from the Lord....We are confident, I say, and willing rather to be absent from the
body, and to be present with the Lord (2 Corinthians 5:1,6,8).

Paul also explained that one day Christ would suddenly
catch to heaven the many Christians who had not died and
were alive at His coming, instantly giving them new bodies
capable of living in heaven, and resurrecting and trans-
forming the bodies of those who had died:

> Now this I say, brethren, that flesh and blood cannot
> inherit ·the kingdom of God; neither doth corruption
> inherit incorruption. Behold, I shew you a mystery
> [revealing a truth unknown in the past]; We shall not all
> sleep [die], but we shall all be changed, in a moment, in the
> twinkling of an eye, at the last trump: for the trumpet shall
> sound, and the dead shall be raised [i.e., resurrected from
> their graves] incorruptible, and we [those alive at that time]
> shall be changed (1 Corinthians 15:50-52).

> But I would not have you to be ignorant, brethren, con-
> cerning them which are asleep [i.e. are dead]..., them also
> which sleep in Jesus [whose souls and spirits have been
> "absent from the body, present with the Lord" in heaven]
> will God bring with him [at His coming]....For the Lord
> himself shall descend from heaven with a shout, with the
> voice of the archangel, and with the trump of God: and the
> dead in Christ shall rise first [i.e., their bodies are resur-
> rected to rejoin their souls and spirits]:
> Then we which are alive and remain shall be caught up
> together with them in the clouds [in transformed bodies that
> can handle such a journey], to meet the Lord in the air: and
> so shall we ever be with the Lord (1 Thessalonians 4:13-17).

Paul is describing what has come to be known as the
Rapture. A common criticism of that doctrine by those who
reject it is the claim that the word is not found in the Bible.
In fact, it is found in the passage above in the Latin Bible.

The phrase "caught up" is *raptus* in Latin, coming from the Latin verb, *rapere*, to carry or catch away. That is exactly what Paul is describing. We don't fly away to heaven on our own; Christ comes and takes us there. He catches us up from this earth. How else could we get into heaven?

Still convinced that Y2K will be a worldwide calamity beyond imagination, Gary North says many Christians, caught in the throes of Y2K, will ask in desperation and disillusionment, "Where was the Rapture? Why is Jesus letting this happen to me? We were promised the Rapture. This is the Great Tribulation." North responds, "It won't be the Great Tribulation, but it will seem like it. A time of great testing is coming."[23]

Testing for *Christians*? *We* were supposed to be in charge by this time, according to what North declared with equal confidence ten years ago. There wasn't a word about Y2K problems, but a thrilling vision of a new America run by Christians. His prognostications then were about as accurate as his Y2K predictions today:

> By 2001, you could be president, thanks to the coming "Second American Revolution" of the late 1990s....You see, as a Christian and a conservative, you'll be part of a very popular bunch.
>
> In fact, voters will be insisting that all leaders...be firmly committed to no-nonsense, Christian values. ...Christians and conservatives will be swept into most elective U.S. offices by ridiculous margins....
>
> Humanism's house of cards is about to collapse. ...[We have] the most dazzling, mind-bending Christian plan of action since Luther swung his hammer at the church door in Wittenberg....I invite you to join us in setting the agenda of world affairs.[24]

As a Reconstructionist leader who believes that the Christian's task is to take over this world and reconstruct civilization according to biblical principles, North ridicules the

Rapture. His hope is in this world, which is why Y2K has become such a burden to him. The Bible offers the "blessed hope" (Titus 2:13) that Christ will suddenly (and it could be at any moment) take His own to heaven to join Him in His Father's house of many mansions. That faith changes one's entire perspective.

The Price of Admission to Heaven

If Christ takes His own to heaven, on what basis are we to be admitted there? Not because of our good works: "all our righteousnesses are as filthy rags" (Isaiah 64:6); "All have sinned, and come short of the glory of God" (Romans 3:23); "Not by works of righteousness which we have done, but according to his mercy he saved us" (Titus 3:5). Even if we could live a perfect life in the future, keeping the law from now on would not gain *extra* credit since it is what the law demands. There is no way, by keeping the law perfectly in the future, to make up for having broken it in the past: "Therefore by the deeds of the law there shall no flesh be justified in his sight" (Romans 3:20).

We could never pay the infinite penalty (eternal separation) demanded by God's perfect justice for our rebellion against Him, which the Bible calls sin. God, being infinite, could pay that penalty, but it wouldn't be just, because He is not one of us. Therefore, in love and mercy, God the Son left His Father's house in heaven to become a man through the virgin birth. He didn't cease to be God and He will never cease to be man: He is the one and only God-man. He alone was able to pay the penalty demanded by His infinite justice, and He paid it fully upon the cross.

It was not the cruelty of man mocking and crucifying Him that saves us; that would only add to our condemnation. While man did his worst in hatred, Jesus Christ, in love we didn't deserve, said, "Father, forgive them." Hanging on the cross, He became the sin offering, paying the penalty we deserved. Before He gave Himself in death into His Father's hands, He cried in triumph, "It is finished!" The debt had been paid in full; and it is *only* on that basis that we can be forgiven by a holy, righteous God: "Being justified [forgiven] freely by his grace through the redemption that is in Christ Jesus:...that he [God] might be just, and the justifier of him which believeth in Jesus....A man is justified by faith without the deeds of the law" (Romans 3:24-26,28).

That is why the Bible repeatedly declares that salvation is a *gift* of God's grace: "the gift of God is eternal life through Jesus Christ our Lord" (Romans 6:23); "For by grace are ye saved...: it is the gift of God" (Ephesians 2:8). A gift cannot be earned, merited, or paid for; it can only be received. We receive the gift of eternal life by faith in Christ, believing that He has provided it and that He offers it to us freely. There is no other way. Jesus Himself said, "I am the way, the truth, and the life; no man cometh unto the Father, but by me" (John 14:6). You can receive that gift from God right now by believing in and receiving Christ.

The Rapture Is Not the Second Coming

In Chapter 6 we dealt with the fact that the Rapture is distinct from the Second Coming. We pointed out that when Christ's feet touch the Mount of Olives at His Second Coming to rescue Israel in the midst of Armageddon, He will bring "all the saints" from heaven with Him (Zechariah 14:4-5). Obviously He must have already taken them to heaven at the Rapture or they could not come from there with Him.

There are many who deny that the Rapture and the Second Coming are two distinct events separated by seven years, during which Christ's bride is with Him in heaven while Antichrist reigns on earth. Their main objection is, *Show us just one verse in the New Testament that refers to* two comings *yet in the future.*

Our response is simple: *Show us one verse in the Old Testament that said the Messiah would come twice.* Every Christian believes that Christ came 1,900 years ago and that He will make good on His promise, "I will come again." Yet nowhere in the Old Testament does it explicitly say there would be two comings. That is why the disciples and the pharisees were equally confused (and why Jews reject Jesus as the Messiah today). They thought (and today's Jews still think) that the Messiah would come only once, to establish peace, deliver Israel from her enemies, and rule the world. Jesus didn't do that, so He couldn't be the Messiah.

But the prophets also said He would be killed ("he was cut off out of the land of the living," Isaiah 53:8; "Messiah [shall] be cut off," Daniel 9:26); indeed, that He would be crucified ("they pierced my hands and my feet," Psalm 22:16; "they shall look upon me whom they have pierced," Zechariah 12:10). How could He establish an everlasting kingdom of endless peace on David's throne ("Of the increase of his government and peace there shall be no end, upon the throne of David...even for ever," Isaiah 9:7) and yet be killed?

There is no way to put into one event and one time frame what the Hebrew prophets said about the coming of the Messiah. He had to come twice: first as the Lamb of God to be rejected by His own people and to die for the sins of the world; the second time as the Lion of the tribe of Judah, to destroy Israel's enemies and to rule and reign forever.

And so it is in the New Testament: there is no way to put into one event and one time frame what Christ Himself and His apostles said about His return. He comes at a time of peace ("As the days of Noe were," Matthew 24:37); but He comes in the midst of Armageddon, the greatest war in human history ("And I saw heaven opened, and behold a white horse; and he that sat upon him was called Faithful and True....And I saw the beast [Antichrist], and the kings of the earth, and their armies, gathered together to make

war against him that sat on the horse, and against his army,"
Revelation 19:11,19). He comes when even the Antichrist
knows He is coming, as the verse just quoted declares; yet He
comes when no one suspects He is coming ("in such an hour
as ye think not the Son of man cometh," Matthew 24:44).
There must be two comings: the Rapture and the Second
Coming.

At the Rapture, Christ comes to resurrect the saints who
have died and to transform the living and catch them up
together to heaven; at the Second Coming He comes *with* His
saints to rescue Israel at Armageddon. At the Rapture, Christ
doesn't come to earth, but catches His own up to meet Him
"in the air" above earth and takes them back to heaven; at His
Second Coming, Christ comes to the earth, destroys Antichrist, and establishes His millennial kingdom on David's
throne, ruling the world from Jerusalem. These *must* be two
events.

The Clear Teaching of Imminency

It is now nearly 2,000 years since our Lord Jesus Christ
promised, "I will come again, and receive you unto myself;
that where I am, there ye may be also" (John 14:3). He made
it clear that He could fulfill that promise at any time and
that His own were to watch for His coming, expecting His
imminent return. Such are the undeniable implications of
the following passages, which ought to shake those who
reject the doctrine of imminency and deny that the church
should be expecting Christ's return at any moment:

> Let your loins be girded about, and your lights
> burning; and ye yourselves like unto men that wait
> for their lord....Blessed are those servants, whom
> the lord when he cometh shall find watching....And
> if he shall come in the second watch, or come in the
> third watch, and find them so, blessed are those ser-
> vants (Luke 12:35-38).

> Watch therefore: for ye know not what hour
> your Lord doth come....Therefore be ye also ready.
> ...Blessed is that servant, whom his lord when he
> cometh shall find so doing [i.e., watching] (Matthew
> 24:42,44,46).

> Watch therefore, for ye know neither the day nor
> the hour wherein the Son of man cometh (Matthew
> 25:13).

> Watch ye therefore: for ye know not when the
> master of the house cometh....Lest coming sud-
> denly he find you sleeping. And what I say unto you
> I say unto all, Watch (Mark 13:35-37).

Such language only fits a coming of Christ that could occur at any moment. That could only be the Rapture of the saints to heaven. It could not refer to the Second Coming at Armageddon, which can't occur until Antichrist has established his kingdom. A major purpose of the Second Coming is to destroy Antichrist: "whom the Lord shall consume with the spirit of his mouth, and shall destroy with the brightness of his coming" (2 Thessalonians 2:8). Furthermore, this coming of Christ (which *must* be the Rapture) could only occur prior to the tribulation period and appearance of Antichrist, or it could not come *at any moment* and would not come *when not expected.*

The scriptures immediately above could not fit a pre-wrath, mid-trib, or post-trib Rapture. If the Rapture cannot occur until Antichrist first appears or until the middle or end of the Tribulation, then the element of surprise is removed, and Christ's admonition that we must watch and be ready at any moment or we will be caught unawares by His return, which will come at "such an hour as ye think not," is inappropriate.

The early church, trusting Christ's promise and heeding His warnings, lived in constant expectation of His imminent return. That fact is quite clear from the following scriptures:

> For our conversation [preoccupation] is in heaven; from whence also we look for the Saviour, the Lord Jesus Christ (Philippians 3:20).

> Ye turned to God from idols to serve the living and true God; and to wait for his Son from heaven (1 Thessalonians 1:9-10).

> Looking for that blessed hope, and the glorious appearing of the great God and our Saviour Jesus Christ (Titus 2:13).

> So Christ was once offered to bear the sins of many; and unto them that look for him shall he appear the second time without sin unto salvation (Hebrews 9:28).

There is no denying, on the basis of the above Scriptures and others, that those in the early church, as Christ Himself and the apostles had taught them, were watching and waiting for Him. Therefore it must have been possible for Him to come at any moment. They would not have been looking for Him—and Christ and the apostles would not have taught them to be in that attitude of expectancy—were it necessary for any event (the coming of Antichrist, Great Tribulation) to precede the Rapture. Furthermore, Christ associated with evil the thought that His return could be delayed, and denounced those who entertained that idea:

> But and if that evil servant shall say in his heart, My lord delayeth his coming; and shall begin to smite his fellowservants, and to eat and drink with the drunken; the lord of that servant shall come in a day when he looketh not for him, and in an hour that he is not aware of (Matthew 24:48-50).

> But and if that servant say in his heart, My lord delayeth his coming; and shall begin to beat the menservants and maidens, and to eat and drink, and to be drunken; the lord of that servant will come in

a day when he looketh not for him, and at an hour when he is not aware, and will cut him in sunder, and will appoint him his portion with the unbelievers (Luke 12:45-46).

The Element of Surprise Doesn't Fit a Y2K Catastrophe

The Bible makes some very definitive statements which require certain inescapable conclusions concerning the period of time leading up to the Rapture. For example, we are repeatedly told that the coming of the Day of the Lord (or the Day of Christ—the two are synonymous) will be "like a thief." In other words, it will come at a time when least expected. As we noted in Chapter 6, Paul had taught this to the Thessalonians whom he had converted out of rank paganism: "For yourselves know perfectly that the day of the Lord so cometh as a thief in the night" (1 Thessalonians 5:2). Peter agrees: "But the day of the Lord will come as a thief in the night" (2 Peter 3:10). No one makes this fact more clear than Christ Himself:

"Therefore be ye also ready: for in such an hour as ye think not the Son of man cometh" (Matthew 24:44); "Be ye therefore ready also: for the Son of Man cometh at an hour when ye think not" (Luke 12:40).

And take heed to yourselves, lest at any time your hearts be overcharged with surfeiting, and drunkenness, and the cares of this life, and so that day come upon you unawares. For as a snare shall it come on all them that dwell on the face of the whole earth. Watch ye therefore, and pray always, that ye may be accounted worthy to escape all these things that shall come to pass, and to stand before the Son of man (Luke 21:34-36).

While the bridegroom tarried, they all slumbered and slept (Matthew 25:5).

Jesus is speaking both of the coming of the Day of the Lord and of His coming which initiates that Day. In these terms He can *only* be speaking of the Rapture because there is no surprise at His Second Coming. Therefore, we must conclude that the Rapture marks the beginning of the Day of the Lord. In these passages, His emphasis is on the element of surprise. Christ is unmistakably telling us that His coming (and the dawning of the Day of the Lord, which begins the Great Tribulation) will be at a time when, if his followers sat down and looked at conditions around the world, they would, on that basis, conclude that He *wouldn't come at that time.*

We say "around the world," because, while the conditions need not be uniform everywhere, they must be universal enough to apply generally to His broad statement, not merely to a specific region. The conclusion, therefore, to which we have already been driven by other Scriptures, seems inescapable: Christ is not coming to take His bride to heaven in the midst of worldwide distress caused by a devastating war or international financial collapse brought on by Y2K, but during a time when life is carrying on in a normal manner.

While there have always been areas of famine or distress, never have these conditions existed at one time all over the world. That is what is unique about Y2K: if it turns out to be as bad as the alarmists say, it will happen all over the world. We are continually told of the interconnectedness of today's world, that even if the United States got its house in order, the crashing of computers elsewhere would drag us down too. Feldhahn says that "the evidence that we will encounter Year 2000 problems is powerful" and that these will take effect "all at once, all around the world."[25] Consequently, if Y2K lives up to expectations, there would be a period of time during which conditions would not be as described at the return of Christ and He could not rapture His bride to heaven. That would violate Scripture.

There will be universal distress simultaneously during the Great Tribulation under Antichrist. Couldn't Y2K, as some believe, be the means of bringing that about? Why couldn't Christ come right now and Y2K be the universal calamity some expect?

Christ could come at any moment. But if the means of ushering in the Great Tribulation and reign of Antichrist is already present and the world is fully informed about it, then we have lost the element of surprise. Remember, the Day of the Lord or of Christ must come as a thief. As we pointed out in Chapter 6, Y2K just doesn't fit.

Convictions and Attitudes at the Midnight Hour

Christ's warning concerning "surfeiting, and drunkenness and the cares of this life" (Luke 21:34) can hardly apply to a time of worldwide distress caused by a Y2K computer collapse. "Surfeiting" is an old English word for overindulgence and gluttony—hardly a danger in the midst of war and economic distress. In the context, then, "the cares of this life" must refer to being occupied with the pleasures and possessions which turn one from heaven to earth. Only during a time of normal life and plenty would one need to resist the temptation to indulge in such sins, not during a world war or universal financial disaster.

The same conditions are implied in Christ's parable of the ten virgins and the warning it carries for those waiting for Christ to rapture His bride, the church, to heaven: "While the bridegroom tarried, they *all* slumbered and slept" (Matthew 25:5, emphasis added). Yes, the five wise virgins do have the oil of the Holy Spirit in their lamps and are therefore seemingly true Christians. But they, too, join the sleep of fools, having grown weary of waiting for the bridegroom to come. That sleep is descriptive of a people contented, at ease, and well fed, not those in the throes of Y2K.

Jesus seems to be describing conditions and attitudes at the midnight hour just before His return for His bride—conditions and attitudes, sadly enough, among the very saints for whom He is coming. He paints this picture not once but many times and in various ways. He also offers a solemn warning that those who lose the eager anticipation of His return and are pleased to imagine that His coming is delayed are likely to fall into the practice of evil. However, if the Rapture cannot occur until something else happens first, such as the appearance of Antichrist or the Great Tribulation, then we have lost imminency, and His admonition against suggesting a delay is meaningless.

Must We Not Face Antichrist?

In spite of the clear teaching of imminency in Scripture, many Christians insist that the church must face Antichrist before the Rapture can occur. Christ's warnings, which we have quoted, never mention Antichrist. He is not warning us in order to strengthen our resolve to resist Antichrist and to stand strong in the face of his persecution and slaughter of Christians. On the contrary, the great danger for Christians at the time of the Rapture is plainly stated to be ease and pleasure. Relying more upon new "revelations" he and others have received than upon the Word of God, Marvin Byers, author, educator, pastor, and missionary, explains why he believes the church must face *and conquer* the Antichrist:

> Hebrews 10:12-13 tells us that...Christ..."sat down at the right hand of God...waiting till his enemies are made his footstool." In answer to the poison and death that Satan injected into humanity, Christ injected His life and power, and now He is waiting for us to use it....
>
> Rather than snatching man away from Satan's grasp, the Lord is offering us His life and power. In this way the same human race that chose to put themselves under Satan's feet will now arise and put Satan under Christ's feet....

> It is evident from 1 Corinthians 15:25-26 and 51-54 that
> there will be no Rapture until all His enemies are placed
> under His feet. The last enemy that will be conquered will
> be death, and Paul says death will be conquered in the
> Rapture. So then, if any enemy remains unconquered by
> the Church in these days, the moment to conquer death
> [i.e., the Rapture] has not yet arrived!
>
> Further, the Antichrist is an enemy that must be con-
> quered before the "last enemy," death, can be conquered
> in the Rapture. The Church has a work to accomplish [to
> face and conquer Antichrist and Satan], and she will not
> leave this world [in the Rapture] until She can say as Christ
> said, "It is finished!"[26]

One need know very little Scripture to see the error of
the above. It borders on blasphemy to teach that Christ is
waiting for the church to put Satan under His feet. Satan
was defeated at the Cross. Indeed, he was "cast out" (John
12:31). Death was, of course, *conquered* in the death and resurrection of Christ, so that enemy is already under His feet
and its final end is assured. Death, however, will persist for
those living on earth even after the Rapture and the resurrection of the church and saints of all ages. Even in the millennial kingdom of Christ there is still death: "for the child
shall die an hundred years old" (Isaiah 65:20); and multitudes will die in the great battle of Gog and Magog at the
end of the millennium (Revelation 20:8,9). Death is not *done
away with* until after the Great White Throne judgment,
when "death and hell were cast into the lake of fire. This is
the second death" (verse 14).

Byers doesn't even mention Y2K and obviously hadn't
heard of it. Instead, he sees the year 2000 as the time of final
victory for the church. Sadly, some of his predictions,
though "confirmed" to many others by revelations and
dreams, have already proven to be wrong. There is not much
time left for Antichrist to appear, take over the world, and
be conquered by the church prior to March 2000—certainly

not the 1,260 days that Byers says this enemy of Christ must reign. Boldly, Byers wrote in 1991 (and must now regret it): "We declare to the Church once again, that September 1989 was the beginning of the last seven years of the Church Age. We further declare that Christ will come *in* His church around September of 1996. He will later come *for* His Church around March of A.D. 2000."[27]

Again the error is obvious. There is no way that Christ can "come *in* His Church"—whatever that may mean. He already indwells every believer. Nor was there any visible change in the church in 1996 other than its continued slide deeper into apostasy, which continues to this day as foretold. Certainly there was no change for the better.

What If Y2K Turns Out to Be a Mouse Instead of a Lion?

For years cult leaders and alarmists have made money and gathered followers through prophecies of disaster on the horizon. Such tactics have been the stock in trade of Mormons and Jehovah's Witnesses from their very beginnings—and their history contains numerous dates, now past, which they confidently prophesied would mark the return of Christ. The approach of the year 2000 may be a last chance for such scams. There are two sides to the coin, however, and Y2K could very well backfire on those who have made too much of it. A recent story recited the fall of a cult leader because the doom prophesied didn't come:

> The bomb shelters were built, the food and clothing were gathered, the weapons were stockpiled, the fuel was stored. But Armageddon never came.
> Elizabeth Clare Prophet, spiritual leader of the Church Universal and Triumphant, had warned back in the 1980s that a nuclear holocaust was coming. But when March 1990 slipped by without the prophesied disaster, her apocalyptic sect went into a skid it is still struggling to halt.

The church is selling two-thirds of its 12,000-acre Royal Teton Ranch on the northern edge of Yellowstone National Park. It is laying off staff members, selling equipment, closing businesses and losing members. Disillusioned after years of costly preparations for a calamity that never came, followers left in droves upon realizing the world would go on....

In the last few years, the church has chopped its staff from 750 to 172. It has shut down its construction department, printing shop, food processing plant, farm and ranching operations, cafeteria, medical office and book distribution center. The shelter is still there, but church officials say the weapons were sold long ago.[28]

There could be similar resentment against evangelicals who were wrong about Y2K and led many astray. As a result of disillusionment, many who once called themselves Christians may turn against Christ, leave the church and return to the world because Christian leaders persuaded them to take unnecessary measures in preparing at great cost in money, time, and energy for something that never happened. The resentment will be even greater for those non-Christians who perceive that the promised help (which they never actually needed) was only a means of attempting to persuade them to believe in Jesus Christ.

When the predicted Y2K holocaust fails to materialize, the world will breathe a great sigh of relief. Fear and deep pessimism will suddenly be replaced by the greatest wave of optimism mankind has experienced in its history. The world will believe that, with the new millennium, a New Age has truly dawned. Who needs God now?

Two things are likely to happen. First, the failure of the Y2K disaster scenario to materialize will be taken as proof that mankind can indeed solve all problems, and having conquered this Goliath, is entering the new millennium with heads held high and limitless possibilities unfolding. And if the Rapture has not occurred by the end of the year 2000, very few will believe in it after that. Why wait any longer?

That neither the Rapture nor the rise of Antichrist and a world government nor Armageddon have occurred will add to the triumph not only of technology over Apocalypse but over Christianity in general and the Bible-believing variety in particular, making it much easier for a new world religion to emerge without being tainted by either. At the same time, however, the desire for success with, and approval by, the world will draw those professing Christians who are so inclined into an even deeper alignment with the enemies of the Cross, all for the good causes of "traditional values," unity, and keeping Christianity from being further maligned.

In our opinion, this is likely what will happen. The alarmists will prove to be wrong. There will be some problems, but not nearly of the magnitude that is being shouted in the media, and especially in private newsletters. Prophecy will be discredited because of its close association with the Y2K fiasco. Sound doctrine will fade even further into the background among evangelicals, and a new ecumenism with deception beyond imagination will take over the scene.

Playing into the Enemy's Hands

Unfortunately, for all the good intentions of those who are trying to alert us to the Y2K problem, paranoia seems to be developing in many as a result, especially in Christians. And, sadly enough, paranoia can cause Christians to act irrationally and even like cultists. In so doing, they play into the hands of the enemies of Christ who are looking for justification to restrict the preaching of the gospel.

Furthermore, some people are not above spreading rumors and deliberately creating antigovernment sentiment. Rumors usually offer what those who heed them want to believe. The following statement, attributed to Attorney-General Janet

Reno, has been circulated widely among Christians and has been accepted as fact. In fact it is a fraud:

> A cultist is one who has a strong belief in the Bible and the Second Coming of Christ; who frequently attends Bible studies; who has a high level of financial giving to a Christian cause; who home schools their children; who has accumulated survival foods and has a strong belief in the Second Amendment; and who distrusts big government. Any of these may qualify [a person as a cultist] but certainly more than one [of these] would cause us to look at this person as a threat, and his family as being in a risk situation that qualified for government interference.

This vicious anti-Christian declaration was supposedly made by Reno in a "60 Minutes" interview. It was brought to the attention of Representative James V. Hansen of Utah, who sent an inquiry to the Justice Department. Its Office of Legislative Affairs responded in a letter dated March 7, 1995, which we quote in part:

> The plain fact is that the quote is a hoax. The Attorney General has never been interviewed on "60 Minutes." She has never discussed cults, or tried to define one....
>
> The quote first appeared, to our knowledge, in the August 1993 *Paul Revere Newsletter* of the Christian Defense League in Flora, Illinois. The information came by telephone from a woman in Florida whose name was not noted. The newsletter subsequently ran a retraction.

A call to "60 Minutes" verified the fact that Janet Reno has never appeared on that program. Unfortunately, such rumors cause some Christians to take defensive actions that may even violate the law. Irresponsible actions by Christian extremists could make it difficult for the rest of us. Rumors of the government using Y2K to suspend the Constitution, to arrest Christians as enemies of the state, of concentration camps already in place, for example, have a peculiar appeal to the credulity of some.

Concerning Y2K, however, Christians are only echoing the same cries of alarm which are being sounded (though hardly heeded) in the secular world. Those who react to these warnings in fear and take extreme measures could shipwreck their own faith as well as that of others when subsequent circumstances prove them wrong, especially if they proclaimed with certainty that they were heeding Bible prophecy or some personal revelation from God.

The One Real Concern Involving Y2K

The sounds of alarm within the church are reaching a crescendo. And the delusion that Christians are supposed to feed the world keeps growing. McAlvany writes, "If you have the financial means to do so...doesn't it make sense to acquire extra dehydrated/freeze-dried food for relatives, friends, people in your church, or associates who cannot afford to do so? Preparation is not just about saving your own skin or your family's. It is about helping those around you who really count. Think about it!"[29]

Yes, *think* about it. *Everyone* counts. We are to love our neighbors as ourselves. As for who is one's neighbor, Christ answered that question by using a publican, a man who was held in general contempt, as an example of one who was a "neighbor" within the meaning of His command.

How wealthy would one have to be to provide for all of one's family and special friends—as well as neighbors—who can't afford to stock up for themselves? And where will all of that freeze-dried food come from when no supplier in that small and specialized industry has the production capacity to meet such demand?

The more successful The Joseph Project 2000 and others like it become in persuading Christians to accumulate food, emergency equipment, and supplies not only for themselves but for others, the greater strain on those suppliers. The greater the strain and growing shortages of certain items and the longer the delivery dates, the higher the level of anxiety. This situation could feed on itself and get out of hand.

And that brings us back to the one real concern associated with Y2K: that we may not even get to the year 2000 before panic-driven runs on banks and food markets could create further hysteria. It will be surprising—even irresponsible—if we don't see an aggressive media campaign by the federal and state governments working together to prevent panic, to assure the public that all will be well. A major purpose of this book is to help in that regard. We hope readers will exert a calming influence.

There are rumors that the National Guard in various states is already being alerted that it may have to be called out at any time. If that is true, there is nothing ominous or insidious about it (preparation for a Clinton takeover, as the fearmongers want us to believe). Rather, these are the prudent measures which responsible authorities ought to take in view of the potential for panic that has already been created by well-meaning "experts" issuing sensational warnings of coming calamity.

What Are We to Do?

In light of the possibility for panic, it would only be prudent to gradually accumulate some extra nonperishable food over the next few months. Every household should always have on hand for any emergency enough food and water to last for at least three or four weeks, which should be sufficient. While dry beans and rice cannot offer the full range of vitamins and minerals we need, they do keep for a long time and provide protein and enough other essentials to sustain a person for some time. Whole grains—wheat, for example—retain their nutritional value longer than flour. Always use the oldest when you draw from these stocks, and replenish them in the ordinary course of life. There are flashlights and extra batteries and kerosene lamps (if you want to go that far) and first-aid supplies to gather.

Of course, if you live in an area of cold winters, you need some extra blankets, warm sweaters and coats, and other clothes. Some people already have wood stoves, and it is only sensible for them always to have at least a year's supply of firewood on hand to prevent running out at the wrong time and having to buy when prices are high, instead of being able to purchase at the bottom of the market. For those who don't have wood stoves, in most cases it would be too expensive to acquire one and remodel the house to accommodate it.

At least one portable radio (with extra batteries) is a top-priority item. And don't forget medications. Over-the-counter medicines can be stocked, but for those that require a prescription the physician probably would not want to give a large supply in advance "just in case." And don't overlook expiration dates on medications and other items where applicable.

It is not our intention to provide a complete checklist of survival items or instructions on how to store food and water. There are specialists who offer all the information one needs in books and on the Internet. We suggest you consult them and use your own common sense in evaluating their advice.

Whatever you do, don't panic. Fear can easily sidetrack Christians from the real tasks in these last days. Stay calm, act rationally, and trust God for His protection and guidance in all things. You can only do so much. Hutchings and Spargimino wisely comment, "Our reaction to the Y2K problem may be worse than the problem itself! If the worst-case scenario develops, will *any* amount of preparation prove sufficient?"[30] Obviously not.

We are not to be anxious for tomorrow but to trust in our Lord for we do not know (nor do the "experts") what a day may bring forth (Proverbs 27:1; Philippians 4:6,7; James 4:13-15). And while we are "anxious for nothing," we are to be prudent and diligent in all that we do, rejoicing in our Lord. Christ gave very specific commands and promises in Matthew 6:25-26,31-34:

> Take no thought [don't be anxious] for your life, what ye shall eat, or what ye shall drink....Behold the fowls of the air: for they sow not, neither do they reap, nor gather into barns; yet your heavenly Father feedeth them. Are ye not much better than they?
>
> Therefore take no thought, saying, What shall we eat? or, What shall we drink? or, Wherewithal shall we be clothed?...for your heavenly Father knoweth that ye have need of all these things.
>
> But seek ye first the kingdom of God, and his righteousness; and all these things shall be added unto you. Take therefore no thought [don't worry about] the morrow: for the morrow shall take thought for the things of itself. Sufficient unto the day is the evil thereof.

May each one of us, in our individual spheres of influence, provide that rational respone to irrational hysteria which will turn back the tide of panic that otherwise could fulfill unfounded fears.

EPILOGUE

As this book was going to press in January 1999, developments on this subject were unfolding much as anticipated. CNN Headline News on January 15, 1999 took its cameras inside a huge underground command station at Dugway Proving Ground in Utah, a nerve center connected to thousands of military computers, and announced that they were all Y2K compliant. The January 1999 edition of *Embedded Systems Programming* carried an editorial which stated, "Ten months ago in this space I asked for those of you who have encountered year 2000 (Y2K) problems in embedded systems you're developing to let me know. In all of the e-mails I received, no one cited a verifiable problem." The articles planned for 1999 (including the December issue) in this premiere publication on embedded systems which goes out to the true experts working in this field will not even address Y2K.

In contrast to this deafening silence among those who know the facts, Christian "experts" continued to sound the alarm. On January 11 and 12, 1999 James Dobson aired on his "Focus on the Family" program a talk by Michael S. Hyatt given to his staff apparently two months earlier. The original talk contained outdated statistics concerning the lack of preparedness of business and government, which were all the more outdated when the programs aired. There was also misinformation of the kind we have pointed out (concerning embedded chips, etc.). The January broadcast recommended and offered Hyatt's book as well as Shaunti Feldhahn's two books and The Joseph Project.

Christianity Today of January 11, 1999 carried a major article on Y2K which attempted to offer a balanced view but contained again the usual misinformation mixed with some calm appraisals and opened the door very wide to the possibility of the worst.

A week later, *Time* for (January 18, 1999) displayed on its cover a fanatical "Christian" dressed in long white robe and wearing a placard proclaiming "The End of the World!?!" The article basically was a spoof on Christian concern over Y2K. As we had feared, the secular world was stepping up its ridicule of the church for its handling of this subject.

In the meantime, improvements continued in every sector, though strangely overlooked by Christians still sounding the alarm.

NOTES

CHAPTER ONE: Worldwide Chaos and Disaster?

1. *Sunday Times*, London, August 3, 1997.
2. Gary North, special report, undated [1997], p. 6 and back cover, promoting his *Remnant Review*.
3. Donald S. McAlvany, *The McAlvany Intelligence Advisor*, February 1998, p. 1.
4. Ibid., pp. 2-3.
5. "Zap! How the Year 2000 Bug Will Hurt the Economy," *Business Week*, March 2, 1998, p. 93.
6. Larry Martin, testimony before the U.S. Senate Subcommittee on Financial Services and Technology of the Banking, Housing, and Urban Affairs Committee, July 10, 1997.
   http://www..senate.gov/~banking/97_07hrg/071097/witness/martin.htm
7. Jack and Rexella Van Impe, "2000 Time Bomb" (video). Available from Jack Van Impe Ministries, Box 7004, Troy, MI 48007.
8. "Programmers Tried to Avert Y2K Glitch," *San Francisco Chronicle*, November 16, 1998, Letters to Business section.
9. CNET News, November 11, 1998.
10. Michael S. Hyatt, *The Millennium Bug: How to Survive the Coming Chaos* (Regnery Publishing, Inc., 1998), front and back, outside of jacket cover.
11. Larry Burkett, Weekly E-mail, November 16, 1998, cited in
    E-mail: y2kconstituent@cfcministry.org
    from Christian Financial Concepts.
12. "Millennium bug cost rising," *The Bulletin* [Bend, Oregon], September 18, 1998, p. A11.
13. *The Wall Street Journal*, November 7, 1998.
14. Ibid.
15. "Weapons agency not 2000-verified," *The Bulletin* (Bend, Oregon), November 28, 1998, p. A1.
16. Steven Levy, "Will the bug bite the bull? Not worried about the Millenium Computer Problem? The Experts Dare to Disagree," *Newsweek*, May 4, 1998.
17. "Y2K, the Storm," *World*, August 8, 1998, p. 9.

18. Rick Cowles, "Transmission and Distribution," *Utilities and the Year 2000.* Available at:
    http://www.addsyst.com/writers/tnd.htm
19. Ross Anderson, cited in Julian Gregori, *What Will Become of Us? Counting Down to Y2K* (The International Crisis Management Center, 1998), p. 67.
20. Ibid., pp. 61-62.
21. Ibid., pp. 63-64.
22. Gary North's Y2K Links and Forums, "Water Utilities Survey Reports Extremely Bad News...." Available at:
    http://www.garynorth.com/y2k/results
23. *North Platte, Nebraska: A Case Study of the Year 2000 Computer Problem.* Available at:
    http://genteel.creighton.edu/y2k.htm#Case Study
24. Robert Lau, cited in Nick Edwards, "Millennium Bug Threatens Financial Chaos," *The Netly News,* October 6, 1997.
25. Cited in North, p. 5.
26. McAlvany, February 1998, p. 3.
27. Ibid.
28. Burkett, Weekly E-mail, November 16, 1998.
29. Ibid.
30. Mike Phillips, "Y2K and Banks," cited in Hyatt, p. 85. Available at:
    http://www.75557.232@compuserve.com
31. *The Wall Street Journal,* November 18, 1998.
32. Ed Yourdon, "Sayonara Washington," cited in Jim Lord's *Year 2000 Survival Newsletter,* sample issue, P.O. Box 84910, Phoenix, AZ 85071.
33. Mark A. Frautschi, "Embedded Systems and the Year 2000 Problem," Shakespeare and Tao Consulting. Available at:
    http://www.tmn.com/y2k
34. Ronald Pacchiano, "Time Will Tell," *Computer Shopper,* December 1998, Special Anniversary Issue, p. 409.
35. Jack Anderson, "Y2K Disaster Preparedness," audiotape of talk given at the Bend Ministerial Association meeting, October 24, 1998. Available from Westside Church, 2051 NW Shevlin Park Road, Bend, OR 97701.
36. Ibid.
37. James Dobson, "Y2K: Expectations and Preparations" (Panel), CT149/22060, October 23-25, 1998. Available from Focus on the Family, (719) 548-4527.
38. McAlvany, February 1998, p. 9.
39. Dobson, op. cit.
40. Ibid.
41. Ibid.
42. Ibid.
43. Ibid.

44. William G. Phillips, "The Year 2000 Problem: Will the Bug Bite Back?" *Popular Science*, October 1998, p. 90.
45. Bruce Webster, in Levy, May 4, 1998.
46. McAlvany, February 1998.
47. The *Los Angeles Times*, November 23, 1998. Available at: http://www.latimes.com/archives/doc/rArchive/temp/ temp.9876
48. Phillips, p. 90.
49. Ibid., pp. 5-20.
50. North, *Remnant Review*, February 1, 1997.
51. McAlvany, February 1998, p. 1.
52. Levy, p. 62.
53. Jonathan Marshall, "Doomsayers Rant, But Year 2000 May Not Be Armageddon," *San Francisco Chronicle*, July 20, 1998, On Economics section, p. D2.
54. Jerry Falwell, *National Liberty Journal*, August 1998, p. 1.
55. Brannon Howse and J. M. Smith, "The Bug that Wouldn't Die: Part II in a Continuing Series," *Jerry Falwell's National Liberty Journal*, September 1998, pp. 10-11.
56. Karl Feilder, *Chicago Tribune*, September 30, 1997.
57. Ibid.
58. McAlvany, op. cit.
59. Hyatt, *Millennium Bug*, back cover of jacket.
60. North, special report [1997], p. 2.

CHAPTER 2: Panic, Stock Up and Arm?

1. Ibid., p. 95.
2. Chuck Missler, *K-Ration Intelligence Report*, June 23, 1998.
3. Senate "Hearing on Mandating Year-2000 Disclosures for Publicly-Traded Companies," November 4, 1997. Cited in Hyatt, p. 233.
4. *Time*, June 15, 1998.
5. Joseph Project 2000 from the Y2K brochure. Available from 6409 Bells Ferry Road, Woodstock, GA 30189-2324, (678) 445-5512; Fax (678) 445-5503. Available at: http://www.josephproject2000.org E-mail: jp2k@mindspring.com
6. Dobson, Y2K panel, quoted in *The Christian News*, November 16, 1998, p. 21.
7. Gregori, *What Will Become of Us?* p. 60.
8. Phillips, "The Year 2000 Problem, p. 91.
9. Gary North, "Blind Man's Bluff in the Year 2000," November 20, 1998. Available at: http://www.garynorth.com E-mail: garynorth@trapped.com
10. Gregori, p. 64.

11. Pacchiano, "Time Will Tell," p. 408.

12. Chuck Missler, "Round Table, Y2K: The Millennium Bomb," tape 2, side 2. Available from Koinonia House, P.O. Box D, Coeur d'Alene, ID 83816-0347.

13. Donald S. McAlvany, "The Millennium Bug: Toward a State of National Emergency and a Cashless Society," *The McAlvany Intelligence Advisor*, April 1998, pp. 1, 2, 8.

14. *The Orange County Register* (California), July 1, 1998.

15. All Politics, July 14, 1998, special report titled "Clinton Urges Americans to Act on Y2K Problem," pp. 2-3.

16. Gary North, "A 24-page report that proves, point by point, that this is no 'Chicken Little' fantasy but a terrifying reality," sent out by direct mail to promote North's *Remnant Review* early in 1998, from insert between pp. 16-17 and p. 25.

17. North, "Blind Man's Bluff."

18. Van Impe, "2000 Time Bomb," video.

19. N. W. Hutchings and Larry Spargimino, *Y2K = 666? How Will January 1, 2000 Affect You?* (Hearthstone Publishing, 1998), p. 66.

20. Phillips, "The Year 2000 Problem: Battling the Bug," p. 90.

21. Jack Anderson, "Y2K Disaster Preparedness" audiotape.

22. Dobson, Y2K panel, October 23-25, 1998.

23. Available at:
    http://www.techstocks.com/~wsapi/investor/s-16203/reply-216

24. Rick Cowles, "Electric Utilities and Year 2000: Real-Life Examples of Date Related Problems for Electric Utilities." Available at:
    http://www.euy2k.com/reallife.htm

25. Steve Hewitt, "Year 2000 Bug, Part 2, Good News and Bad," *Christian Computing Magazine*, 10, no. 10 (October 1998). Available at:
    http://www.gospelcom.net/ccmag/y2k/octy2k.html

26. Ibid.

27. Steve Hewitt, "Y2K, The Challenge Ahead, Part 3," November 1998. Available at:
    E-mail: steve@ccmag.com

28. Anderson, "Y2K Disaster Preparedness" audiotape.

29. McAlvany, February 1998, p. 9.

30. Anderson, "Y2K Disaster Preparedness" audiotape.

31. Ibid.

32. StepWise Solutions promotional information packet for Automated Hybrid-Radix Tool for Year 2000 Remediation. Available from StepWise Solutions, Watermill, NY, (516) 726-0010.

33. Dobson, Y2K panel.

34. *The Wall Street Journal*, November 20, 1998, cited in Burkett, Weekly E-mail, November 30, 1998.

35. Hewitt, "Year 2000 Bug, Part 2."

36. Hewitt, "Year 2000 Bug, Part 1," September 1998. Available at:
    http://www.gospelcom.net/ccmag/y2k/sepy2k.html
37. "Social Security Administration: Significant Progress Made in Year 2000 Effort, but Key Risks Remain," Report AIMD-98-6, 10/22/97. Available at:
    E-mail: info@www.gao.gov
38. Anderson "Y2K Disaster Preparedness" panel.
39. Hewitt, "Year 2000 Bug, Part 2."
40. Gary North's Y2K Links and Forums; "Category: Power Grid," November 19, 1998.
41. North, "Blind Man's Bluff." Available at:
    E-mail: garynorth@trapped.com
42. StepWise Solutions, Hybrid-Radix Tool.
43. David Hayes *(Kansas City Star)*, "Some Experts Say It Is Time to Chill About Y2K," *San Francisco Chronicle*, November 16, 1998.

CHAPTER 3: Could It Really Be That Bad?

1. Julian Gregori, *What Will Become of Us?* p. 66.
2. Michael Diamond, "Wall St. Passes Y2K Test Without a Glitch," *USA Today*, July 14, 1998, p. 1A.
3. "Zap! How the Year 2000 Bug Will Hurt the Economy" (Cover Story), *Business Week*, March 2, 1998, p. 93.
4. Nicholas Zvegintzov, "The Year 2000 as Racket and Ruse," *American Programmer*, February 1996.
5. Bill Gates, quoted by Bruce Chapman, "Crash 2000," *Seattle Post-Intelligencer*, June 14, 1998.
6. Joel Willemssen, before Subcommittee on Government/ Management, Information, and Technology of the Committee on Government Reform and Oversight. Field Hearing on "Oversight of the Year 2000 Problem: Lessons to Be Learned from State and Local Experiences," September 3, 1998. GAO/T-AIMD-98-2781. Available at:
    http://www.house.gov/reform/gmit/hearings
7. Zvegintzov, "Racket and Ruse."
8. "The Real Year 2000 Nightmare: Manufacturing Systems," *Industry Week*, January 5, 1998. Available at:
    http://www.industryweek.com/specialseries/networkedcorp/010598/index/html
9. Ibid.
10. Ibid.
11. "Horn's Subcommittee Report: U.S. Will Not Meet Deadline," October 17, 1998, Link:
    http://www.house.gov/reform/gmit/y2k/y2kreport/summary.htm
12. Hutchings and Spargimino, *Y2K=666?* pp. 73-74.
13. Ellen M. Steinlauf, letter to author, November 27, 1998 (on file).

14. "Boeing Gets Intelligence Community Y2K Ready," *Boeing News* 57, no. 45 (November 13, 1998): A11. Available at: http://www.boeing.com/companyoffices/aboutus/y2k/pubs/981131.htm

15. From the desk of Don McAlvany, "Y2K: How Big the Crisis?" (extract), November 20, 1998. Available at: http://www.mcalvany.com/samples/HBC_W.html

16. *Washington Post,* June 12, 1998.

17. *The Orlando Sentinel,* November 2, 1998.

18. Hewitt, "Year 2000 Bug, Part 1."

19. "Weapons agency not 2000-verified," *The Bulletin,* November 28, 1998, p. A1.

20. North, "Blind Man's Bluff," November 20, 1998.

21. Don McAlvany, "The Millennium Bug: Electrical Power Grid at Risk" Extract available at: http://www.mcalvany.com/samples/PWR_W.html

22. Dobson, Y2K Panel, audiotape.

23. McAlvany, "The Millennium Bug": Electrical Power Grid at Risk." Extract available at: http://www.mcalvany.com/samples/PWR_W.html

24. Hewitt, "Y2K, the Challenge Ahead, Part 2." Op. cit.

25. Ibid.

26. Gregori, "What Will Become of Us?" p. 121.

27. Ibid, pp. 111-123.

28. Hewitt, "Y2K, The Challenge Ahead, Part 3," November 1998.

29. Ibid.

30. Ibid.

31. Ibid.

32. Wired News (November 10, 1998), cited in Larry Burkett's Weekly Y2K Fax, November 23, 1998.

33. Phone interview, November 25, 1998 (on file).

34. "Industry Wakes Up to the Year 2000 Menace," Fortune Features, April 27, 1998. Available at: http://www.pathfinder.com/fortune/1998/980427/imt.html

35. Phillips, "The Year 2000 Problem," p. 90.

36. Fortune Features, p. 3.

37. "Boeing Gets...Y2K Ready."

38. Hewitt, in Dobson, "Y2K" panel.

39. Ibid.

40. Hewitt, "Y2K, The Challenge Ahead, Part 3."

41. Jim Lord's Year 2000 Survival Newsleter, sample issue, undated, early 1998.

42. Hewitt, "Year 2000 Bug, Part 1," September 1998.

43. Burkett, Weekly E-mail, November 16, 1998.

44. *World,* October 17, 1998, p. 28.

45. Falwell, *National Liberty Journal*, November 1998, p. 7.
46. Ibid., p. 8.
47. *World*, August 15, 1998, p. 16.

CHAPTER 4: A Calm Appraisal

1. Greg Miller, "Debunking Year 2000's Computer Disaster," *Los Angeles Times*, November 3, 1997, p. A1.
2. Alex Patelis, cited in Marshall, "Doomsayers Rant," p. D2.
3. Ibid.
4. Phillips, "The Year 2000 Problem," p. 90.
5. Fred Moody, "Don't Believe the Hype: It's Y1K All Over Again," *ABC News* commentary, November 13, 1998. Available at:
    http://www.abcnews.com/sections/tech/FredMoody/moody64.html
6. The Y2K Weatherman. Available at: http://Y2KWatch.com
7. Moody, "Don't Believe the Hype."
8. Hewitt, in Dobson, "Y2K" panel.
9. Ibid.
10. Y2K Weatherman, November 24, 1998.
    E-mail: Y2kwman@yahoo.com
11. Ed Yardeni, "Y2K: An International Perspective," conference sponsored by Center for Strategic and International Studies, October 1998.
12. Gary North, "A Billion Lives Lost if Things Go Fairly Well," *The Christian News*, October 12, 1998, p. 8. Available at:
    http://www.garynorth.com
13. Joel Ackerman, Conference on Millennial Planning for Hospital Managers, Orange, CA. Archived in:
    http://www.latimes.com/archines/doc/rArchives/temp/temp.9876
14. Eileen P. Gunn, "A New Legal Target: The Millennium Bug," *Fortune*, April 27, 1998. Available at:
    http://www.pathfinder.com/fortune/1998/980427/feal.html
15. Zvegintzov, "The Year 2000 as Racket and Ruse."
16. "Y2K Is Months Away, but Sharks Are Circling: The President gets ready to launch a preemptive strike against Y2K lawsuits," *Time Daily*. Available at:
    http://cgi.pathfinder.com/time/daily
17. Central Electric Cooperative (Oregon), *Central Issues*, November 1998, p. 40.
18. Bonneville Power Administration Internet summary sheet, October 7, 1998. Available at:
    http://www.bpa.gov/Corporate/C1/Y2K/Y2K.html
19. COM/Electric, "COM/Electric Is Readying for Year 2000." From http://www.comelectric.com/corp/weby2k.htm

20. Western Area Power Administration, "Facts: Western Power Administration, Year 2000." Available at:
http://www.wapa.gov/cso/y2k/factsmay.htm

21. National Power PLC-United Kingdom. Available at:
http://www.national-power.com/investor/anrpt1998/internal.htm

22. U.S. Senate hearing. Available at:
http://webserv.vnunet.com/_user/plsql/
pkg_vnu_news.right_frame?p_story=56468

23. Ibid.

24. Greg Miller, "Debunking Year 2000's Computer Disaster," *Los Angeles Times*, November 3, 1997, p. A1.

25. Ibid.

26. Copy of interview on file.

27. Ibid.

28. Copy of interview on file.

29. Anderson, "Y2K Disaster Preparedness" audiotape.

30. "Boeing Gets...Y2K Ready."

31. "TI posts 'Year 2000 Ready' product status on the Web," *Texas Instruments Integration*, October 1998, p. 1. Available at:
http://www.ti.com/year2000

32. Ibid.

33. Boeing and the Year 2000 Challenge, "The Boeing Approach to the Year 2000 Challenge," undated [June 19, 1998], p. 1 of 2.
Available at:
http://boeing.com/companyoffices/aboutus/y2k/pmo
approach/htm

34. Ibid.

35. Reuters News Service, November 3, 1998.

36. *EDN*, October 22, 1998, p. 84.

37. USCG Navigation Center. Available at:
http://www.navcen.uscg.mil/gps/geninfo/y2k

38. Copy of November 1998 interview on file.

39. Stan Runyon, "Program addresses Y2K for HP instruments," EDTN network. Home Page:
http://www.edtm.com/news/nov23/112398tnews5.html

40. Gregori, *What Will Become of Us?* p. 8.

41. Ibid., p. 12.

42. Steve Greg, speaker, October Bend Ministerial Association, audiotape.

43. Gregori, *What Will Become of Us?*, p. 121.

44. *Business Week*, March 2, 1998, p. 96.

45. Diamond, "Wall St. passes Y2K test," p. 1A.

46. From StepWise Solutions, Hybrid-Radix Tool.

47. McAlvany, op. cit., April 1998.

CHAPTER 5: The Church's Final Hour? or Greatest Folly?

1. From an advertisement for *Y2K News* Magazine in Falwell's *National Liberty Journal*, November 1998, p. 7.
2. Drew Parkhill, "Disaster Preparedness," BMS-Y2K, November 14, 1998, audiotape #1444. Available from Westside Church, 2051 NW Shevlin Park Road, Bend, OR 97701.
3. Jack Anderson, "Y2K Disaster Preparedness" audiotape, October 24, 1998.
4. Ibid.
5. Steve Hewitt, "Y2K, The Challenge Ahead, Part 3,"
    http://www.gospelcom.net/ccmag/articles/covr1198.html
6. *World*, August 22, 1998, as cited in Pastor Charles Pack's *The Spirit of Prophecy*, September/October 1998, p. 8
7. Adelle M. Banks, *Religion News Service*, "Moderation Urged on Ministries in Responding to Millennium Computer Bug," *The Christian News*, November 16, 1998, p. 19.
8. Gary North's Institute for Christian Economics (ICE) newsletter, November 1998.
9. "Y2K Disaster Preparedness," audiotape, October 24, 1998.
10. Gordon McDonald, "Y2K Update," *Personal Update*, October 1998, p. 17.
11. Anderson, "Y2K Disaster Preparedness" audiotape, October 24, 1998.
12. Ibid.
13. Phil Arms, "Y2K...What They're Not Telling You," two audiotapes. Available from Phil Arms Ministries, P.O. Box 770, Alief, TX 77411.
14. Jerry Falwell, *National Liberty Journal*, November 1998.
15. Brannon Howse, "A Biblical Response to Y2K," *National Liberty Journal*, October 1998, pp. 1, 7.
16. Parkhill, "Disaster Preparedness" audiotape, November 14, 1998.
17. Anderson, "Y2K Disaster Preparedness" audiotape, October 24, 1998.
18. Parkhill, "Disaster Preparedness" audiotape, November 14, 1998.
19. Ibid.
20. Dobson, Y2K panel, October 23-25, 1998.
21. Hewitt, "Y2K, The Challenge Ahead, Part 3," November 1998.
22. Ibid.
23. Dobson, Y2K panel, October 23-25, 1998.
24. Ibid.
25. Ibid.
26. Letter on file.
27. Jon Little, "Preparing for the Unknown," *Anchorage Daily News* Peninsula Bureau, Nikiski, Alaska. Available at:
    http://www.adn.com/stories/t98112980.html

28. "Moderation Urged." pp. 19,21.

29. Parkhill, "Disaster Preparedness" audiotape, November 14, 1998.

30. Ibid.

31. Ibid.

32. Anderson, "Y2K Disaster Preparedness" audiotape, October 24, 1998.

33. Christian Broadcasting Network, December 2, 1998. Available at:
    http://www.cbn.org/the700club

34. Ibid.

35. Ibid.

36. Sonya Bruce, "Y2K Readiness: Northwest Utilities Plan Ahead,"
    Bulletin, Northwest Public Power Association, November 1998,
    pp. 13-17.

37. Banks, "Moderation Urged," p. 19.

38. North's ICE newsletter, November 1998.

39. Anderson, "Y2K Disaster Preparedness" audiotape, October 24, 1998.

40. Norm Coleman, *Star Tribune,* St. Paul, Minnesota, December 3, 1998.

41. Anderson, "Y2K Disaster Preparedness" audiotape, October 24, 1998.

42. Shaunti Christine Feldhahn, *Y2K The Millennium Bug: A Balanced Christian Response* (Sisters, OR: Multnomah Publishers, 1998), p. 216.

43. Dobson, "Y2K: Expectations and Preparations" panel, October 23-25, 1998.

44. Burkett, quoted in Feldhahn, "*The Millennium Bug.*"

45. Quoted from The Joseph Project 2000 website promoting the book,
    Y2K: The Millennium Bug by Shaunti Feldhahn. Available at:
    http://www.josephproject2000.org/preparation.htm

46. Feldhahn, *Y2K, The Millennium Bug,* excerpted from Chapter 10.

47. Anderson, "Y2K Disaster Preparedness" audiotape, October 24, 1998.

48. Feldhahn, The Joseph Project 2000 brochure.

49. Feldhahn, *Y2K, The Millennium Bug,* pp. 118-119.

50. Dobson, "Y2K" panel.

51. Anderson, "Y2K Disaster Preparedness" audiotape, October 24, 1998.

52. Jerry Falwell's *National Liberty Journal,* December 1998, p. 20.

53. Quoted from The Joseph Project 2000 website promoting
    Feldhahn's *Y2K: The Millennium Bug.*

CHAPTER 6: A Biblical Rejection of Y2K Disaster

1. Van Impe, "2000 Time Bomb" video.

2. As cited on *ABC News* commentary, November 13, 1998. Available at:
   http://www.abcnews.com/sections/tech/FredMoody.moody64.html

3. Hutchings and Spargimino, *Y2K=666?* p. 72.
4. Albert James Dager, "Y2K, Y2Worry," *Media Spotlight*, volume 21, no. 3, p. 22.
5. The Y2K Weatherman, November 30, 1998.
    E-mail: Y2kwman@yahoo.com
6. Banks, "Moderation Urged."
7. Chuck Missler, "Round Table, Y2K: The Millennium Bomb," Tape 2, side 2. Available from Koinonia House, P.O. Box D, Coeur d'Alene, ID 83816-0347.
8. Ron Reese, "Danger! Worldwide Depression! Computer Bug (Y2K) Crisis Nears!" A tract printed and distributed by Maranatha Ministries, 1201 Idle Hills Rd., Brooklyn, MI 49230.
9. Van Impe, "2000 Time Bomb" video.
10. Ibid.
11. Dobson, "Y2K" panel.
12. Ibid.
13. Ibid.
14. Ibid.
15. Roy Maynard, "Binary blowout?" *World*, August 22, 1998, p. 17.
16. David Wilkerson, "America's Golden Calf Is Coming Down!" *Times Square Church Pulpit Series*, undated (c. August or September 1998), p. 2.
17. Dobson, "Y2K" panel.
18. Ibid.
19. Lynn Vincent, "Backward Christian Soldiers?" *World*, August 22, 1998, p. 16.
20. Paul Marshall, with Lela Gilbert, *Their Blood Cries Out: The Worldwide Tragedy of Modern Christian Who Are Dying for the Faith* (Word Publishing, 1997), pp. 139-43. See also *Christians in Crisis* newsletter (every issue reports on such atrocities); for free subscription call (800) 286-5115.
21. Hewitt, "Year 2000 Bug, Part 1."
22. *The Wall Street Journal*, November 10, 1998.
23. Jerry Falwell's *National Liberty Journal*, September 1998, p. 1 ·
24. Cited in Banks, "Moderation Urged."
25. Stated in Van Impe, "2000 Time Bomb."
26. For full substantiation of this amazing prophecy, see Dave Hunt, *A Cup of Trembling: Jerusalem in Bible Prophecy* (Eugene, OR: Harvest House, 1995).

CHAPTER 7: A Contrary Scenario

1. *San Francisco Chronicle*, November 16, 1998.
2. Greg Miller, "Debunking Year 2000's Computer Disaster," *Los Angeles Times*, November 3, 1997, p. 1A.

3. Ibid.
4. Testimony of Sally Katzen before the U.S. House of Representatives Subcomittee on Government Management, Information, and Technology of the Committee on Government Reform and Oversight, July 10, 1997. Available at:
    http://www.comlinks.com/gov/kat710.htm (October 24, 1997)
5. *San Francisco Chronicle*, November 16, 1998.
6. Oracle Corporation. Available at: http://www.oracle.com/year2000
7. "NRC's Year 2000 Activities," November 17, 1998. Available at:
    http://.nrc.gov/NRC/NEWS/year2000.html
8. Ibid.
9. NRC Testimony Before Congress. Available at:
    http://www.nrc.gov/NRC/TESTIMONY/y2ktest.html
10. Tom Raum, "Year 2000 Council Created," ABC News. Available at:
    http://www.techDailyNews/y2k_council0204.html
11. Television news interview broadcast on CSPAN, July 2, 1998.
12. Dallas Semiconductor Corp., "Year 2000 Compliance," statement on Y2K for its products. Available at:
    http://www.dalsemi.com/info/y2k
13. Dallas Semiconductor letter to customers dated May 1, 1998, from Kevin Self, Senior Applications Engineer, (927) 371-3870
    E-mail: kevin.self@dalsemi.com
14. *The Christian News*, November 1, 1998, p. 21.
15. *San Francisco Chronicle*, November 16, 1998.
16. "Y2K, the Storm," *World*, August 8, 1998, p. 9.
17. *Time*, June 15, 1998.
18. From a copy of President Clinton's executive order dated February 4, 1998. Available at:
    http://www.itpolicy.gsa.gov/mks/yr2000/exord.htm
19. *Time*, June 15, 1998.
20. *The Bulletin* (Bend, OR), December 7, 1998, p. A5.
21. Hyatt, "Why I Am More Pessimistic Than Ever," November 30, 1998. Available at:
    http://www.michaelhyatt.com
22. "Cyberscope," *Newsweek*, December 1, 1998.
23. Rosemarie Yu, "Coming Clean on Y2K," *Business 2.0*, January 1999, p. 33; Hewitt, "Year 2000," Part 2, op.cit.
24. Leora Lawton, "Counting Down to the Year 2000: Ready or Not," *Circuits Assembly*, December 1998, pp. 28-32.
25. Dallas Semiconductor, "Year 2000 Compliance."
26. Patrick L. Porter and Deborah Radcliff, "At Chase Manhattan the Task Amounts to 200 Million Lines of Code." *Software Magazine*, March 1997
27. Ibid. Available at:
    http://www.sentrytech.com
28. Ibid.

29. Testimony of Irene Dec, House Committee on Ways and Means, Hearing on the Year 2000 Computer Problem, May 7, 1998. Available at:
> http://www.house.gov/ways_means/oversight/testimony/ 5-7-98/5-7dec.html

30. Hyatt, *The Millennium Bug*, inside front of jacket.

31. November 25, 1998. Copy of interview on file.

32. CNET news, June 17, 1998, from a Reuters report.

33. *Datamation Global 100*, July 1997.

34. *Fortune*, March 3, 1998.

35. *Asian Business*, May 1, 1998.

36. *Los Angeles Times*, November 23, 1998. Archived at:
> http://www.latimes.com/archives/doc/rArchive/temp/temp. 9876

37. Ibid.

38. *Los Angeles Times*, November 23, 1998, pp. C1, C6.

39. Phillips, "The Year 2000 Problem," p. 89.

40. Ibid., pp. 92-93.

41. Oracle Corporation. Available at:
> http://www.oracle.com/year2000

42. Benny Evangelista, "Y2K Kink Dissected at Comdex: Computer Trade Show Explores Y2K Problem," *San Francisco Chronicle*, November 17, 1998, pp. B1, B10.

43. Ibid.

44. Ibid.

45. Ibid.

46. "Y2K, the Storm," *World*, August 8, 1998, p. 9.

47. Miller, "Debunking," p. A2.

48. FDIC Brochure, "The Year 2000 Date Change: What It Means to You and Your Insured Financial Institution."

49. Bank of the Cascades special letter to customers, undated.

50. *Hemisphere:* December 1998, pp. 16,18.

51. Jeff Jinnett testifying before U.S. Senate Subcommittee. Available at:
> http://webserv.vnunet.com/www_user/plsql/ pkg_vnu_news.right_frame?p_story=56468

52. Hyatt, *The Millennium Bug*, p. 215.

53. North, op. cit.

54. *Los Angeles Times*, August 16, 1982.

CHAPTER 8: The Christian Response

1. Dager, "Y2K, Y2Worry?" p. 20.

2. Dobson "Y2K" panel, October 23-25, 1998.

3. Gregori, *What Will Become of Us?* pp. 138-140.

4. Parkhill, "Disaster Preparedness," audiotape #1444, November 14, 1998.

5. Ibid.

6. Hewitt, "Y2K, The Challenge Ahead, Part 3"; Mark A. Kellner, "Y2K: A Secular Apocalypse? *Christianity Today,* January 4, 1999, p. 60.

7. Anderson, "Y2K Disaster Preparedness" audiotape, October 24, 1998.

8. Maynard, "Binary Blowout?" pp. 13-14.

9. Quoted in Feldhahn, *Y2K The Millennium Bug,* p. 41.

10. Larry Burkett, "Y2K Position Paper." Available at:
     http://www.cfcministry.org/library/Y2K/cfcY2Kposition.htm

11. Larry Burkett, Weekly E-mail, November 16, 1998.
     E-mail: Y2KConstituent@CFCMinistry.org

12. Anderson "Y2KDisaster Preparedness," audiotape, October 24, 1998.

13. Feldhahn, *Y2K, The Millennium Bug,* p. 110.

14. Nicholas Zvegintzov, "The Year 2000 as Racket and Ruse," *American Programmer*, February 1996.

15. Ibid.

16. *Globe and Mail* (Toronto, Canada), November 2, 1998.

17. Michelle Locke, The Associated Press, "Food Hoarding Climbs with Concern over Y2K," *The Bulletin* (Bend, OR), December 7, 1998, p. A5.

18. Ibid.

19. Dobson, "Y2K" panel.

20. Locke, "Food Hoarding Climbs."

21. Gregori, "What Will Become of Us?" p. 111.

22. Dager, "Y2K, Y2Worry," p. 23.

23. North, "The Millennium Bug."

24. From an ad for "The Blueprint Series" of Reconstructionist books mailed out by Gary North in 1987.

25. Feldhahn, *Y2K, The Millennium Bug,* pp. 16, 109.

26. Marvin Byers, *The Final Victory: The Year 2000*, Foreword by General Jose Efrain Rios Montt, ex-president of Guatemala (Companion Press, 1991), pp. 126-27.

27. Ibid., p. 371.

28. *The Kansas City Star,* April 5, 1998, p. A30.

29. *The McAlvany Intelligence Advisor,* August 1998, p. 26.

30. Hutchings and Spargimino, *Y2K=666?* p. 115.

INDEX

If you would like to receive a free monthly newsletter featuring timely articles by Dave Hunt and informative answers to readers' questions, and offering hard-to-find resource materials, write:

THE BEREAN CALL
P.O. Box 7019
Bend, OR 97708

You may also visit our website at:

www.thebereancall.org

or (for orders only) call
1-800-937-6658